# Nationalism
# and Sexuality

# Nationalism and Sexuality

Respectability and Abnormal Sexuality
in Modern Europe

## George L. Mosse

HOWARD FERTIG · NEW YORK

Hardcover edition originally published
by Howard Fertig, Inc. in 1985.

Library of Congress Cataloging in Publication Data
Mosse, George L. (George Lachmann), 1918–
    Nationalism and sexuality.
    Includes bibliographical references and index.
    1. Sex customs—Europe—History.   2. Sexual ethics—
Europe—History.   3. Middle classes—Europe—Conduct of
life.   4. Sex customs—Germany—Case studies.   5. Fascist
ethics.   6. Sex customs—Great Britain—Case studies.
I. Title.
HQ18.E8M67   1985      306.7'094      84–6082
ISBN 0-86527-429-0 (pbk)

Design by Albert Burkhardt

First Howard Fertig, Inc. Paperback printing 1997
5 4 3 2 1

Manufactured in the United States of America

# Foreword

This work does not pretend to be a general history of respectability, nationalism, normal or abnormal sexuality, although these are the materials with which it deals. Instead, the book seeks an understanding of how such themes functioned to shape society's attitudes toward the human body and its sexuality. Many aspects of the history of sexuality are not in fact discussed at all. For example, I will have much to say about the role of medicine in shaping perceptions and policing sexuality, and do not mean to disregard the startling advances in hygiene which took place at the same time. Equally, the new joy in the human body that emerged at the turn of the nineteenth and twentieth centuries, the aesthetic appreciation of human beauty, is discussed from a functional point of view, as it relates to nationalism and respectability, and not for its undoubted impact upon the avant garde of arts and letters. The movement for women's rights will also concern us: yet though it touched most aspects of women's lives, only its relationship to nationalism and respectability will occupy us here.

We are concerned with the attitudes of society toward sexuality, and though these placed harsh demands upon those who wanted to be respectable, they did not fill middle-class society solely with bored husbands, frustrated wives and frightened outsiders. Many people must have lived satisfactory and fulfilled private lives, though we can never know with any certainty the balance between happiness and despair among respectable men and women. However, it is not our purpose to investigate private lives but public attitudes. The terms "middle classes" and "bourgeoisie" used throughout this book are troubling in that they refer to diverse groups of the population, from retail merchants to academics and high civil servants. Yet these terms will take on sharper contours through the integrative function which respectability served as against those who did not fit in with society's behavioral norms.

The history of those inside society, of the family, of heterosexual men and women, is by now rather well documented, and I have drawn as much as possible upon this literature. Here I must thank Sterling Fishman in particular for helping to guide me through the material. The history of those on the fringes or outside society is much more difficult to reconstruct. It is a hidden story which is only now in the process of being recaptured. Without the great kindness of James D. Steakley in letting me share some of his vast knowledge, crucial passages of the book dealing with gay and lesbian history—and much more besides—could never have been written. Academic conferences are only too rarely learning experiences, and it is therefore with real pleasure that I acknowledge my debt to the participants in the first International Conference on Gay Studies and Women's Studies at the University of Amsterdam in June 1983.

The importance of Sander L. Gilman's work for my own is reflected in the pages that follow, and so are the conversations I have had with Robert Jay Lifton over the years. Anson Rabinbach deserves thanks for letting me share his knowledge of barely discovered fields of history. I have greatly benefited from discussions with my students in the seminars on the history of sexuality at the University of Wisconsin and the Hebrew University of Jerusalem. Howard Fertig, once again, questioned my argument all the way and thus helped to give the book such clarity as it may possess, while Ann Adelman and Barry Youngerman further refined the text. Marilyn Baumgarten typed and retyped the manuscript with exemplary skill and patience. Regardless of how useful this book may prove to be in advancing historical knowledge, my own work as a historian has been much enriched by becoming familiar with the research of those working at the frontiers in all these aspects of human knowledge.

# Contents

# Illustrations

(following page 96)

1. *The Consequences of Masturbation* (1830), painted for Dr. R. L. Rozier's *Des Habitudes Secrets.* From Albert Moll, *Handbuch der Sexualwissenschaften* (Leipzig, 1921).
2. *Queen Luise Surrounded by Her Children* (1808). Reproduced as a postcard, "Aus grösser Zeit" (n.d.).
3. *Queen Luise and the Future Emperor William I* (1897), by Fritz Schaper. Statue in private collection; picture reproduced in Jutta von Simson, *Fritz Schaper 1841–1919, Materialen zur Kunst der Neunzehnten Jahrhunderts,* Vol. 19 (Munich, 1976), Abb. 25.
4. *Bust of Queen Luise* (1810), by Gottfried Schadow. From Paul Seidel, "Königin Luise im Bild ihrer Zeit," *Hohenzollern Jahrbuch,* Vol. 9 (1905), 148.
5. *Liberty Leading the People at the Barricades* (1830), by Eugène Delacroix. Reprinted by permission of the Musée du Louvre, Paris.
6. *La République,* by Léon Alexandre Delhomme. Reprinted by permission of H. Roger-Viollet, 6 rue de la Seine, Paris.
7. *Germania* (1835), by Philipp Veit. Reprinted by permission of the Städelsches Kunstinstitut und Städtische Gallerie, Frankfurt-am-Main.
8. *The German Woman at War.* Postcard issued by the Bavarian Committee for Volunteer Nurses (n.d.)
9. *Monument to the Fallen,* by Menfer. Monument at the University of Bonn; picture from: *Deutscher Ehrenhain, für die Helden von 1914/18* (Leipzig, 1931).

# Nationalism
and Sexuality

## CHAPTER I

# Introduction: Nationalism and Respectability

## I

This book is concerned with perceptions of sexuality, but also with the state and the nation. It seeks to trace the relationship between nationalism, the most powerful ideology of modern times, and respectability, a term indicating "decent and correct" manners and morals, as well as the proper attitude toward sexuality. The respectabilities we now take for granted, the manners, morals, and sexual attitudes normative in Europe ever since the emergence of modern society, have a history in which nationalism played a crucial role. Ideals that we may regard as immutable were novel some two hundred years ago, and just as modern nationalism emerged in the eighteenth century, so the ideal of respectability and its definition of sexuality fell into place at the same time.

Setting modern attitudes toward behavior and the human body in perspective may help to explain why these attitudes have lasted so long, meeting all challenges; and here nationalism gave essential support and much needed sustenance. Analyzing the relationship between nationalism and respectability involves tracing the development of some of the most important norms that have informed our society: ideals of manliness, which will loom so large in these pages; and their effect on the place of women; and insiders who accepted the norms, as compared to the outsiders, those considered abnormal or diseased. Analyzing the history of sexuality in the context of the concerns of respectability and the preoccupations of nationalism can help us to realize where we stand, how we got there, and how we might change.

Within the developing framework of nationalism and respectability, sexuality will be our special concern because it is basic to human behavior and preoccupied the moral concern of respectability. But it also informed aesthetic sensibilities; ideals of human beauty and ugliness stood at the boundaries of erotic passion. Throughout the following pages we seek to show how concepts of sexuality haunted bourgeois society and nationalism, to be acknowledged yet curbed, deflected from the physical onto an ideal stereotype of male and female beauty.

Our study concentrates upon Germany, partly because here we witness the ultimate consequences of trying to direct and control human sexuality: the concerted effort under National Socialism to regenerate respectability. But we shall also be concerned with England, providing important parallels and contrasts to Germany. Both of these nations were Protestant powers, and the overriding importance of the eighteenth-century Protestant revival—whether in the form of Pietism or Evangelicalism—for the history of respectability cannot be ignored. To be sure, respectability eventually spread throughout Europe; a bourgeois movement at first, it soon encompassed all classes of the population. Yet it seems proper to make a beginning by examining the relationship between respectability and nationalism in those two nations that led the way to an alliance between them, an alliance that regarded control over sexuality as vital to the concept of respectability, indeed, to the very existence of bourgeois society. At times other nations, France and Italy, for example, will be drawn into the argument wherever this seems appropriate. Moreover, toward the end of our story England will recede into the background and Italy will come to the fore. National Socialism, which provided the climax to the alliance of nationalism and respectability, must be seen against the background of fascism rather than against that of a nation that refused to join in this experience.

Our discussion has been deliberately narrowed in order to obtain a better focus: from the history of respectability and nationalism in all its ramifications to the more specific relationship of that history to sexuality and to the human body; from all of Europe to Germany and England, with some examples taken from France and Italy. By such specific analysis we can better assess the actual functioning of sexuality in society, and also the role which nationalism played in the development and maintenance of bourgeois respectability.

That modern nationalism emerged at a certain point in history—the late eighteenth and early nineteenth centuries—is generally recognized, but the history of respectability has only recently received attention. Yet manners and morals, as well as sexual norms, are part of the historical process; in fact, they changed markedly during this very age. We must appreciate the relativity of such values in order to understand how they came to be allied with nationalism. What one regards as normal or abnormal behavior, sexual or otherwise, is a product of historical development, not universal law. Thus, for example, it has recently been shown that homosexuality was tolerated and even respected among important and influential circles in the early Middle Ages, and only later considered dangerous to Church and state.[1] Even during the eighteenth century the pederastic encounter between a priest and a young boy could provide material for comedy.[2] By the start of the nineteenth century, however, readers would not have been amused, but would have insisted that the priest was sick and must be punished.

The word of God itself was not immune to change. In 1782, Sarah Kirby Trimmer, an English lady who was concerned with the Christian upbringing of children, edited the Bible in order to bring it in line with the new ideal of respectability, and others soon followed.[3] The term "to bowdlerize" entered the English language at that time, meaning the expurgation of books by omitting or modifying parts considered indelicate. Thomas Bowdler himself edited the *Family Shakespeare* (1818) in such a manner as to omit all those passages "which cannot with propriety be read aloud in a family." After all, "Shakespeare had gratified the bad taste of the age in which he lived," was himself untutored, and thus at times gave way to "unbridled fancy." So Hamlet's question to Ophelia, "Lady, shall I lie in your lap?" was expurgated and in its place a stage direction substituted that told Hamlet to lie down at Ophelia's feet. Obviously, Lucio's lines from *Measure for Measure* had to go: "a little more leniency to lechery would do no harm . . . it is impossible to extinguish quite . . . til eating and drinking be put down."[4]

Only two centuries ago, customs that we now view with incredulity prevailed among the aristocracy, and not among that class alone. For example, at Holkham, the country seat of the earls of Leicester, ennobled in the eighteenth century, the chamberpots sit in a cupboard in the dining room. They are now merely a tourist attraction, but barely two hundred years ago they would have been used during dinner, perhaps more regularly than the knife and fork. But then, during that same dinner—say toward the end of the eighteenth century—a true gentleman in some aristocratic circles would have been expected to fondle the bosom of his beautiful female partner.[5]

To be sure, there were always conventional standards of behavior. But the respectability that determines modern ideas of sexuality is based on attitudes not generally accepted before the last century. The concept of respectability was itself part of new ways of regarding the human body and sexuality that triumphed only during the nineteenth century.

Manners are not always based upon attitudes toward sexuality, and many of those manners that were said to civilize man developed apart from sexual patterns of behavior. It would be difficult to connect the evolution of table manners, say, and even courtesy, to the history of sexuality. But respectability came to rule behavior patterns in all these areas, and was based on a consistent attitude toward the human body, its sensuous qualities and its sexual functions. "Decency" referred to table manners and decorum as well as to modesty, purity, and the practice of virtue. Thus manners and morals cannot be separated. Both were intrinsic aspects of man's control over his sexual passions.

Modern manners and morals, as we shall soon show, were to a large extent the products of late seventeenth- and eighteenth-century religious revivals. What Norbert Elias has called the "civilizing process" had begun to evolve long before,[6] as feudal society changed to court society and the middle classes began to assert themselves. But this process was greatly accelerated by the rise of Pietism in Germany and Evangelicalism in England. The refinement of court society had prepared the way for modern manners, more at the table than in sexual behavior; but they became a way of life only during the religious awakening.

This climax coincided with the triumph of the middle classes and proved congenial to their needs and fears. The middle classes can only be partially defined by their economic activity and even by their hostility to the aristocracy and the lower classes alike. For side by side with their economic activity it was above all the ideal of respectability which came to characterize their style of life.

Through respectability, they sought to maintain their status and self-respect against both the lower classes and the aristocracy. They perceived their way of life, based as it was upon frugality, devotion to duty, and restraint of the passions, as superior to that of the "lazy" lower classes and the profligate aristocracy. Thus, the definition of the bourgeoisie used in this book arises out of the growth of respectability itself, which in interaction with their economic dynamic, their fears and hopes, created a lifestyle that first became largely their own and eventually that of all settled and ordered society. Although the evolution of respectability had begun long before, as we noticed, the religious revivals of the eighteenth century played a crucial part in locking it into place for that time and for the future as well.

In fact, the libertinage of court society served Pietists and Evangelicals as a foil to the pure and chaste behavior they preached. Catholic moral theology had always condemned excess, but even while so doing, it judged the individual sexual act rather than drawing consequences for an entire personality or way of life. Such moral theology focused upon those sexual acts which hindered human reproduction—the wasting of male sperm or abortion. These were deadly sins, while other expressions of sexuality were treated with greater leniency and understanding.[7] Protestantism had split into many national and religious components during and after the Reformation, components by no means agreed on that strictness of moral purpose which had informed the rebellion against the papacy. The Protestant religious revival of the eighteenth and early nineteenth century changed all that, and returned to Protestantism a moral fervor which united Lutherans, Anglicans, and Calvinists against an unregenerate world. Evangelicalism and Pietism did not include all, or perhaps even most of the Protestants in their nations; but through their dynamic appeal to the middle classes, they managed to change the moral climate in England and in the Protestant north of Germany.

Behavior was an expression of inward piety—that moderation and control over the passions which the religious revival proclaimed and which fitted so well the lifestyle of the middle classes. Thus, August Hermann Francke, a founder of German Pietism, warned students in 1722 to shun idle conversation and curiosity on their travels in order to remove all pretext for scandal. Indecent posture and gestures were to be avoided, as well as unnecessary laughter.[8] Most forms of profane entertainment and personal ornamentation were condemned. Equally, English Evangelicalism was imbued with a deep sense of the sacredness of all ordinary relations and common duties of life. Sexual relations between men and women were stripped of sensuousness; marriage and the family were to be based on the joint practice of piety.[9] Sins, real or imagined, were to be atoned through single-minded concentration on one's vocation in life. John Wesley taught men to look into their own hearts in order to find those truths and values which contemporary society had forgotten. Evangelicalism provided an intensely emotional ethical code for much of the English nation, and Pietism performed the identical function for Lutheran Germany.[10]

The French Revolution reinforced this moral and religious revival, for it was seen by many Englishmen and Germans as the judgment of God upon the profligate ways of the nobility. The Annual Register of London observed in 1798 that "The French Revolution illustrates the connection between good morals and the proper order and peace of society more than all the eloquence of the pulpit and the disquisition of moral philosophers have done for many centuries."[11] "The French Revolution," we read in The Public Ledger of 1816, "with all its constant horrors, was preceded by a total revolution of decency and morality. . . ."[12]

The wars against the French Revolution and Napoleon were waged on behalf of patriotism and morality, both of which determined the direction of the new national self-consciousness. English Evangelicals writing anti-Jacobin pamphlets castigated supporters of France as enemies of Church, state, and morals. English ballads written during the wars which failed to mention king and country were reprimanded as "impious and indecent."[13] The wars unleashed purity crusades, meant to support the war, stop revolution at home, and spread the Evangelical gospel at one and the same time. This even though in some of these crusades the Evangelicals were a minority.[14]

In Germany, the national consciousness sparked by the wars of liberation against Napoleon was also linked to an improvement of morals. Thus the poet Theodor Körner called upon Germans to recapture that morality which the loose-living French had corrupted. The symbol of Prussia defeated by Napoleon was Queen Luise, exemplifying virginity and purity. After her death in 1810 she was regarded as a secular saint, her death mask stylized into a picture of the Madonna (see plate 4). New ideals of manliness and virility destined to play a vital role in the development of ideas about sexuality and respectability spread the message that things Germanic were inseparable from middle-class morality. Here, as we shall see, during the wars of the French Revolution, the ideal of manliness came into its own. And Ernst Moritz Arndt, the prophet of German nationalism, returning from the Battle of Leipzig (1813) against Napoleon, exclaimed—with an emphasis worthy of note—"I return from a bloody quarrel fought out among men (*Ich komm aus blutigem Männerstreit*)."[15]

The reality of the French Revolution was quite different from the imputation of vice by its enemies. The Jacobins were in fact puritans, not easily distinguished in this respect from Evangelicals and Pietists. St. Just proclaimed that republics are forms of government based upon virtue. Prostitution and pornography were prosecuted, for the Jacobins believed that the elimination of vice was an integral part of the defense of the Revolution and the nation. To be just, as Robespierre told his fellow citizens, meant to be stern, and he condemned his enemies, the Girondins, as a political sect "which wants nothing but happiness and is dedicated only to pleasure."[16] True, the Jacobins, unlike their foreign adversaries, stood within the tradition of the Enlightenment; but while that tradition refused to regard the entire human body with shame,[17] it nevertheless drew a sharp line between virtue and vice, normal and abnormal behavior. The Jacobins even dropped their initial attempt to legislate equality for illegitimate children.[18] Marianne as Liberty, the symbol of the Revolution, at first portrayed partially undressed, soon became fully clothed and serene (see plates 5 and 6). The Revolution was itself a stage in the rooting of respectability in France, just as by revulsion against it the Revolution encouraged the practice of virtue among its enemies.

Romanticism also made its contribution to the establishment of respectability. The romantic rebirth of the medieval ideal put forward an image of order to set against the chaos of modernity. Sir Walter Scott defined chivalry as individual freedom in the service of the social order. Through its loyalty, its heroism, and its manner and morals, "chivalry distinguishes the gentle knight from the churl or the savage."[19] Here was an example of an age when society with its manners and morals was still intact—romantics confused their own concept of respectability with the customs of a more primitive time. Loyalty to the state was for Sir Walter Scott an integral part of chivalry, kept alive through colorful ritual and the charisma of monarchy.[20] Rebecca, the heroine of Scott's *Ivanhoe* (1820), a book read with equal interest in England and Germany, defended both her womanly virtue and her personal dignity, while the popular example of Robin Hood remained loyal to the true king and repulsed the usurper. Here virtue, personal dignity, and loyalty exemplified a coherent order of the kind to which the bourgeoisie aspired, and one that was constantly endangered by outsiders who rejected both respectability and an ordered society. Romanticism, through such medieval imagery, reinforced the onslaught of respectability, whose driving force was the religious revivals and the French Revolution working within the imperatives of the new bourgeois society.

Respectability became entrenched during the first decades of the new century. It triumphed within the life span of one generation. Harold Nicholson has recounted that in the second decade of the nineteenth century, Sir Walter Scott's great aunt felt ashamed to read a book "which sixty years ago I have heard read aloud for larger circles, consisting of the first and most creditable society in London."[21] The free flow of passion and fantasy in the exuberant English novels of the previous century was now seen as symbolic of the threat to the existing order of things: "Good society hates scenes, vetoes every eccentricity of manners and demonstrativeness of demeanor as bad form."[22]

The triumph so quickly won proved enduring. In his summation at the trial of Oscar Wilde for sodomy at the end of the nineteenth century, the judge pointed out that while, as far as he knew, neither Sir Walter Scott nor Charles Dickens had ever written a single offensive line, there were eighteenth-century novels which were painful for persons of modesty and decency to read.[23] Respectability was now taken for granted, and Oscar Wilde was not to be its only victim. Ford Madox Ford, that superb observer of English society, wrote in 1913, as the Victorian age was supposedly drawing to a close, that "society . . . can exist only if the normal, if the virtuous, and the slightly deceitful flourish, and if the passionate, the headstrong, and the too-truthful are condemned to suicide and madness."[24] The First World War was to change little: the ideal of respectability continued to inform society as it had for Sir Walter Scott's great aunt, oblivious of Ford's irony and regard for the bitter truth.

Respectability had first accompanied the triumphant bourgeoisie and served to legitimize and define the middle classes as against the lower classes and the aristocracy. In the nineteenth century, it was to serve the needs of a class seeking stability amid changes it had itself initiated. The travails of industrialization seemed unending; so did the need to keep control in a nervous age, to find firm structures for a bewildering world. Again and again we will find men and women reaching out to grasp a "slice of eternity," whether embodied in nature, the nation, or religious belief, in order to counteract "the vibrations of modernity."[25] The nineteenth-century struggle to control sex—beyond those controls already attempted by the various churches—was part of a larger effort to cope with the ever more obvious results of industrialization and political upheaval.

In order to establish controls, to impose restraint and moderation, society needed to reinforce the practical techniques of physicians, educators, and police. But their methods had to be informed by an ideal if they were to be effective, to support normality and contain sexual passions. In most timely fashion, nationalism came to the rescue. It absorbed and sanctioned middle-class manners and morals and played a crucial part in spreading respectability to all classes of the population, however much these classes hated and despised one another. Nationalism helped respectability to meet all challenges to its dominance, enlarging its parameters when necessary while keeping its essence intact. We shall discuss later the most serious challenge to respectability before the First World War: the revolt of the younger bourgeois generation. The crucial role of nationalism in helping to meet and redirect such challenges is one of the main reasons why the manners and morals which triumphed at the beginning of the nineteenth century have endured so long.

Nationalism is perhaps the most powerful and effective ideology of modern times, and its alliance with bourgeois morality forged an engine difficult to stop. In its long career, it attempted to co-opt most of the important movements of the age, to absorb all that men thought meaningful and held dear even while holding fast to certain unchanging myths and symbols. It reached out to liberalism, conservatism, and socialism; it advocated both tolerance and repression, peace and war—whatever served its purpose. Through its claim to immutability, it endowed all that it touched with a "slice of eternity." But however flexible, nationalism hardly wavered in its advocacy of respectability.

The two histories thus become enmeshed. Nationalism helped control sexuality, yet also provided the means through which changing sexual attitudes could be absorbed and tamed into respectability. In addition, it assumed a sexual dimension of its own, coming to advocate a stereotype of supposedly "passionless" beauty for both men and women. The aesthetics of nationalism and respectability will occupy us at some length, for the nineteenth century was an ever more visually centered age, when attitudes toward society and the nation were often expressed in aesthetic terms.

The alliance between nationalism and respectability was forged, and its fate determined, from the very beginning, when both were emerging as the eighteenth century drew to a close and maturing in the few decades that followed. That it was indeed an alliance, and not a complete merger, must be made clear from the start. Each of the concepts had its own separate origins and identities before the two joined forces for mutual support. In fact, one strand of nationalism, which aimed to revitalize politics and society, persistently sought to modify respectability. But while we shall refer to this point of view from time to time, its force, at least in western and central Europe, was soon spent after the revolutions of 1848.

The distinction between normality and abnormality was basic to modern respectability; it provided the mechanism that enforced control and ensured security. We shall see how medical definitions of normal and abnormal sexuality accompanied the rise of respectability, and how those distinctions which had been used rather more loosely by Christian moral theology became firm and unbending matters of sickness and health. To a large extent the physician took over from the clergy as the keeper of normalcy. It is not atypical that Thomas Bowdler himself, who began his career by expurgating Shakespeare in 1818, was both a doctor and an Evangelical. The appearance and character of each individual was classified as normal or abnormal: nervousness was supposedly induced by the practice of vice, while virility and manly bearing were signs of virtue. Nationalism adopted this ideal of manliness and built its national stereotypes around it.

Sexual intoxication of any kind was viewed as both unmanly and inherently antisocial. Those who could not control their passions were either considered abnormal to begin with or would inevitably drift into abnormality. Richard von Krafft-Ebing exemplified the attitudes prevailing by the end of the nineteenth century: if the normally constituted civilized being was not capable of mastering his sexual urges as soon as they came into conflict with the demands of society, then family and state, the foundations of the legal and moral order, would cease to exist.[26] Nationalism reinforced such control by redirecting men's passions to a higher purpose and by projecting a stereotype of human beauty which supposedly transcended sensuousness.

Masturbation was thought to be the root cause of all loss of control, indeed, of abnormal passion in general. It was said to reflect an over-heated imagination, inimical to bourgeois sobriety, and was supposed to induce nervousness and loss of energy. Not only did it put forward a stereotype opposed to all that was manly and virile, or womanly and chaste, but masturbation was considered an antisocial act. The masturbator practices a lonely vice, we hear over and over again; he loves no one and is dead to the call of family, nation, and humanity.[27] If masturbation became common, it would "menace the future of modern societies; therefore, it is urgently necessary for us to try to extirpate this public calamity."[28] Moreover, the masturbator's presumed passion for secrecy, it was asserted, easily led him to practice homosexuality, another secret vice thought to be flourishing in the dark recesses of the city. That one abnormality led to another was common wisdom supported by the medical profession; masturbation even brought on various forms of insanity.[29] Worse yet, the love of secrecy and the practice of vice not only made men and women outsiders in respectable society but was a danger to the security of the state. At a time when conspiracy theories of history were popular, the masturbator was viewed as a readymade conspirator against the state.

The evil of masturbation was, in fact, one of the principal themes of a privately owned wax museum opened in Paris in 1775 by Jean François Bertrand-Rival (also simply known as J. F. Bertrand) which lasted into the first decade of the nineteenth century. This graphically documented what was to become a general prejudice: that masturbators, like those infected with venereal disease, were pale, hollow-eyed, weak of body and spirit—the antithesis of the emerging national stereotype. They were alien to the ideals of manly combat and social conquest.[30] Recommending his museum to the protection of Napoleon, Bertrand saw marriage and the family as the chief bulwark against vice, licentiousness and disease being spread by "vicious bachelors."[31] In pursuit of modesty and decency, his watchwords, he refused to spare the sensibilities of the school-children who visited his museum. Most of the figures were portrayed as near death, exhausted by masturbation or an excess of sexual pleasure. One young masturbator was shown to have lost his penis, while the waxen image of a young woman's ulcerous vagina was meant as a warning against unquenchable sexual appetite. The museum was a success, at least with the headmasters of some of Paris's most prestigious schools, even though at one time vandals destroyed all of the figures.[32] This then was the first "museum of respectability," a fit introduction to a visually centered age. Not only does it point to a restrictive sexual morality, but the underlying principle that guided Bertrand in exhibiting his collection of figures exemplified the way in which bourgeois youth was introduced to the new-found morality of its elders. Youthful passions, so Bertrand tells us, "are better contained by the image of horrible sickness, than by the pleasant picture of health."[33] Moral terror was to accompany the rise of respectability.

Few had paid attention to masturbation before 1760, when Dr. Simon André Tissot's L'Onanisme pointed out its supposed dangers. Voltaire popularized Tissot, and Rousseau joined in the chorus.[34] Tissot's book was translated into English (1772), where it superseded Dr. Bekker's Onania, or the Heinous Sin of Self Pollution (1710), originally published in London, a book whose warnings had gone largely unheard. Tissot himself was one of the most distinguished physicians of his time, teaching medicine at the universities of Lausanne and Pavia, advocating inoculation against smallpox, a new and controversial medical practice, and writing popular medical tracts stressing the importance of personal hygiene. Fighting against masturbation, he appealed to the harmony of nature instead of biblical examples.[35]

Tissot was a Deist, a man of the Enlightenment, himself a fervent admirer of Rousseau. Man is created virtuous by God, and each individual must heed His call. This entailed sexual restraint as well as upholding the sanctity of marriage and the family. The masturbator, according to Tissot, threatened the division between the sexes: he was pale, effeminate, devoid of energy. The "natural harmony" which the Enlightenment advocated in this instance supported the ideal of respectability.[36]

A French physician, R. L. Rozier, summed up the viewpoint of men of science abreast of their time at the turn of the eighteenth

and nineteenth centuries when he wrote that "morality and humanity demand protection [against the vice of masturbation] and
medicine has to respond to their wishes"[37] (see plate 1). Vice and
virtue became a matter of health and sickness. To remain healthy
entailed a willingness to follow the dictates of nature, which supported the new respectability. Sickness was a consequence of crimes
against nature, which if they could not be cured, must lead to decline and death. The Enlightenment and the science of medicine
sharpened the distinction between vice and virtue, insider and outsider, which the religious revival had also encouraged.

During the early nineteenth century, the normal and abnormal
were irrevocably fixed—each encompassing a set of morals, manners, looks, and intellectual qualities. The antithesis of abnormality could be found in the new national stereotypes. The manly Englishman or German showed the restraint and self-control so dear
to the middle class. Manliness meant freedom from sexual passion,
the sublimation of sensuality into leadership of society and the nation. A renewed emphasis on masculinity had been part of both the
Evangelical and the Pietistic revivals. John Wesley, for example, believed that only true men could express that gravity which symbolized the solemnity of the spirit.[38] This ideal of masculinity was
reinforced by the wars against Napoleon. In Germany, virility was
exalted by the fraternity movement and the Gymnasts, both movements of national renewal directed against the French occupation
of Prussia, both supposedly distinguished by emphasis upon the
beauty of body as well as physical prowess. Manliness was not just
a matter of courage, it was a pattern of manners and morals. Masculine comportment and a manly figure exemplified the transcendence of the so-called lower passions.

Manliness as an outward symbol of the inner spirit had medieval
roots in the ideals of knighthood, whose symbols were employed in
daily speech, defining male attitudes toward women, as well as in
the popular culture surrounding modern wars. Chivalry in battle
was a sign of national superiority.[39] But above all, manliness was
based upon the Greek revival which accompanied and comple-
mented the onslaught of respectability and the rise of modern
nationalism.

Greek sculpture as described by J. J. Winckelmann in his *Geschichte der kunst des Altertums* (*History of Ancient Art*, 1774)
was the model. Lithe and supple figures, muscular and harmo-

nious, became the symbols of masculinity, the nation, and its youth. But the beauty of Greek sculpture was considered a sexless beauty. The very whiteness of the figures, which Winckelmann had stressed, was supposed to strip them of sensuousness, as Walter Pater tells us later in the nineteenth century. Winckelmann, to cite Pater once more, linked physical beauty with serenity.[40] There is no connection, a French commentator of the period tells us, between perfect beauty and the desire to perform sexual acts with such beauty. He cites Winckelmann, the poet August von Platen, and Michelangelo as authorities for this view;[41] in fact, all three were homosexuals, but their sexuality although quite well known at the time, was ignored in order to use their ideal of beauty. There is some irony in the fact that Winckelmann, the homosexual, made Greek art fit for the middle classes and supplied the model for the male national stereotype. Yet what could better represent the supposed immutability of morals and of the nation than the noble simplicity and quiet greatness he saw in Greek art?

Such a concept of beauty stripped youth of passion. Many writers in England, Germany, and France at the turn of the eighteenth and nineteenth centuries were fascinated by the newly rediscovered statue of Laocoon being strangled by snakes. Here was a singular example of self-restraint, calm in the face of unbearable pain. Such a figure, these writers tell us, transcends the individual and his passions. Winckelmann summed up his idea of Greek beauty in lines actually written about a Greek torso, but applicable to all classical sculpture: "The quiet and repose of the body reveals the lofty and harmonious spirit of he who braves the greatest dangers for the sake of justice, who provides for his country's defense and brings peace to its subjects."[42] Friedrich Schiller in his influential *Über die ästhetische Erziehung des Menschen* (*The Aesthetic Education of Mankind*, 1795) praised such beauty for ennobling the sexual act, otherwise merely instinctive, and saw in classical beauty the consummation of man's humanity.[43]

The Greek ideal which fascinated these men was abstract and generalized, fit to become a symbol. Winckelmann had encouraged such abstraction by asserting that the absence of any individual or accidental traits was essential to the beauty of Greek sculpture.[44] Yet this symbol did not go unchallenged, for the nakedness of Greek sculpture might undermine respectability. For example, while Hegel praised the classical ideal of beauty as uniting body and mind, he held that it must be cleansed of sensuality by covering the sex organs and other potentially prurient parts of the body.[45]

Historicity, too, was involved in the argument about what classical beauty might represent. Herder, with his commitment to historicity as part of the awakening national consciousness, wrote that Greek artists "did not know how we [i.e., Germans] existed in the past, in what historical period we lived, and what it was that gave us the miserable notion that we wanted to live in a different period, among a different people [i.e., the Greeks] and different sky."[46] Friedrich Schlegel put it plainly when he wrote that national consciousness was the sine qua non of all art.

The reply of Goethe and other champions of Winckelmann was that the purpose of art was to represent mankind.[47] Classical beauty transformed the individual into a universally valid and immutable symbol. Thus, when a monument to General Blücher, who had played a crucial role in Napoleon's defeat, was to be erected, Goethe wanted it to represent a naked Hercules, while Christian Rauch proposed to show the figure in contemporary garb. Rauch won out in this case by appealing to the German national consciousness. "Classical imitations," he wrote, "seem to have nothing in common with us."[48] Yet despite the popular appeal to history, in a century which unlike the Enlightenment was preoccupied with its roots, Germanic symbols never managed to obliterate the appeal of the ancients. The reason for the survival and strength of classical symbols is not difficult to explain, for while historical symbols were necessary in order to arouse national self-consciousness, the nation had to annex a "slice of eternity" in order to take on the appearance of an immutable force that could provide security and shelter. The classics for one served this purpose well.

The historical dimensions of nationalism found many forms of symbolic expression, from books and paintings to ceremonial and folk dancing.[49] The Gothic element played an important role in this symbolism, and medieval figures like the "Bamberger Reiter" (the horseman guarding the Cathedral of Bamberg) remained exemplary of the German soul. But the Greek model also occupied a crucial place in national self-representation, inspiring, for example, the design of many national monuments and, significantly for our argument, providing the stereotype of the ideal German male. Women, as we shall see, were represented through medieval symbols rather than by the lofty and harmonious spirit of Greece. The nakedness of Greek male sculpture as part of national self-representation did not cease to be troubling, and its latent threat to respectability will occupy us throughout this book. A comment by the art historian Wilhelm Lübke made in 1869 was generally accepted not only for sculpture but for some painting as well: ". . . just as sculpture must recall the reality of flesh and blood, it must rid [the figure] of all accidents of individuality in order to give the work the stamp of a higher purpose . . . because of this aim the human body will always appear in a noble and lofty nakedness."[50]

This ideal of classical beauty was co-opted by nationalism, just as nationalism would annex many other political movements and philosophies over the years. The nation was attempting to provide symbols with which the people could identify. The national flag, the national anthem, the national monuments all date from the beginning of the nineteenth century, and so do the male and female national stereotypes. Such national symbols were part of the urge to see and touch, to participate in a reality that was becoming ever more complex and bewildering. The visual self-representation of the nation was just as important as the much cited literature of nationalism.

The nation protected the ideal of beauty from the lower passions of man and helped transform it into a symbol of self-control and purity. The national stereotype and the middle-class stereotype were identical. In the case of the female, the stereotype, whether Germania or Marianne, easily conformed in matters of respectability to the Madonna-like ideal associated with Queen Luise of Prussia.[51] The beautiful male was more troubling: modeled upon Greek sculpture, he was potentially a homoerotic symbol. Masculinity provided the norm for society; its symbol had to send out clear and unambiguous signals. Therefore, nationalism tried to exorcise homoeroticism from masculine beauty and to make it respectable. It also attempted to absorb all the latently erotic aspects of personal relationships among men, as the history of friendship will show us.

Nationalism and respectability assigned everyone his place in life, man and woman, normal and abnormal, native and foreigner; any confusion between these categories threatened chaos and loss of control. The clear and distinct roles assigned to men and women were basic—they will occupy us throughout our study. John Wesley, typically enough, had already expressed this division through his stereotypes of men and women. Masculinity meant depth and seriousness, while the feminine was shallow and often frivolous.[52] The fate of the image of the hermaphrodite or androgyne (part man and part woman) during the nineteenth century is the most startling illustration of the importance of fixed and unchanging sex roles as part of the fabric of society and the nation. In the first half century, the androgyne was still being praised as a public symbol of human unity. But by the end of the century the image, with its confusion of sex roles, had turned into a monster, so that young Aubrey Beardsley, the artist, could use it in that way in order to shock English middle-class sensibilities.[53] In 1903, Otto Weininger, in his much read *Geschlecht und Charakter* (*Sex and Character*), made confusion of sex roles the cutting edge of his anti-Semitism. Jews behaved like women rather than men, being unable to control their passions. The same accusation was popularly leveled against other outsiders, as well as against those whose behavior and sexual practices were considered abnormal.[54]

Alongside the idealization of masculinity as the foundation of the nation and society, woman, often accused of shallowness and frivolity, was at the same time idealized as the guardian of morality, and of public and private order. "Establishing order and quiet in a man's family," we hear at the end of the eighteenth century, "is a better means of keeping a husband than good looks."[55] As a national symbol, woman was the guardian of the traditional order. Always, women exemplified virtue. Dr. R. L. Rozier summed up this function of the feminine image when he wrote that beauty and decency cannot be separated in a woman, and the fact that he made this comment in his *Lettres Medicales et Morales* (*Medical and Moral Letters*, 1822) brings to mind once more the medical sanction of morality.[56] Samuel Richardson's virtuous *Pamela* (1740), obsessed with her chastity, always moralizing, influenced not only England but Germany as well.[57]

Woman was not confined to the family, yet the roles assigned to her were conceived of as passive rather than active. She was to be a guardian, protector, and mother. Bertrand, whose museum provides such a good example of the rooting of respectability, put it graphically: strength is a manly prerogative, while women must exemplify beauty and decorum.[58] Man was active and woman passive, and the two roles must not be confused. Such sentiments will be often repeated throughout these pages; they would have sounded absurd to the aristocratic women of the eighteenth century, for many of whom beauty meant license. That a man allowed his body to be used like that of a woman was part of the traditional attack on homosexuality,[59] now reinforced by the emphasis on manliness and virility as symbols of respectability.

Woman as a national symbol was the guardian of the continuity and immutability of the nation, the embodiment of its respectability. It is significant that the poets of the German wars of liberation against Napoleon took Hermann or Arminius as their symbol rather than Germania. The German who had defeated the Roman Legions was an apt symbol for those who "fought among men," as Arndt had put it, at a time when the modern ideal of manliness was being born. Germania was often depicted with a medieval castle above her head, draped in long robes, looking backward into the past, while Britannia, dressed in armor, evoked antiquity (see plate 7). Both were usually seated. If Marianne was scantily dressed during the French Revolution and again in 1830 leading the mob in Delacroix's famous painting, as soon as she became a national symbol she covered herself in chaste and acceptable fashion (see plates 5 and 6). Family ideal and public symbol reinforced one another.

The triumph of the nuclear family, reflected so well by Bertrand, coincided with the rise of nationalism and respectability. The intimate modern family developed in the eighteenth century, superseding older ideas of kinship. This family remained patriarchal, as the institution of marriage was strengthened through compulsory church weddings and registration. The nuclear family did encourage sentimental bonds between men and women, for marriage was no longer looked upon as principally a commercial transaction, while at the same time it defined their roles more sharply than in the larger unit defined by kinship (which continued to prevail in the countryside). Industrialization and the division of labor were crucial here, for no longer were business and home under one roof. The mistress of the house who had made accounts, dealt with apprentices, or sold wares now only supervised the domestic staff.[60] The distance between the place of work and the home became a sign of prestige. By the end of the century, Theodor Fontane writing in 1892 made the garden between the Treibels' villa and the factory a symbol of bougeois pretension. The nuclear family kept order by assigning to each member his or her own place.

Domesticity characterized the ideal modern family, the "warm nest" into which one could retreat from the pressures of the outside world. In 1839 the novelist Bertold Auerbach wrote that family celebrations should replace purely religious festivals.[61] But families were not really as self-contained as all that, and the saying that a man's home is his castle was never more than a pious wish. The state reached in to regulate marriage and divorce. True, a certain reluctance to intervene in the most private recesses of family life was illustrated by the failure to pass an incest law in England until 1908, though in Germany the state had few scruples.[62] Yet formal legislation tells us little about the true function of the family as one of society's policemen of sexuality. That this function was in fact exercised on children is quite clear. The whole system of education both inside and outside the family had become geared to the teaching of virtue and the avoidance of vice, as so-called character-building and the inculcation of respectability for the most part took priority over book learning. The disciplinary function of the father seems central to the maintenance of hierarchy and order in the family and thus of respectability. It is relevant to recall that in the eighteenth century a father's curse upon a wayward child was thought to bring about that child's physical and mental ruin. Restif de La Bretonne in 1779 wrote the "history of a man whom the curse of his father plunged into libertinage."[63] As a rule, the curse was exercised upon that son or daughter who failed to choose an approved partner in marriage or who had deviated from acceptable sexual norms.

Although we know too little about the strengths and weaknesses of this policing function, it saw to it that respectability was not threatened. The many bowdlerized "Family Shakespeares" and "Family Bibles" appeared during the very period when the nuclear family was becoming dominant. They were designed to preserve middle-class life from temptation. The family gave support from below to that respectability which the nation attempted to enforce from above.

National ideals must have penetrated the family as well, although again we know very little about this process. Just how the father used appeals to nationalism in order to strengthen his patriarchal powers we can only glimpse in the novels of the age and the memoirs of those who revolted against such discipline. The family was supposed to mirror state and society; conservatives like W. H. Riehl in his *Die Familie* (*The Family*, 1854) emphasized its hierarchical structure and praised it for maintaining order. Through the rule of the father as patriarch, the family educated its members to respect authority: "the German state will harvest the fruit sown by such a family."[64] Earlier, Friedrich Ludwig Jahn, the founder of the Gymnasts and the fraternity movement, had called the family the fountainhead of the national spirit.[65]

At times, exalted notions of manliness and virility might clash with the family ideal. And in fact the glorification of the community of men, which we shall often encounter, did lead some to the conclusion that society was carried upon the shoulders of unwed males. Nevertheless, the prevailing sentiment was that the family was a cheap and efficient surrogate for the state, controlling the passions at their source. Clearly, the family was the policeman on the beat, an indispensable agent of sexual control as directed by physicians (more often than not, the family doctor), educators, and the nation itself. Any threat to its survival endangered the nation's future. Such fears about the family, and therefore the nation, were closely involved, as we shall see, in the concern over population growth.

## II

Our study concentrates on Germany, using other countries, particularly England, for comparative purposes, and to give an added dimension. The eighteenth-century Protestant revival affected these two countries directly, leaving a unique impact on the tenor of life that other regions did not share; of course, the substance of bourgeois morals and sexuality, which are our concern, spread throughout Europe. The difference in tone between Protestant and Catholic nations was well reflected in the love-hate relationship of so many Germans and Englishmen with the so-called Catholic South. When German writers like Thomas Mann equated the South with sin and immorality, or English popular literature swarmed with "dagos" and "Portuguese" villains, the North–South contrast was merely one more device to shore up respectability. Those who were the prisoners of respectability in the Protestant North projected their forbidden sexual fantasies upon foreign nations and regions. The Catholic South, in reality as respectable as the North, fulfilled this purpose; so did the Arabian Desert and its inhabitants, as we shall see later. "Their spirit is free, their steps are unconfined, the desert is open . . .",[66] so Edward Gibbon idealized the Arabs in his *History of the Decline and Fall of the Roman Empire* (1776–88).

A further distinction between Catholic and Protestant nations involves the national iconography which is so important for our argument. There is a surprising similarity between the English and German national stereotypes, their ideals of masculinity and of the role of women. While these ideas were in all likelihood shared to some degree by Catholic countries as well, they surfaced only occasionally, and must have been less widespread. To be sure, Marianne is similar to Germania or Britannia as the chaste guardian of her nation. But the male stereotype, along with its homoerotic overtones, is more difficult to find in Italy or in France. As no comparative histories of sexuality or national iconography exist, it was necessary to start with two nations that shared an Evangelical tradition and a similar iconography, however great the differences between their respective nationalisms and political structures.

Yet there is one striking difference. Whereas in Germany Pietism had a direct impact upon the inward direction of nationalism, the effect of Evangelicalism on English nationalism was much less direct. But then England was united and powerful while Germany was still struggling for national unity. In any case, it is the similarities that are more striking, for the differences between England and Germany are well enough known; indeed, they have become part of English national myth.

The shared moral heritage of England and Germany, their crusade against the French Revolution, brought to these countries the triumph of respectability as a means of controlling the passions, thereby encouraging ideals of human beauty, friendship, and love that supposedly transcended sexuality. However, the nineteenth century was not untouched by tolerant attitudes commonly associated with more recent times. Indeed, Michel Foucault maintained that the greater freedom of discourse about sexuality in the nineteenth century meant that the era was less obsessed with repressing sexuality than had been thought.[67] From the latter part of the nineteenth century there was certainly more frank talk about sexuality than ever before, and what was considered abnormal penetrated closer to the surface of society. But Foucault's conclusion would have been rejected by those contemporaries who were more often than not frustrated in their fight to wring even a few concessions from society. Furthermore, as we shall see, even feminists, homosexuals, and lesbians proclaimed their adherence to the basic norms and stereotypes of respectability, wanting only to bend the bars of their cage, not to unhinge them.

## CHAPTER 2

# Manliness and
# Homosexuality

## I

The ideal of manliness was basic both to the self-definition of bourgeois society and to the national ideology. Manliness was invoked
to safeguard the existing order against the perils of modernity,
which threatened the clear distinction between what was considered normal and abnormality. Moreover, manliness symbolized the
nation's spiritual and material vitality. It called for strength of body
and mind, but not brute force—the individual's energies had to be
kept under control. The quiet grandeur of Laocoon was the ideal.

Women also played a symbolic role in the national mystique; indeed, they furnished the national symbols like Germania and Marianne. But these female symbols were, as we have seen, sedate
rather than dynamic. They stood for immutability rather than progress, providing the backdrop against which men determined the
fate of nations. The stereotyped embodiment of manliness was
modeled on an ideal of male beauty born in the eighteenth-century
Greek revival, while the image of woman in German or English national iconography was frequently fashioned after traditional portrayals of the Virgin Mary.

Manliness drew upon the aristocratic ideal of knighthood as a
pattern of virtue in a changing world and a model for some of its
behavior. Nevertheless, it was a bourgeois concept. During the
wars of the French Revolution, citizen armies replaced profession-
als, as in England and Germany many middle-class volunteers
rushed to the colors, inspired by love of their nation and a desire to

prove their manhood. This unprecedented phenomenon assured a prominent place for the ideal of manliness in the self-image of the bourgeoisie, just when that class was reaching for power. The poets of the German wars of liberation glorified manliness; and dramas such as those of Klopstock and Kleist about the *Herrmannschlacht* (the victory of Arminius over the Roman Legions) emphasized male strength, dominance, and cruelty.

Manliness, we must remember, reinforced the division of labor which was a requisite of bourgeois society not only in economics but in social and sexual life as well. The roles of the sexes had to be clearly differentiated, while children were assigned a separate sphere of their own. The division of labor within the family and the distinction between masculinity and femininity were perpetually reaffirmed as imperatives of the modern age.

Richardson's *Pamela* had insisted upon such a hierarchy, which was constantly reaffirmed during the German wars of liberation. Some volunteers, among the most articulate, dedicated their swords to Queen Luise of Prussia like knights to their ladies, and Theodor Körner rhymed that those who refused to volunteer would never again be kissed by a German girl, enjoy German song or German wine.[1] The role of women is made perfectly clear, as we shall see later, and this point of view did not change with the passage of time. In 1911, the physician Albert Moll, for all of his sympathy with the movement for women's rights, still lamented that women were becoming increasingly like men and men like women; sexual differentiation had to be maintained if culture was to flourish.[2] And Havelock Ellis, the most tolerant of sexologists, was alarmed to observe that the masculine-feminine dualism was in jeopardy.[3]

The orderly division of labor—and with it a settled family life— were thought to be vital in view of the rapid changes that occurred long before the movement for women's rights, at a time when respectability and modern nationalism were becoming established and the industrial revolution was affecting all of Europe. If the bourgeoisie had created the social dynamic of modernity, it also sought to keep it under control. Respectability, refined in the religious revivals of the eighteenth century, was to be the ideology that held this structure together.

All those who attacked the norms of bourgeois behavior or trespassed beyond the circumscribed limits of male or female activity were considered abnormal—strangers outside the tribe—and judged to be a threat to society. Habitual criminals or so-called sexual perverts belonged to this category, of course, as did foreigners (for many Germans, the French lacked manliness), and Jews, who were sometimes accused of confusing gender roles.

Sexual perversion was thought to be almost as threatening to middle-class life as the restlessness of the lower classes, and much more so than the arrogance of the aristocracy. Homosexuals provide a particularly useful example of how the line between normal and abnormal was to be ever more closely drawn through the rise of respectability and its emphasis upon manliness. They were thought to symbolize not only the confusion of sexes but also sexual excess—the violation of a delicate balance of passion. "The energy that the primitive male animal puts almost solely into sex," Lord Baden-Powell told his young Boy Scouts immediately after the First World War, "in the human, is turned into all sorts of other activities, such as art, science. . . ."[4] The homosexual was, in this context, considered primitive. During the early nineteenth century he was associated with rebellion of all kinds; in England, for example, he was accused of giving aid and comfort to the enemy during the wars of the French Revolution.[5]

It is illuminating to analyze the changing attitude toward "perverts" of the Catholic Church, in contrast to the Protestantism which so largely determined German and English respectability. Catholic theology, in the years before manliness had become so important, had drawn no immutable line between normal and abnormal. Homosexuality was condemned as an act committed against the divine order and therefore against nature. Homosexual acts led to divine retribution, not only rebellions and revolutions, but natural catastrophies such as the destruction of the city of Lot because some of its inhabitants had practiced this unnatural vice. The term "homosexual" derived from medicine and only slowly replaced the traditional "sodomite" during the second half of the nineteenth century. Still, Catholic moral theologians had traditionally emphasized the biological factor of homosexuality, asking if the practice of homosexuality had in its positions imitated heterosexual sexual behavior, what role the man had played in the act (men taking female positions were often punished with greater severity than those who had taken the male position), and, most important, whether the act had been consummated. The Catholic gradation of sin worked here as well, even if within the framework of a general condemnation of this so-called unnatural vice.[6]

Alphonso Maria de Liguori, whose eight-volume *Moral Theology* (1749–53) became normative for father confessors, drew a sharp distinction between mortal and venial sin. In order to determine whether a mortal sin had been committed, Liguori asked whether so-called abnormal sexual acts were performed habitually and whether they were part of a search for pleasure and enjoyment (which, depending on the person's intention, could be a mortal sin) or merely accidental, such as a nightly pollution (which could be forgiven). Masturbation, with its spilling of seed, could be a deadlier sin than homosexuality, provided that this had not been physically consummated.[7] Though Liguori in general agreed with Protestants in his rejection of the nude human body as a temptation to vice, he can be interpreted as refining this general principle of Christianity.[8]

Protestants knew no such distinctions blurring the line between normal and abnormal sex. John Calvin, commenting on the Book of Isaiah's harsh judgment of dissolute and arrogant women, warned that God would punish not only the women and their husbands, but also the state that tolerated such behavior.[9] All sexual acts outside marriage or for purposes other than procreation were unequivocally condemned; it was sinful even to contemplate them. To be sure, Protestantism also practiced casuistry in its practical instructions to men and women on how best to adjust to life in this world. But the Protestant Church's moral realism concerning what the state and its rulers could do contrasted sharply with its unqualified demands on the actions—and thoughts—of the individual. The concept of "holy pretence" or the "good deceit"[10] applied only to public policy, as when, for example, Joshua laid an ambush at God's command in order to save his people.

In 1608 the Puritan William Perkins, taking aim at Catholic casuistry, wrote that for the individual, "whatsoever wanteth conformity to the law of God is sin, whether it be with the consent of will or not."[11] Thus Protestant inflexibility in judging individual behavior had a long tradition by the time Pietism and Evangelicalism emerged to tighten the reins still further. This moral rigor had played a key part in the onslaught of respectability and helped to differentiate the intensity of bourgeois morality between Protestant and Catholic countries. Indeed, Liguori's so-called sexual permissiveness caused great offense in Protestant circles and was cited throughout the nineteenth century in attacks against the Catholic Church. Catholic permissiveness, it was said, was ruining the moral fiber of the German people, and so undermining the well-being of the nation.[12]

Yet by the second half of the nineteenth century, even the Catholic Church had become considerably more rigorous about any form of sexual behavior that could endanger the sanctity of marriage and the family. In Belgium, Catholic bishops issued a declaration against onanism, meaning all forms of *coitus interruptus*, in 1909, an example later followed by other national churches. Catholic bishops in Germany joined the struggle against a declining birth rate—to bear children was both a Christian and a patriotic duty.[13] These stands helped draw a sharper line between normal and abnormal sexuality, although the Catholic Church still displayed somewhat more tolerance in defining actual sinfulness. One orthodox Catholic condemnation of irreligion and the Enlightenment was willing to concede that the pleasures of this world could be enjoyed in moderation.[14]

The stricter Evangelical and Pietist view drew reinforcement from the medical profession. Indeed, as the nineteenth century progressed, it was the doctors who did the most to stimulate awareness of homosexuality as a social concern;[15] to some extent they replaced the ministers of religion as the guardians of normality. "We are responsible," the editor of the English medical journal *The Lancet* proclaimed in 1819, "for the employment of our peculiar authority in promoting the purification and well-being of human society."[16] Toward the end of the nineteenth century one of Proust's homosexual characters summed up the increased role of the medical profession in the policing of sexuality: ". . . my confessor could find nothing to say to me, and my doctor told me that I was insane."[17]

The medical analysis of homosexuality during the nineteenth century helped demarcate a clear boundary between normal and abnormal sexuality. Forensic medicine came to the aid of judges and juries trying to enforce the laws against sodomy by developing a stereotype for use in identifying homosexuals.

If at the beginning of the nineteenth century the Enlightenment had encouraged the decriminalization of homosexuals—the *Code*

*Napoléon* of 1810 punished only the seduction of minors and forcible rape—so toward the end of the century the law was tightened once more. England was never touched by the *Code Napoléon;* there the death penalty for homosexuals was abolished only in 1861, and in Scotland not until 1889. German states like Bavaria followed the example of the *Code* and condemned the confusion between immoral acts committed by individuals and crimes committed against the state. Sexual morality was a private concern as long as it did not interfere with the rights of others. But Prussia, Napoleon's old enemy, did not follow suit; while the death penalty was abolished from 1851 onward, homosexual acts were punished by prison and the loss of civil rights. This Prussian provision became the law of the *Reich* in 1871 after German unification, as paragraph 175 of the new criminal code.

In England the abolition of the death penalty was followed in 1885 by the Criminal Law Amendment, which punished all homosexual acts whether committed in public or private. Such acts were referred to as "gross indecencies," which gave wide latitude to judges. The tightening of laws was justified in England as in Prussia not on religious but on secular grounds. Though medicine might no longer justify the punishment of homosexuals, the people's sense of justice demanded it.[18]

But medicine did in fact justify the criminalizing of homosexuality, as the Church had done previously. It attempted to identify offenders for the law courts and judges. And this medical construct of homosexuality came in turn to determine how society itself perceived the homosexual. The developing stereotype drew elements from earlier notions about sexual deviance. According to Tissot's *L'Onanisme,* the "maladie des nerves" that led to masturbation caused all sorts of other physical illnesses as well, and depleted the soul's spiritual faculties; masturbation itself led to imbecility.[19] We have mentioned how the specimens at the Paris Wax Museum in the late eighteenth century served as object lessons of the destructive effects of sexual excess.[20] The fatigue and nervous disposition supposedly caused by such excess were now seen by the medical profession as endangering manliness. The medical imagination became preoccupied with the non-manly man—a category not limited to homosexuals. Physicians and educators were obsessed with the personal sexual habits of those in their charge. Masturbation and homosexuality were not regarded as inborn but were attributed to bad thoughts and bad nerves. In fact, during the nineteenth century most diseases were traced to deterioration of the nerves; so at times were political and social problems.

The Outline of Forensic Medicine, written by the physician Johann Valentin Müller in 1796, exemplified the attitudes of medicine toward those who sinned against convention. Müller refused to distinguish between different kinds of homosexuality, or to consider some less abhorrent than others. Vice, no matter how practiced or consummated, had personal and public consequences. Like most medical men who wrote about homosexuality in those days, his object was to help courts recognize "perverts" so they could be sentenced. In what was to become the standard approach in such texts, he began with the supposed physiological causes of homosexuality and proceeded to describe its outward signs. External appearance, it was assumed, always betrayed the private practice of vice; telltale traits included reddened eyes, feebleness, fits of depression, and negligence about personal appearance—the subject's head tended to hang down listlessly.[21] Müller attempted to interconnect all the principal sexual perversions, contending, for example, that masturbation led to homosexuality, an idea to which R. von Krafft-Ebing much later, in his famous *Psychopathia sexualis* (1892) would give additional sanction.[22]

With one perverse practice sliding into another, the gap between normality and abnormality grew ever more immense. Müller viewed the "disease" of unconventional sex as dangerous to the health of the state.[23] His arguments resurfaced often during the nineteenth century as justifications for the punishment of vice. Sodomy and masturbation led to impotence and thus to depopulation; the secrecy that accompanied deviant sexuality resembled a conspiracy sowing hatred against the state; men and women who practiced such vices lacked either moral sense or civic responsibility; and their souls were as incapable of spirituality as their bodies were slack and without tone.[24]

A half century later Ambroise Tardieu, in his *Crimes Against Morals from the Viewpoint of Forensic Medicine* (1857), stressed a feminine appearance and diseased body as outward signs in a male homosexual, whose "disease" he attributed to uncontrolled imagination and fantasy.[25] Johann Ludwig Caspar, perhaps the most famous authority on forensic medicine in mid-nineteenth-century Germany and influential in other nations as well, refused to blame homosexuality for other bodily ills, but he still described homosexuals as bizarre in appearance and bodily movement.[26] Finally, Dr. P. Möbius, in *Geschlecht und Entartung* (*Sexuality and Degeneration*, 1903), pitted the physical stereotype of the sexual deviant against "the healthy human being," whom he described as "mostly lithe and tall; his face is never ugly."[27] Health is equated with manliness. Adolf Hitler would constantly use the phrase "lithe and tall" when describing the ideal German.

Long before Möbius, the picture of disease and depravity had been set off against the emerging national stereotypes of manliness, symbolized by sun-drenched Greek statues whose vigor and energy were balanced by a fine harmony and sense of proportion. Those who worked to create the stereotypes saw the beautiful male body as a manifestation of the manly virtues. Winckelmann's ideal of Greek beauty was integrated into the scheme of bourgeois values associated with restraint, chastity, and purity. The classical hero had nothing in common with Müller's homosexuals or, for that matter, with the stereotypes of other groups often placed outside the confines of society—Jews, the insane, or criminals, all men and women exhausted from constant motion, lacking either ideals or the will to carry through purposeful activity.[28]

Yet Greek models and bourgeois respectability were not always so easily integrated. Both Hölderlin and Schiller linked their cult of Greek beauty not to the family but to male friendship, the *Männerbund* whose popularity was never to vanish in nineteenth-century Germany.[29] Schiller's unfinished play about the Order of St. John of Malta (*Die Malteser*), on which he worked from 1788 to 1803, was to exemplify heroic action in a Greek mode. It featured two knights whose passionate friendship found its fullest expression in carnal homosexual love. When the work was finished by others many years after Schiller's death, and finally performed in 1865 and again in 1884, the scenes focusing on the love between the two knights were dropped, and a minor theme from Schiller's draft, involving a Greek girl, was amplified.[30] The cult of male friendship which had loomed so large among eighteenth-century German writers was now looked upon with increasing suspicion, even though love among men had usually been considered as devoid of sensuality, unlike that between men and women. Some still considered such a *Bund* a precondition to German unity, agreeing with Fichte that true love must transcend personal relationships in order to embrace the nation;[31] but the intimacy of such friendships and their sentimental vocabulary came under attack as respectability and the concept of normalcy triumphed. Further attempts to strip male friendships of all erotic content will occupy us later.[32] Here we must note that despite the potential danger of homoeroticism, Greek ideals of friendship and beauty were not discarded, but rather adapted to heterosexual love.

Above all, in the first decades of the nineteenth century, male beauty symbolized timeless order and promised to heal a sick world. Friedrich Schiller in 1795 had seen beauty as saving men from the extremes of brutality or exhaustion.[33] Among others, Friedrich Theodor Vischer, the most important German aesthetician of the nineteenth century, assigned to beauty and manliness the task of preventing chaos.[34] Order and harmony were supposed to keep the passions in check. Some of Rupert Brooke's popular poems before and during the First World War treated the combination of beauty and order as peculiarly English;[35] but the Germans had already appropriated this ideal as their own. And in France, the writer Henry de Montherlant summed up such ideals after the First World War when he described how he became "drunk with order" when contemplating the male body, steeled by sport and displaying its muscles.[36] For Brooke, both intellectuals and homosexuals lacked cleanliness of body and mind; they were "half-men with their dirty songs and dreary."[37] Brooke's preoccupation with cleanliness and purity was typical of the "generation of 1914," which hoped that war could rescue the nation from moral decay.

The idea of masculinity, including its borrowed Greek standards of male beauty, was drafted by European nationalisms into service as national symbol or stereotype. The Greek ideal was stripped of any lingering eroticism, while its harmony, proportion, and transcendent beauty were stressed. Masculinity was expected to stand both for unchanging values in a changing age and for the dynamic but orderly process of change itself, guided by an appropriate purpose. The ugly counter-image of the nervous, unstable homosexual and masturbator, whose physiognomy was ever more sharply delineated thanks to medical science's attribution of moral and aesthetic values, became an important symbol of the threat to nationalism and respectability posed by the rapid changes of the modern age (see plate 13).

Nationalism looked back for inspiration to preindustrial values, anchoring its ideals within the immutable forces of history, nature, and timeless beauty. Modernity, which the bourgeoisie had been so instrumental in creating, now seemed a menace to stability. The normal–abnormal dualism, already interpreted in aesthetic and medical terms, took on an added dimension—the genuine as against the artificial, organic as against stunted growth.

From the nineteenth century on, the guardians of nationalism and respectability felt menaced by the big city, the apparent center of an artificial and restless age. Such cities were thought to destroy man's rootedness. They led to alienation—and unbridled sexual passion. It was further said that the extremes of luxury and poverty to be found in cities favored the practice of sexual deviance. Caspar used that argument in explaining why sodomy flourished (as he claimed) in Italian cities;[38] he also accepted the stereotyped contrast, all too common in Germany, between the sensual South and the disciplined North. Somewhat later, Alois Geigel, another expert on forensic medicine, made the same point: big cities encourage vice.[39] When court cases concerning homosexuality were reported in the London press, the analogy to the biblical cities of Sodom and Gomorrah was almost always drawn.[40] The dark and secret recesses deep within the "jungle of cities" were usually considered breeding grounds of homosexuality and masturbation. Sexual deviance was once again linked to conspiracy, darkness, and stealth. The village or small town close to nature possessed no dark bowels within which vice could flourish. It symbolized those eternal values that stood outside the rush of time. Here the nation and manliness were at home; here one could still recall the healthy, happy past. The city was home to outsiders—Jews, criminals, the insane, homosexuals—while the countryside was the home of the native on his soil. Such notions, common by the middle of the nineteenth century, were to be repeated almost word for word by Heinrich Himmler during the Third Reich.[41]

Every stereotype and myth must have a kernel of truth to be believable. A homosexual subculture did indeed exist in big cities like Berlin and London, as many readers learned from the newspapers—or from the propaganda of purity crusades. One impressionistic survey, quoted by the homosexual rights leader Magnus Hirschfeld in *Berlins Drittes Geschlecht* (*Berlin's Third Sex*, 1904), catalogued the clubs, restaurants, hotels, and bathhouses frequented by Berlin homosexuals. Hirschfeld actually quoted the survey in order to testify to the respectable behavior of the clientele.[42] Hirschfeld's own book was part of a series of works called "Documents of Life in the Big City," which explored the milieu of bohemians, dance halls, and the like. Berlin was presented as the home of all those living on the fringes or outside respectable society.

The Berlin physician and pioneer sexologist Iwan Bloch, writing in his influential *Das Sexualleben unserer Zeit* (*Sexual Life of Our Times*, 1906) about the "vibrations" emitted whcn men and women tried to enter the modern age, listed the temptations of the big city, ballrooms, dance floors, and cabarets, all existing only to kill time; they are described as little more than glorified bordellos.[43] The link between cities and illicit sexuality was thus carried over into the twentieth century. For Bloch, the inner strength that was essential if sexual excess was to be avoided required a sense of rootedness and restfulness. A properly functioning soul would keep sexuality under control.[44] Modernity, on the other hand, encouraged homosexuality and masturbation, which Bloch, like many of his predecessors, long believed were acquired tastes found mainly among those who had given in to temptation.[45]

As sexual abnormality came more and more to be seen in this alien context, far removed from the nourishing soil of the countryside, nationalists felt that the line between normal and abnormal had to be tightly drawn if the nation was to be protected against its enemies. In the second half of the nineteenth century, Darwinist ideas amplified the nationalist animus against the abnormal. Such ideas were thought applicable to the management of human society, just as the medical theorists had provided a quasiscientific justification for sexual rigor. Natural selection, which Darwin had seen at work among animals, would reward a healthy national organism free of hereditary disease and moral weakness. On the simplest level, this meant dedication to reproduction. *The Lancet* opposed contraception when its use was debated in 1870 because "a nation fruitful in healthy organisms must, in the struggle for existence, displace and swallow up a nation that is abandoned to conjugal onanism."[46] But even more important, if only the fittest survived, demographic growth would depend on the elimination of those vices that sapped men's virility, led to physical illness, and weakened the power of the will. Typically, Iwan Bloch thought that "perverts" could be cured by fortifying their willpower;[47] Alois

Geigel, writing about homosexuality, asserted that industrious and free nations had to encourage moral purity in their struggle to survive.[48] Even those who advocated greater freedom for homosexuals felt compelled to attribute to them a respectable manliness, with physical and mental characteristics that would aid the national struggle for survival. As we shall see, Benedict Friedländer, a pioneer of homosexual rights, felt obliged to deny that decriminalizing homosexuality would damage the ability of the race to wage war. A lively debate had raged long before the First World War: Would greater freedom for homosexuality endanger Germany's military strength?[49] All agreed that it was essential to the health of the nation to maintain the ideal of masculinity in opposition to sensuality and effeminacy. Richard von Krafft-Ebing called masturbators cowardly and lacking in self-confidence. He asserted flatly that periods of moral decadence in the life of a nation were always accompanied by effeminacy, sensuality, and luxury.[50]

Bloch, who approved of masturbation if practiced in moderation, nevertheless saw it as a potential danger to society. The masturbator, he tells us, becomes lonely and shy and loses the natural enthusiasm of youth; his nervousness is apt to damage his heart. "The struggle against masturbation is a fight for altruism."[51] Masturbation was the foundation upon which all sexual perversion was thought to rest, so that what was true for masturbators held true for homosexuals as well. In short, such men and women were a danger to the national community.

Nationalist attacks on nonprocreative sexual practices were at times based on arguments that went beyond health to appeal to the pragmatism of the industrial age. Tissot had already condemned masturbation partly because it was a "besoin sans besoin"—a need that served no useful purpose[52]—in contrast to the manly, purposeful action necessary to the health of society and the state. A physician during the reign of Louis Philippe in France had argued that wasting one's sperm through masturbation was like throwing money out the window.[53]

With the struggle for national survival seen in terms of steadiness of purpose, of moral and physical health, the concept of "degeneration" emerged as the antithesis of manliness. It was first formulated by Benedict Augustin Morel in 1857 as the medical label for a process by which men and women were destroyed through what Morel termed "moral and physical poison." This deviance from the norm, as Morel called it, could be brought about by such poisons as alcoholism and the use of opium, by debilitating diseases like malaria, but also by the social environment, a nervous temperament, diseased moral faculties, or inherited bodily and mental weakness. Several of these poisons usually combined in order to begin the relentless process of degeneration.[54] Morel gave the term "degeneration" a medical meaning, but it derived from his interpretation of the Book of Genesis. Adam before the fall was the ideal human, the measure of man. However, as a result of the fall from Paradise, human beings can no longer escape external influences such as climate or nourishment, or the poisons, diseases, and environmental factors that carry some men furthest away from the ideal type. They have degenerated from the standard once set.[55] Characteristically for the process of diagnosing the outsider, a train of thought based upon subjective belief was transformed into medical knowledge.

Max Nordau, himself a physician, was the chief popularizer of degeneration as a medical concept. In his *Entartung* (*Degeneration*, 1892), he used it to sharpen the distinction between normal and abnormal, between the bourgeois virtues which led to progress and the vices which led to the extinction of the individual, the family, and the national community. "We distinguish the healthy from the diseased impulse," Nordau tells us, "and demand that the latter be combated." The legitimacy of all desires must be judged by the standards of society. "The activity imperiling society offends against law and custom, which are nothing but an epitome of the temporary notions of society concerning what is beneficial and what is pernicious to it."[56] Hence to offend even against transitory norms of society was "repulsively immoral,"[57] and while Nordau did not explicitly mention homosexuality, surely all deviant sex would imperil society. Those who did so were outsiders whose asymmetry of face and cranium were said to reflect the imbalance of their mental faculties.[58]

Nordau's preoccupation with the exhaustion of the nerves and lack of self-discipline was rooted in a fear of the new speed of time: steam and electricity, he writes, have turned everyone's life upside down, while railway travel has ruined the nervous system. But the fight against degeneration would be won by those with strong nerves, clear heads, dedication to hard work, and a strict control over fantasy and imagination—the familiar criteria for manliness.[59] The degenerate, on the other hand, was easily identified by his deformed body. Thus the concept of degeneration lent greater authority to forensic medicine in pointing to the outward signs of abnormality, and in making private vice a public matter. By the end of the nineteenth century, Darwinism and degeneration had sharpened public attitudes toward the abnormal that had existed for over a century.

The concepts of degeneration and manliness were taken up by European racism, as we shall discuss later in some detail. Here it is necessary to point out that the stereotyped depiction of sexual "degenerates" was transferred almost intact to the "inferior races," who inspired the same fears. These races, too, were said to display a lack of morality and a general absence of self-discipline. Blacks, and then Jews, were endowed with excessive sexuality, with a so-called female sensuousness that transformed love into lust. They lacked all manliness. Jews as a group were said to exhibit female traits, just as homosexuals were generally considered effeminate. The spawn of dark, dank alleys, estranged from the healing power of nature, alien to the world of Greece, such outsiders were thought to engage in secret conspiracies.[60]

Abnormality then could be interpreted in medical terms as well as those of race. Marcel Proust, homosexual and part Jew, wrote in *Remembrance of Things Past* (1913–27) that homosexuals, like Jews, were invested by their persecutors with all the moral and physical characteristics of a race.[61] And indeed, he believed that both the Jew and the homosexual felt themselves to be "one of a brotherhood," and intuitively recognized other members of their group.[62] He thought that homosexuality was an "incurable" disease. *Remembrance of Things Past* is pervaded by a sense that the persecuted collaborate with their persecutors, as Proust himself did when he portrayed the homosexual as degenerate and feminine in appearance. His hatred of his own "secret vice," his outrage at being called feminine, and the duel he fought with another homosexual who had questioned his manliness, all show Proust trying to escape the "cursed race."[63] Such a response was not uncommon among homosexuals.

Self-hate was equally familiar among Jews. It was the reaction of outsiders trying to get inside and finding the door locked for no conceivable fault of their own; of people who wanted to be normal but who found themselves trapped into abnormality, tolerated only as long as their vice had the charm of unfamiliarity. Swann, the Jew of *Remembrance of Things Past*, was welcomed among the Guermantes as an exotic plant, until he became a Dreyfusard and seemed to be threatening their political and social position.

## II

The medical stereotype of homosexuality had fixed the homosexual in place during the nineteenth century: his so-called abnormality was no longer confined to individual sexual acts, but was part of his psychological makeup, his looks and bodily structure. The concept of homosexuality had become absolute, the antithesis of respectability. But medical men did claim to be scientific, studying individual cases of homosexuality, and eventually this claim led to a reconsideration of homosexuality itself by those physicians who attempted to rise above that moral prejudice which had informed their colleagues during the nineteenth century. A new science of sexology made its appearance at the turn of the nineteenth and twentieth centuries, no longer the handmaiden of forensic medicine. Such medical inquiry could lead to a reconsideration of homosexuality; and medicine, instead of serving to narrow the limits of normalcy, might serve to modify the boundaries between the norm and what was considered abnormal.

The changing attitude toward homosexuality of the Viennese physician Iwan Bloch was symptomatic of the difference sexology might make in the way homosexuals were viewed by society. At first, before he extended his investigation of homosexuality, he had held the conventional belief that homosexuality was an acquired taste encouraged by bad examples—men wearing long hair and kissing each other. Bloch joined in the condemnation of Oscar Wilde, and affirmed that male friendships must be devoid of erotic feelings.[64] But his hostility to homosexuals, still firm in 1903, had become ambivalent by 1906. Now most homosexuals were to be accepted as legitimate members of society, although others continued to exemplify human degeneration. For those born with such an inheritance, congenital homosexuality was normal rather than abnormal, and should be accepted by society and the state. Homosexuals who had acquired this sexual taste—pseudo-homosexuals, Bloch called them—were "*Wüstlingspederasten*" (libertine pederasts), who continued to exemplify the restlessness and excess of modernity.[65] Making the distinction between true and pseudo-homosexuals was one way of trying to preserve the categories of normalcy and abnormality while attempting to legitimize homosexuality.

Richard von Krafft-Ebing, perhaps the most celebrated sexologist at the turn of the century, showed a similar change in attitude. He was attacked by Magnus Hirschfeld, the most radical sex reformer of the time, for his claim that he could recognize homosexuals by physical signs of degeneration, believing homosexuality to be an illness not unlike masochism and sadism.[66] Krafft-Ebing in his famous *Psychopathia sexualis* of 1877 had stated that a constant war must be waged against men's instincts. Sexual excess encouraged nervous tension, while big cities led to the decline of the family and nations—all sentiments common during the century.[67] Yet, with the passage of time and further study, Krafft-Ebing was ready to make some concessions to homosexuality. In 1901, he summarized his life's work in Magnus Hirschfeld's own journal, dedicated to sex reform, surely in itself a declaration of purpose. Sexual deviance, he wrote, was not the fault of the homosexual. Homosexuality, though against natural law and a form of degeneration,[68] was nevertheless compatible with intellectual excellence and highly developed spiritual faculties. Homosexuality could be acquired by some, and in others it was a malfunctioning of the human organism; its victims deserved pity, not scorn.[69]

Havelock Ellis took a more straightforward stand. Like Hans Blüher, the theoretician of the German Youth Movement and male society to whom we shall return in the next chapter, Ellis believed that homosexuality, by directing men's energies toward public rather than private concerns (after all, homosexuals could have neither wife nor family), made human civilization possible. While the homosexual must not flaunt his sexuality before normal society, he should nevertheless be protected. He might even possess greater worth than the normal person (though Ellis also has much to say in praise of family life). Essentially, Ellis held that sexual acts were a private matter, not subject to public judgment.[70] Yet, interestingly enough, he was not at ease in his collaboration with John Addington Symonds, not only because Symonds's open homosexuality might compromise the scientific claims of *Sexual Inversion*

(1897), but also because he was uncomfortable with abnormal sexuality.[71]

Sigmund Freud was a part of this group of sexologists, whose work he knew well and who influenced his own psychoanalytic theories. Contemporaries were particularly struck by the simple, detailed, and precise way in which Freud described sexual practice, refusing to use the customary Latin.[72] However, Freud was not willing to grant legitimacy to either homosexuality or lesbianism. Freedom to range equally over male and female objects, he wrote, was possible only in childhood, or during primitive states of society and early periods of history. In adult life, such a range was regressive.[73] Maturity meant restriction and definition of the sexual aim, that is to say, heterosexuality. He rejected Hirschfeld's claim that there existed a third sex, which should claim equal rights with the other two, and he did not use Krafft-Ebing's construct of a female soul in a male body, despite the fact that he recognized congenital homosexuality and opposed the criminal prosecution of homosexuals.[74] Nevertheless, compassion did not serve to mitigate stern judgments based upon his medical theory. Homosexuals were sick, and had no place in either maintaining or furthering modern culture. Civilization was founded on the renunciation of instincts, as Freud wrote in 1908, and it was chiefly family feeling with its erotic roots which induced individuals to make such a renunciation.[75] Freud's attitude toward homosexuality was part of his attempt to adjust men and women to existing society, to try to meet society's discontents—an effort that became increasingly urgent after the First World War.

Magnus Hirschfeld was the most straightforward, treating homosexuality as the "third sex," an intermediate stage between the masculine and the feminine. As such, he held, it was a natural and legitimate variant. Homosexuals looked and behaved normally, and should never be treated as though they were abnormal. Hirschfeld made no distinction between true and pseudo-homosexuality.[76]

For all their undoubted attachment to contemporary manners and morals, Bloch, Ellis, Hirschfeld, and Freud as well, changed the way in which homosexuality was discussed. They challenged the assertion that homosexuals were insane or decadent with the claim that unduly rigid standards of morality were keeping homosexuals from leading normal and productive lives. Yet when sexologists described such lives, they confined themselves, for the most part, to contributions to the arts and literature. The homosexual as aesthete had made a deep impression at the *fin de siècle*, whether summed up by Oscar Wilde in England or by Philipp Count zu Eulenburg in Germany, who composed music and played the piano at the court of Emperor William II until he and the emperor were involved in a homosexual scandal. Homosexuals were granted intellectual excellence, but the list which doctors like Bloch compiled to prove this point contained for the most part artists, poets, and philosophers. There was barely a statesman, and no generals or captains of industry; the men of action were missing.[77]

Manliness was still largely denied to homosexuals: did they not contain a female soul in a male body, as Krafft-Ebing claimed?[78] Admittedly, the link between homosexuality and feebleness of mind had now been branded as false. It was no longer thought that congenital homosexuality spread disease. Homosexuals were assigned an honorable, if unmanly, place in society. But in spite of the sexologists' good intentions, they remained creatures apart, outsiders to a society in which manliness played such a crucial role. As it was, even those changes in the status of homosexuals that sexologists advocated were slow to influence the moral prejudices of medicine, which would remain largely in place for another half century.

## III

Those outsiders who tried to win acceptance by finding some way toward social norms can provide us with a mirror image of society as its would-be imitators saw it, heightened and sharpened by their striving toward respectability. Not all outsiders wanted to become insiders, but those who made the attempt can deepen our understanding of the meaning of manliness for both nationalism and bourgeois society.

First of all, homosexuals tried to counteract the stereotype of promiscuity by claiming sexual moderation. Magnus Hirschfeld, during his tour of homosexual Berlin in 1904, paused repeatedly to point out that sex was no more an obsession among homosexuals than it was in "normal" society.[79] The quest for sexual purity was, after all, a central demand of respectability; it was eventually endorsed by almost all those who defended homosexuality. Such defenders also sought to convey images of virility. Thus in *Corydon*, intended only for a small, select audience, André Gide wrote in 1911 about pederasts like himself: "if I insist on their physical looks, it is only because it does matter if they carry themselves well and are virile."[80] Significantly, these words were written by the author who was probably the first to assert in public that homosexual experience can bring joy and happiness, as for example when Michel saw the boy Baktir in *The Immoralist* (1911).[81]

Homosexuals used various strategies in trying to prove their manliness. They often asserted that their spirit of comradeship made them the best soldiers. Ancient Greek battles in which male lovers fought side by side seemed to prove the point. Benedict Friedländer argued that homosexuality was necessary in any well-functioning army. He maintained that homosexuals were uniquely capable of transcending sexuality, thus rendering them particularly manly.[82] His book *Die Renaissance des Eros Uranos* (*The Renaissance of the Eros Uranos*, 1911) accepted all the normative definitions of manliness and respectability. Friedländer was not alone in making such arguments, but he took his praise for martial values one step further by embracing racism. Attacks on homosexuals, he wrote, were led by Jews determined to undermine Aryan virility and self-awareness.[83] Friedländer, although he was himself a Jew, was a well-known friend of Eugen Dühring after the former socialist had become one of the most violent of racists.[84] Racism was a heightened form of nationalism. Friedländer may well have thought that by embracing it he was doing all he could to court acceptance, although it had not yet by any means become the dominant mode of thought among German nationalists. The spectacle of one outsider attempting to buy his entrance ticket to society at the expense of another is common enough. For Friedländer, the Jews were assigned the very stereotype which society had created for homosexuals. Those twice locked out of normative society had an especially difficult stand, which led some like Friedländer to redouble their effort at acceptance, while others, like Magnus Hirschfeld, homosexual and Jew, became strong advocates of human rights. Marcel Proust, half Jew and homosexual, seems to have felt more kindly toward the Jew Swann than toward his homosexual Baron de Charlus.

Jews also wanted to enter society and fervently embraced its norms. They sought to escape the stereotype of the outsider which society had foisted upon them by emphasizing their commitment to respectability and manliness. German Jews were fond of evoking participation in Germany's wars, not only to prove their citizenship but also to demonstrate heroism and manly comportment. Highlighting this quest, Max Nordau at the Second Zionist Congress of 1898 called for the creation of "muscle Jews" as against pale-faced and thin-chested "coffeehouse Jews." Later, he expressed the hope that "our new muscle Jews" might regain the heroism of their forefathers.[85] Zionists and assimilationists shared the same ideal of manliness. But Jews never directed the weapon of racism at others in order to facilitate their own acceptance into society.[86] Not only had they experienced racial persecution but, in any case, they could not claim membership in the Aryan race. Most homosexuals lacked the experience of this specific persecution and, if they wished, could consider themselves part of the Germanic race.

The use of racism to gain respectability was a constant theme of the first homosexual journal in Germany, Der Eigene (The Personalist), published by Adolf Brand between 1896 and 1931. Boasting only a few thousand readers up to the First World War, its monthly circulation soared to about 150,000 during the Weimar Republic.[87] Even before the paper published a supplement called Rasse und Schönheit (Race and Beauty) in 1926, Germanic themes had informed much of its fiction, as well as images of naked boys and young men photographed against a background of Germanic nature. One poem, written by Brand himself and entitled "The Superman," praised manliness, condemned femininity, and toyed with anti-Semitism, apparently because of the poet's quarrel with Magnus Hirschfeld, a rival for leadership of the homosexual rights movement.[88]

Brand opposed Hirschfeld's medical approach to homosexuality. Homosexuals did not represent a freakish third sex but were the flower of manliness—Der Eigene advocated a revival of the Greek ideal of beauty and perfection.[89] Brand emphasized sexual purity; he saw "male love as an important factor in all cultural activities."[90] The bizarre climax of Der Eigene's struggle for acceptance was its condemnation of Weimar tolerance—the very tolerance that had allowed the journal to flourish. Der Eigene supported the nationalist right. Germany, in all its manly purity, would rise again and put an end to the moral corruption of the postwar world.[91] Were the Nazis honoring this support for the political right when they failed to prosecute Brand?[92] As we shall see, Heinrich Himmler's view that homosexuality necessarily destroys the "*Männerstaat*" (the state as an expression of manliness) came to prevail, and the Nazis eventually decided to put an end to that threat.[93]

Even among those homosexual apologists who avoided racism, a certain male assertiveness prevailed. Examples can be found in Germany, and also in England where nationalism and racism were not so closely allied. Sir Richard Burton, almost certainly himself a homosexual, remarked with pleasure when translating the *Arabian Nights* into English during the 1880s that, "in the East men respect manly measures" and had not been corrupted by the philanthropic and pseudo-humanitarian behavior common among western governments.[94] T. E. Lawrence, as we shall see, would later project a similar contrast between a supposedly masculine East and the effeminate West.[95] To cite one more example, Hector Hugh Monroe, better known as Saki, a popular writer, again a homosexual, approved of society's prejudice against Jews and effeminate men. He also maintained that "nearly every red-blooded human boy has had war, in some shape or form, for his first love. . . ."[96] He himself enlisted in the First World War although over forty years old, and was killed at the front.

These amplified mirror images of society point to a tragic self-hate, and testify to the pressure society put on those who differed from the accepted norms. None of these efforts really helped win acceptance for homosexuals; they did, however, keep the pretense of normality alive for men like Burton or Munroe, who were in fact disqualified from membership by their secret sexual promiscuity.

Yet the very age of the *fin de siècle* which saw these efforts at homosexual assimilation also witnessed a revolt by avant-garde writers and artists opposed to bourgeois respectability. There was a parallel rebellion within the younger generation of the middle class to which we turn in the next chapter, but it was not to prove as far-reaching. What concerns us here was a passive protest—artistically inclined men and women following their own reveries, withdrawing into a life of the senses, always in quest of artistic beauty. Such beauty, whether of people or objects, at times projected strong erotic feelings. These artists and writers turned the word "decadence" into a badge of pride and the label for a movement, considering it the first step in a much needed reversal of prevailing social values. The decadent milieu provided some homosexuals and lesbians with their first opportunity to integrate into a cultural pattern without having to deny their identity. Both Oscar Wilde and the French lesbian writer Renée Vivienne found comfort there. The way of life exemplified by writers like Camille Huysmans or Baudelaire offered a sanctuary of airless candlelit rooms permeated by the smell of incense, filled with erotic dreams of human and artistic beauty. Refusing to assimilate into respectable society, the decadents proclaimed that they represented the nearly perfect society of the future in which the worship of masculinity and virility would be unknown.

When, as a lark, Oscar Wilde in collaboration with some of his friends decided to write a largely pornographic homosexual novel, *Teleny, or The Reverse of the Medal* (privately published in 1893), they endowed their hero, Teleny, with a "heavenly figure" and "youth, life and manhood,"[97] but they also placed him in a decadent setting. They catalogued the exotic decor of Teleny's apartment, behind whose locked door he indulged his bizarre, opulent tastes and lustful ways. The novel is set in France; indeed, it was written under the spell of Huysmans and Baudelaire. Yet the ambivalence homosexuals felt about decadence informs the work through the contrast between Teleny's way of life, which points up the need for decadence as an element of personal identification against a hostile society, and his appearance, which reflects the preoccupation with manliness. The novel condemns the "sickening faces of effete, womanish men."[98]

Teleny's highly refined artistic sensibilities represent the alliance between homosexuals and artists that was part of the world of decadence. "Homosexuality is the noble disease of the artist," declared Théophile Gautier, while the more sober Krafft-Ebing wrote in 1898 of the medically proven connection between "homosexual decadence" and artistic feeling.[99] Homosexuality was taken to indicate a heightened sensibility—a central component of the concept of decadence. Decadents were wont to proclaim that "man is growing more refined, more feminine, more divine."[100]

The languid youths of the new artistic fashion of the *fin de siècle*, the Art Nouveau or Jugendstil, with their soft rounded lines, were effeminate rather than manly. Growing old had to be avoided, as Oscar Wilde demonstrated so well in his *Picture of Dorian Gray* (1891); but death was the final sensuous experience, the necessary climax of a life fully lived. The decadent symbol of a young boy expiring with a rose in his hand combined the languid beauty of youth with the final sensuous experience. For the self-conscious decadent, greater sensitivity was the by-product of an ebbing life-force, and with it came a craving for extreme and new situations, for artificial stimulants and strong nervous sensations.[101] If the men of this subculture were said to be pale, unmuscled, and dedicated to an aesthetic type of purity, so be it. In this milieu, lesbians and homosexuals could find a community of the like-minded and transcend the stereotype of homosexuality, not by adopting the ideal of manliness but by challenging the very existence of normalcy.

The decadent response was largely confined to France and England. A group of English homosexuals even attempted to revive decadence after the First World War.[102] Germany produced few advocates of the stature of Wilde, Beardsley, or Baudelaire, though the Expressionists and Thomas Mann's *Buddenbrooks* shared some of their attitudes. In that country, the focus of cultural dissidence shifted to youth in rebellion against the manners and morals of parents and school. This youthful revolt was neither as deep nor as cynical as that of the artists and writers in England or France.

The German Youth Movement, which started among schoolboys in a Berlin suburb in 1901, soon spread through most of the country. At first it was merely an association which allowed boys to roam the countryside without adult supervision and to create their own mode of life. But while the teen-aged boys who joined the movement, all sons of the prosperous middle classes, were out for adventure and fun, the youth movement soon became politicized and endowed with aims transcending those of "youth among itself." The older comrades and adult leaders presented it as a quest for the "genuine" in nature and the nation—as an élite of males that would give a fresh impulse to German national consciousness. The theoreticians of the movement denied that conventional organizational ties could bind a group together in a common purpose. They invoked instead the power of male eros in order to create a true camaraderie—the cell from which the nation might be renewed.[103] The youth movement was a *Männerbund*, a community of males; girls were only later allowed to form their own separate youth movement organizations.

The leaders of the movement, urban youth, were impressed by the harshness and independence of elemental nature, and sounded a note of physical and emotional toughness which permeated the movement and helped shape its ideals of manliness and physical beauty.[104] With their emphasis upon instinct, these young people took unaffected pleasure in bodily contact, as a former member tells us, in tumbling, walking arm in arm, or putting their arms around one another.[105] Its ideal of manliness was clearly expressed and refined in the literature of the movement. The German ideal of manliness, as a journal close to the movement put it, meant the practice of self-control, steeling the body in order to be best at sports and games, to be chivalrous toward girls while refusing to squander one's sexuality—the greatest gift nature can bestow upon a man in the prime of life.[106] This ideal was illustrated by the stylized male figure clad solely in loincloth that adorned the cover of each issue of the *Vortrupp* (*The Vanguard*), as this influential journal was called (see plate 12). Typically, this stereotype was then set against the "ugly human being" of modernity, disfigured by disease, debauchery, a hypocritical way of life, and narrow professionalism. This is the stereotype of the outsider, the foil of Germanic manliness.[107]

The adherents of the German Youth Movement pitted their "genuine" values against the supposed artificiality of bourgeois life; they sought moral and physical health in the context of their voluntary yet cohesive community and in a more meaningful nationalism. They found roots in their own camaraderie, in the unspoilt Germanic landscape, and in the nation as inner experience. Although the advocates of decadence claimed to despise health, roots, and nature, the two movements did have one important attitude in common. They both took part in the rediscovery of the human body at the end of the nineteenth century, sharing a new joy in the way it felt and functioned. Thus both groups challenged bourgeois respectability, with its sense of shame and its secretiveness about bodily functions. Nevertheless, there were profound differences even here. German youth saw the male nude body as the temple of manliness, while for most decadents it exemplified an almost feminine sensuousness.

The *fin-de-siècle* rediscovery of the body was the most serious challenge respectability had to face since its crystallization nearly a century earlier. The challenge of youth was perhaps the more disturbing to bourgeois society. Decadent artists and writers were merely a coterie of outsiders, isolated examples of "men gone bad." But the rebellious youth were considered the élite of their generation, the children of the middle classes. They viewed themselves as healthy, not corrupt, and were attempting to reorder their lives within the confines of the nation. Consequently, their love of their bodies was a much greater threat to middle-class values, especially in the context of the so-called life-reform movements, which advocated nude bathing, nude sports, and the cult of the sun.

The rediscovery of the body by the youth movement was made in the name of true manliness. Not the least of its frightening aspects was that it drew out implications which had been present all along in Winckelmann's own homoeroticism, in the nudity of Greek statues, and in the virility of the national stereotype. The wall between normal and abnormal was destined to remain standing; but it was to be severely shaken and the gate would never again be securely locked.

## CHAPTER 3

# The Rediscovery of
# the Human Body

## I

While writers and artists of the decadent movement sought to express their own identity against the norms of bourgeois society, another kind of challenge to respectability was being mounted in both Germany and England. This was not to be a modernist revolt, but rather one of men and women rediscovering their bodies as part of a search for the genuine as against the artificiality of modern life, of unspoilt nature embattled against modernity. Its champions refused to hide their bodies as society demanded, and instead sought to expose them to the healing power of the sun and the rhythms of nature. The quest for the natural, the exaltation of nature, had been an important bourgeois impetus; but now this was turned back upon the bourgeoisie itself in order to challenge its respectabilities. Those who led this revolt were for the most part young, and their rebellion went beyond books and journals to inspire youth movements, sport, and eventually an entire new national consciousness.

The human body as rediscovered by this new generation of rebels at the *fin de siècle* differed from the new feeling of sensuousness which had prevailed among the decadents, but also from that of the realistic nudes painted by Ingres, Manet, or Hans von Marés. Their nude women were voluptuous, tempting, but remote—posed so as to be officially admired but not appropriated as a part of one's individuality. Such "framing" can be used to capture a rapturous moment in painting or in photography; yet this moment, the pose, remains strangely detached from reality. Gert Mattenklott has shown[1] how the poet Stefan George wove a myth around his personality by issuing stylized, carefully posed photographs that documented the master's inaccessibility (see plate 18).[1] Some female nudes, those of Courbet, for example, titillated the male imagination, and together with a good many lithographs may have served as a kind of pornography until picture postcards usurped this function. The rediscovery of the human body, which seriously challenged respectability, was not supposed to encourage sensuousness but was part of a longing for the genuine which was set in opposition to prevailing moral attitudes. Thus bourgeois children attacked their elders for being hypocrites whose public respectability was accompanied by secret fornication. This hypocrisy was symbolized by the sense of shame over the human body and the fear of nudity, which seemed a vital component of respectability but was now branded as both artificial and unnatural.

The urge to rediscover the human body was especially strong in Germany. Even at the beginning of the nineteenth century, the German Gymnasts were dressed in special uniforms which allowed freedom of bodily movement, but which many contemporaries saw as endangering the norms of respectability. Moreover, these uniforms were frequently defended by invoking the beauty of the human body through analogy with the athletes of Greece.[2] The invocation of Greece can serve as a reminder that Winckelmann's nude sculpture had already become a part of middle-class respectability. Indeed, those rediscovering their bodies at the end of the nineteenth century would continue to invoke Greek models as examples of physical beauty stripped of all sensuousness and sexuality. Much later, during the Weimar Republic, a German judge, when confronted with pictures believed to be lewd, would tell the defendants that if he himself wanted to see a nude body, he would buy a piece of Greek sculpture. Photography, in his opinion, was not able to spiritualize the human form.[3] It is well to bear this in mind when we come to discuss the primacy of sculpture in National Socialist iconography.

Greece was conjoined with nature. The urge to be natural, to integrate oneself with an unspoilt setting, was thought to free the human body of its sexuality. Indeed, writings by nudists usually contained references to both Greece and nature. Both created links toward the acceptance of a living, human nudity, from the end of the nineteenth century on. At a practical level, the German Youth

Movement and the older organizations of Gymnasts now started to combine athletic exercises with roaming the countryside.[4] The Gymnasts were the national stereotype in the making—manliness and morality perceived as a reflection of unspoilt nature and the beauty of Greece.

The early nineteenth century had regarded the sun as bad for one's health.[5] Nevertheless, the analogy between the sun, light, and national regeneration was present even then in Germany, and the blondness and blue eyes of both German and English stereotypes reflected such ideals.[6] The "culture of sun and light," as nudism was first called in Germany, was founded at midcentury but did not make its mark until the 1890s. By the end of the nineteenth century, regeneration through the sun had become a continuous quest. The bronzed body was thought to be especially beautiful— a contrast to the ideal whiteness Winckelmann had admired in Greek sculpture a century earlier. Eventually the sun was accepted as the great healer, and exposure to sunlight became part of the cure for tuberculosis. To hide the body from the sun in shame could now be branded as a sign of moral and mental sickness, of the conspiracy by which the ruling classes suppressed the natural instincts of man.[7]

Nudism was part of the broad German "life-reform" movement, which attempted to return to the so-called genuine forces of life: to regenerate man and society through vegetarianism, anti-alcoholism, nature-healing, land-reform, and the advocacy of garden cities. Cities were condemned as breeding grounds of immorality and moral sickness, and were said to induce bodily ills, all arguments we have met before.[8] Preoccupation with making nudity respectable was constant. The growth of the nudist movement as part of life-reform coincided with the rise of photography even as photographs were becoming the mainstay of pornography. The attack upon nudism centered upon the movement's magazines, designed to spread its cause, filled with photographs of nude men and women. Here the life-reform advocates were under constant pressure to demonstrate how their nudes differed from those that catered to the lower instincts of man.

Nature came to the rescue, for people of flesh and blood could not be sculpted into symbols. Greece certainly continued to provide an idealized physical beauty, yet an immensely popular film like *Paths to Strength and Beauty* (1925), which helped to transmit life-reform to postwar Germany, opened in a Greek gymnasium and then moved on to athletic exercises performed in a natural setting. The "genuine" was of crucial importance to nudity as part of the life-reform movement, and here nature predominated over Greece. What counted in the end was the "framing" of the nude body by nature. Thus an article on "Nudity and Photography" in one of the early journals of the nudist movement (1903) distinguished between nudity and the undressed body: the latter was the subject of photography; the former a "holy mystery" and the "crown of creation." Nudity as distinct from mere lack of clothes must be represented as part of the pure, reverential contemplation of nature (see plate 16).[9]

Nudity was acceptable only, so one leader of the movement tells us, when seen in an unspoilt natural setting:[10] meadows, gardens, or against the background of the sea—"the elemental, eternally alive, always liberated."[11] A typical example of such framing and its interpretation was a nude girl pictured in the magazine *Die Freude* (*Joy*) shortly after the war. The girl is surrounded by flowers, symbols of innocence and purity we shall meet again when discussing the place of women in the world of respectability. The caption of the picture is "Magic Blossoms," and the text states that the truly beautiful body, because of its purity, makes one forget its nakedness, for outward beauty points to an inner purity of mind.[12] It was hoped that such purity would elevate nudity into a spiritual principle. Here photography was indeed a necessary means of communication. The beautiful body, so we read in one of the early journals of the youth movement, *Die Schönheit* (*Beauty*) of 1903, is a work of art. Whoever possesses such a body does not own it: it belongs to all men.[13]

The worship of the sun played a role here as well. In a book that summarized the course of the movement since its inception, sunbathing was rejected. Rather, the sun must be used to harden the body through movement (see plate 15).[14] A posed nude, in spite of its framing, was thought dangerously close to lewd pictures, and there was further debate as to how such a nude, even if sun-drenched and placed in a natural setting, might be distinguished from the nude models preferred by pornography. One answer, interestingly enough, advised the use of glossy paper, which would heighten the artistic merit of the female nude without arousing lust.[15] The debate about the framing of nudes that accompanied the nudist movement from its inception through the 1920s in Germany raised the issue of how best to distinguish between art and pornography. The issue was never properly resolved, and courts even in the late 1920s had difficulty in defining the distinction. However, most nudist magazines and journals of the youth movement took it for granted that the portrayal of sun-drenched bodies in their proper natural setting would transform them into symbols of strength, beauty, and sexual innocence. Artists close to the youth movement at the start of the twentieth century flooded their nudes in sunlight and surrounded them with natural symbols. The painter Fidus (Karl Höppner), who was popular with the youth movement, expressed his own love for the nude body through sunlit figures of boys and girls, framed by flowers, often symbolic of the artist's Theosophical beliefs. These ideals would be strengthened by the First World War, when nudity, sun, and water would become symbols of cleanliness, beauty, and innocence amid death and destruction. The hero of one of the most popular books to emerge from the war in Germany, Ernst Wurche in Walter Flex's *Der Wanderer Zwischen Beiden Welten* (*The Wanderer Between Two Worlds, 1917*), reveals his chastity and strength as he emerges from water into a sun-drenched landscape. "I wish that there was a painter among us," one of his comrades exclaimed as Wurche stood before him, "in all his slender purity, dripping water, shining with sun and youth." [16] The "two worlds" of Flex were those of the youth movement and the war, bridged by the figure of Wurche. Water and sunlight became important symbols during the war in England too, as we shall see. [17]

The metaphors of sun and nature linked the rediscovery of the body to the national stereotype. The birth of national stereotypes was based on a blend of Greek models and worship of the sun and sky; blond hair, blue eyes, and a white skin were regarded as marks of a superior people in both England and Germany. This stereotype was perfected throughout the nineteenth century and came to full flowering during the First World War when it was based on something like a national consensus. Figures like Rupert Brooke in England and Flex's hero, Ernst Wurche, in Germany corresponded in every detail to the stereotype. They were also pastoral figures, once again exemplifying the nation. [18] The nation was represented by preindustrial symbols, for they pointed to an immutability not granted to the appurtenances of modernity. The native sky, mountains, valleys, and flowers, rather than the "artificial" streets or mansions of the city, guaranteed the immutable existence of the nation and its people.

The fact that national symbolism and the setting of nudity coincided was no accident. While some elements of the life-reform movement tended to sympathize with the political left and with pacifism, its nationalist wing obtained a disproportionately large influence. The workers' nudist movements, which had a considerable membership split between various left-wing associations, saw the emancipation of the human body from constraints as part of the liberation of the proletariat.[19] But the political right took the opposite approach. Nudity, so it was said, furthered the regeneration of the race, reconciled social differences, and ranked the Volk according to its character and physique. And nudism, as one of its strongest advocates wrote at the start of the twentieth century, was not to be blamed for lustful thoughts; the blame rested on those degenerate men and women without soul who had such thoughts.[20] Nudist literature emphasized the contrast between rootlessness and materialism on the one hand and true spirituality on the other. One official history of the movement blamed the supposed decline of art into sensuousness after the First World War upon the war profiteers, the newly rich and crooked.[21] Materialism was at the root of modernity, the enemy of that morality which distinguished nudism from pornography. Advocates of nudism insisted that the sexual act in marriage was not to be filled with erotic joy, but performed strictly for the purposes of procreation. These ideas had been an integral part of the volkish right long before the rediscovery of the human body.

Richard Ungewitter, one of the founders of the nudist movement and a leader of its right wing before the war, exemplifies the volkish connection. He saw such movements as furthering the emergence of a racial élite in Germany which would put an end to degeneration and its threat of revolution. Just as foreigners must be expelled from the country, so "foreign bodies" must be eliminated from the human body. This led to the championing of vegetarianism and the banning of smoking and alcohol. Ungewitter had nothing but contempt for the medical profession, which not only rejected such life-reform but, by prescribing birth-control devices, contributed to Germany's decline. Birth control had encouraged an explosion of illicit sexuality, which would be passed on from parent to child and finally lead to death by exhaustion. Illicit sex included masturbation as well as sex between men and women practiced for pleasure rather than procreation.[22] Indeed, the magazine *Die Schönheit* warned its readers of the dire consequences of masturbation, which weakened the muscles and led to cowardice. Masturbation continued to be the deadly enemy of manliness. Christianity was Ungewitter's enemy as well, because of its prudery. If German women were allowed to look at nude German men, they would not lust after members of exotic foreign races.[23] Such ideas may seem bizarre, but they reflect in extreme form the beliefs that were circulating within all these movements. Respectability and nationalism were linked to form a bulwark against sexual passion, a danger always present in nudist thought and imagination.

Heinrich Pudor, another high priest of nudism, was, if possible, even more exacting. He moved in extreme right-wing circles at the turn of the century, going so far as to advocate the use of physical force against Jews—not a general volkish demand at the time.[24] Pudor claimed that he invented the term *"Nacktkultur"* (nude culture) in 1908 in order to protest against the confusion of nudism with pornography. Nudity as practiced in the big city, in theaters and by artificial light, merely titillated the senses. Nudist culture could only exist either in the privacy of the home or within a natural setting out in the sunlight. In that way it fulfilled its moral purpose.[25] He was highly indignant when, as he put it, some of his followers either became homosexuals or confused nudism with nightlife (*Nacktkultur mit Nachtkultur*). It takes a truly noble character like Tolstoy, Pudor wrote, to experience nudity in all its chasteness.[26] Few such characters were to be found, and those exclusively on the volkish right. Pudor's successor after the First World War was Hans Surén, who shared his racism, but attempted to link nudism firmly to gymnastics in order to make the Aryan body more beautiful. We shall encounter him again in our discussion on fascism and sexuality.[27]

The tables were now turned. For Pudor, it was not nude women but those who were clad who induced male lustfulness. Veiling the human body was said to whet the sexual appetite, and bourgeois dress invited immorality.[28] The *Vortrupp* wrote in 1913 that modern clothing hid the faults of the body, making it more difficult to find the right marital partner.[29] Choosing healthy partners was thought to be vital for the future of the race and nation. Girls, however, in an apparent contradiction, often wore "reform dress," which gave them room to breathe but hid their bodies. Here the opposition to confining garments had the reverse effect. A girl's body must be hidden, not so much because she was the chaste mother of the race but because of the rebellion against the corset, which had been obligatory for respectable ladies but was now thought unhealthy since it was tight and uncomfortable to wear. The youth movement had introduced airy and more functional clothes, which nudism and life-reform movements adopted.[30] Such flowing and airy garb hid the female body, but it also became symbolic of the opposition against changing women's fashions, which in turn were thought to be a part of the city life and therefore artificial. The fact that such clothes would make it more difficult to find healthy partners was ignored, probably because female nudism existed side by side with reform dress. Indeed, female nudes continued to be a staple of life-reform magazines. Boys, by and large, were encouraged to show themselves as God had made them—young Greeks become German. Pudor's fears of homosexuality and lustfulness demonstrate the constant effort of these movements to keep the distinction between normal and abnormal intact as part of their striving for respectability.

Such men illustrate the attempt to integrate nudism with respectability which was at the root of the nudist movement. For the majority of those involved, linking nature to the national mystique served to reinforce the effort to transcend sexuality and sensuousness. Nationalism during the nineteenth century annexed many of the social, economic, and cultural movements that engaged the enthusiasm of men and women, including nudism and life-reform. The nation, in turn, strengthened those forces used for setting off the nude body, giving nature a new kind of immutability. The rediscovery of the human body was stripped of its menace to respectability, just as nationalism deprived female national symbols of their real and potential sensuousness, as we shall see when discussing Marianne, Germania, and Queen Luise of Prussia in a later chapter.[31]

The German Youth Movement was one of the most significant organizations through which the rediscovery of the body became part of an important new reality. The youth movement attempted to live close to nature, to develop a genuine comradeship, and to take fresh pleasure in the rediscovery of the human body. But, most important, this lifestyle became part of the search for a new Germany, free of hypocrisy and cant, inner-directed, and symbolized by nature, camaraderie, and physical beauty.

The youth movement began its search for a genuine community as its members roamed the countryside trying to rediscover the inner feelings they felt they had lost in the city. Boys took up sunbathing and nude swimming, and the steeled, bronzed body became part of the movement's ideal of manly beauty. Again, the Greek example was referred to, and naturalness stressed over artificiality. Shame had no place here: "nudity equals truth,"[32] as they put it. To such tenets, German youth added the assertion that unity of body and soul must prevail. These young people saw themselves as alienated from the society of their parents. The cure they sought took the form of a communal affinity encompassing all aspects of life.

Those who have analyzed the youth movement have sometimes found eroticism at its core in the attitude of a male society that at first excluded women and only later accepted them with extreme reluctance. According to Hans Blüher, who based his book *Die Rolle der Erotik in der Männlichen Gesellschaft* (*The Role of the Erotic in Male Communities*, 1917) on his experiences in the youth movement, the homosexual alone creates human communities and states, and exemplifies a principle of association which extends beyond and complements the family. His libidinal energies are fulfilled in the male community, the only kind of association Blüher recognized. Although Blüher believed that homosexual acts were occasionally practiced by leaders and followers of the youth movement, this was of little importance to him, for he held that homosexuality represented spiritual principles—heroism, leadership, and communality.[33] To be sure, it seems absurd to treat the roaming of boys from thirteen to nineteen years old as a paradigm. The influence of Sigmund Freud in such thinking is obvious: sexuality becomes the foundation of all other aspects of life. If Freud was attacked by some for his failure to recognize the difference between love and sexuality, the spirit and the body,[34] the youth movement at times also blurred such distinctions, for it yearned for a fully furnished house, an all-encompassing community.

In spite of its higher purpose, the German Youth Movement was at first perceived as a threat to respectability, especially as nude swimming, sports, and even dancing spread beyond the movement. The exclusion of girls from several of the most important groups gave credence to the suspicions of homosexuality. Pudor had already deplored the infiltration of homosexuals among his followers, and when the *Altwandervogel* (a branch of the original roamers) was rocked by a homosexual scandal in 1911, the whole movement felt threatened. This accusation was leveled against the rich Hessian landowner Wilhelm Jansen, who had become both father-confessor and friend to many youths and thus aroused the envy of other leaders. Jansen and his friends did see in the male body the fulfillment of the Greek ideal of beauty and had made a cult of nudity—for example, introducing the practice of nude bathing into the movement.[35] Jansen was expelled from his group and with some of his followers founded a smaller camaraderie, corresponding to his ideal of youth devoted solely to the cultivation of the group spirit through friendship which, for some, did not lack in eros.[36]

But the so-called Jansen affair was significant because it demonstrated that imputations of homosexuality were never far from those male groupings that combined camaraderie with practices taken from the nudist and life-reform movements. The question whether Blüher or the accusations against Jansen were correct is of little importance when set against the fact that fear of homosexuality haunted all such movements.[37]

The rediscovery of the human body combined with the exclusively male nature of the early youth movement did raise the specter of homoeroticism, even homosexuality. Those who tried to recapture their own bodies as well as nature from the hypocrisy and artificiality of bourgeois life, as they saw it, also wanted to find refuge in a true community of affinity. They began to perceive the nation as such a community. Moreover, the nation helped to spiritualize their new sensuality, to integrate new discoveries into older respectabilities.

Thus the members of the youth movement, like the nudists and the life-reformers, sought to strip their own relationships of an eroticism that might get out of control and to direct their community of affinity toward a higher purpose instead. They sought an inner patriotism more genuine than the saber rattling of their elders. Germanic nature and the Germanic soul would stop male friendships from sliding into sensuality. In spite of Blüher's book and Jansen's supposed sexual transgression, the youth movement was puritan from its very beginnings. Illicit sexuality of any kind was looked upon as distracting boys and girls from the development of their true inner selves as well as from service to the community. Early marriage and chastity before marriage were recommended in order that selfish lust might not get the better of the spirit of camaraderie.[38] The movement was as concerned with the decline of morality as were its elders.

# II

At the same time that the youth movement was dreaming its dream of a "genuine" nation, the search for national regeneration was proceeding from a different direction, though also from out of a *Männerbund* filled with a homoeroticism more thinly veiled than that of the youth movement. Stefan George drew into his coterie some of the best minds in Germany. The poet as intuitive seer was not a new concept at the *fin de siècle*; men like Nietzsche, Richard Wagner, and Gabriele D'Annunzio had already looked upon themselves as prophets of a personal renewal that would change the nation as well. This claim must be seen against the background of a continuing romantic impetus and a renewed emphasis upon the irrational essence of man. Indeed, from 1904 on, George and his circle, not unlike the youth movement, wanted to return to the purity of nature. And although they tended to exalt primitive forces, such fervency was tempered by the belief that male beauty as it had existed in Greece would redeem Germany. Because of his growing admiration for Hellenic culture, George's work eventually recaptured a certain balance and harmony as he turned away from nature into his own circle, to belief in the rebirth of physical and inner beauty.[39]

Stefan George believed that beauty of soul was mirrored in physical beauty. Early in life he began to contrast the beauty of the human body to dead wisdom.[40] Such beauty came alive for George in one young boy, Maximin, whom he presented to his followers almost as a living god; and after the boy's early death in 1905, the myth of Maximin became symbolic of heroic youth—what George called the "secret Germany" to come. Maximin's death strengthened George's sense of mission. In his most famous cycle of poems, *Der Siebente Ring (The Seventh Ring,* 1907), he sounds a strongly eschatological note: salvation lies in that which is imminent, to be expounded by an élite under the leadership of the prophet. This book of poems spread George's fame and many a volunteer carried it into the First World War as a fount of hope and dedication, though George's élite was hardly geared for war or battle.

The disciples were largely selected because of their looks. Later, George would sit behind the window of his house in Heidelberg and seek to enlist any young man whose bearing and figure seemed to reflect his ideals. Such disciples swore an oath of obedience; they promised to live chaste and frugal lives, without luxury or indulgence.[41] But George dominated his circle, encouraging a leadership mystique that wrapped all his movements in secrecy. He cultivated a remoteness, a gaze into the distance, which endowed photographs of the poet with something of the qualities the pictures of saints possess (see plate 18).[42]

No doubt Stefan George was a major poet in the German language. But it was the cult and its aim which fascinated those men who, in George's words, were the "direct nobility," an order templar in the body politic. It was this order's task to guard the "secret Germany" until the time was ripe and the *Reich* could be reborn through beauty of body and soul. When the heroic age dawned, Germans would remember their great men and follow their example.[43] The new leader—at times described as an emperor—would surround himself with disciples, living symbols of beauty like the boy Maximin; the rest of the German people would exercise self-discipline and gladly serve. At the beginning of the century, George's circle mixed pagan elements with the Greek: Dionysian festivals, talk about the "lightening of the blood." But in the end (as we have seen), Greece with its ideal male beauty and harmony prevailed.

The materialism and ugliness these disciples saw all around them fueled the retreat into neo-romanticism and irrationalism, into the worship of the poet-as-prophet and the redemptive power of beauty. Gabriele D'Annunzio had written at the opening of the twentieth century that "the fortunes of Italy are inseparable from the fate of beauty, of whom she is the mother."[44] There was no need to construct blueprints for the new nation to come. George and D'Annunzio were not alone in believing in salvation through prophecy. On the political right, too, there were those who proclaimed that if Germans would only become artists, or find their racial soul, all would be well. Eventually, such inherently vague concepts of national revival, based on myth and symbol rather than workable plans for the future, were adopted by fascism. D'Annunzio inspired many of the rites and ceremonies through which Italian fascism was projected, and the Nazis were not totally mistaken in thinking that they could make use of George. They forgot, however, that for him popular mass movements were the enemy of that aristocracy chosen to guard the secret Germany.

Stefan George's influence was spread by intellectuals, academics and writers who felt concern for Germany's future, who liked to consider themselves as an élite chosen for their manly beauty, and for whom George's remote leadership, wrapped in mystery, produced a necessary focus and discipline. Men as diverse as Friedrich Gundolf, the literary scholar at Heidelberg, of Jewish descent, and Werner von Stauffenberg, who in 1944 was to make an unsuccessful attempt on Hitler's life, were among George's disciples. But so was Ernst Bertram, the philosopher, who collaborated with the Nazis. George himself died in 1933 in self-imposed exile from the Third Reich, sending his refusal to serve as president of Goebbels's Academy of Letters through a Jewish disciple.[45]

If male camaraderie proclaimed its power of regeneration through the youth movement, and the poet-as-prophet was well known at the time, still the George circle presented an exceptional phenomenon. Here homoeroticism was the principal agent of national renewal, certainly one of the most startling consequences of the rediscovery of the human body. Never would homoeroticism and nationalism be so plainly linked, stand so starkly exposed to view. Homoeroticism must be clearly distinguished from homosexuality in this instance. George's remoteness, his poetic ecstasies, and even the early festivals of the group centering upon Maximin can be interpreted as sublimating sexual desire. Women had no place in the George circle, and he never really forgave his disciples for marrying. Curiously enough, almost all of those who have written about Stefan George and his circle have downplayed its stark homoeroticism and concentrated instead upon George's poetry and his love of Greece, itself an interesting example of how to treat the homoerotic male as a national hero.

Yet, in this instance, the purging of the classics by respectability had not quite succeeded, and George was closer to Winckelmann himself than to the later German disciples of Greek sculpture. His élite threatened to rupture the alliance between nationalism and respectability through its emphasis on Greek beauty as a living eros, uniting those select few who could redeem the "secret Germany." They would have rejected any imputation of decadence, and indeed their harmony of form, clarity of expression, and devotion to the national purpose had no part in the decadent movement. Gabriele D'Annunzio's mystic ecstasies, his erotic abandon, were foreign to them.[46] His exuberant Italian nationalism forms a contrast with their serious and intense attempt to lift the curtain on the true Germany. Yet there was much of the theatrical, of the pose, in the George circle as well. The master himself liked to be photographed dressed up as Goethe, and often a flickering light cast its odd shadow upon the master's face. Dressing up in costume was popular among the disciples, and the stilted language—used not only in the poetry but also at times as a form of address—adds to an impression of artificiality that was appropriated by some elements of decadence. Nevertheless, decadence did not determine their outlook as it did that of D'Annunzio or Oscar Wilde.

The rediscovery of the human body was tamed in Germany, caught up in such immutable forces as nation, nature, or the harmony and balance of Greek beauty. Yet one young group of artists and writers, loosely labeled "Expressionists," at the beginning of the twentieth century sought to express their individual passions and instincts in a totally undisciplined way compared to either the youth movement or the George circle. Claiming that nothing was fixed in the world, they wanted "to grasp everything while it was in motion."[47] Expressionism was, above all, a continuous quest for new experiences by an avant garde which took seriously Nietzsche's saying that "ordered society puts the passions to sleep."[48] Thus, Wedekind in his play *Frühling's Erwachen* (*Spring's Awakening*, 1891), allowed his schoolboys to experience all forms of sexuality— masturbation, heterosexual promiscuity, and even a short episode of homosexual lovemaking between the boys. Other writers called for the murder of all the bourgeois, which meant their own fathers, and indeed they wrote plays about patricide. Theirs was a wholesale onslaught upon respectability and everything it stood for.

Yet the Nietzschean ecstasy could not be maintained. After the First World War, many Expressionists sought refuge in socialism or the far right, which shared their emphasis upon the soul and the instincts. But whereas in 1914 three quarters of the Expressionists had been under thirty, now they were aging.[49] Some did continue the impetus into the Weimar Republic, especially in painting and film; but little was left of the cry for sexual liberation.

## III

In England, the rediscovery of the body was not associated with the revolt of youth or with attempts to renew the nation, as in Germany, but instead influenced existing élites and literary sensibilities. At the same time, homoerotic experiences were personalized to a greater extent, without attributing any mystical force to the power of a beautiful body to determine future salvation.

England did not need to rediscover the human body to the same extent as Germany. Homoerotic themes were already much closer to the surface than they were elsewhere, encouraged by the male education of the public schools, followed by Oxford or Cambridge. There were few life-reform, nudist, or youth movements to help control the homoeroticism of the British male. Ever since the 1870s, a tradition of homoerotic poetry absent in Germany had existed.[50] This was not part of any movement, but a highly individual experience. To be sure, it might project the same images as in Germany, for example in Frederick William Rolfe's *Ballad of Boys Bathing* (1890), with its "white boys, ruddy, tan and bare" suffused like the cool water by the "setting sun and golden glare."[51] But only during the First World War when the boys had become soldiers did such poetry move more into the mainstream of literary England to take on national overtones as well. Unlike Germany, the beautiful male was not symbolic of the nation or the national landscape, but simply part of an individual's literary sensibility.

In England, too, in the last decade of the nineteenth century nudity became part of a back-to-nature movement. Once again this was not organized but advocated, for example, by Edward Carpenter, a utopian socialist and practicing homosexual who called for a return through nature to a true community among men. Nudity played an important role in Carpenter's thought as symbolizing not only the genuine but also the equality which must prevail in a just society. "Man clothes himself to descend, unclothes himself to ascend," he wrote in his *Civilization, Its Cause and Cure* (1889); he must "undo the wrappings and mummydom of centuries" in order to advance to a new Eden. Exposed to the sun, both mind and body would become clean and radiant.[52]

Moreover, whereas in Germany Heinrich Pudor, and the nudist, life-reform, and youth movements were all apt to favor the political right, Carpenter was a socialist. Nudity symbolized what he called the "gospel of individual regeneration," which would lead to social and economic reform, and also abolish discrimination against homosexuals.[53] Carpenter's influence was small at the time, but there were others who began to testify to their interest in the nude human body. The respectable academician Henry Tuke loved to paint naked boys bathing, although the figures were idealized, supposedly remote from any overt sexuality.[54] A whole series of paintings and poetry thinly disguised the new-found joy in the nude body as a homoerotic experience. The link between the beauty of ephebes and the pastoral was obvious; it had already provided a theme of homoerotic poetry, just as it would inform the body of so-called soldiers bathing poetry in England and Germany during the First World War.[55]

The triad of youth, nudity, and sunlight would continue to fascinate Englishmen, for example, in the war hero Rupert Brooke's "general sunniness."[56] At that time, the English and the German national stereotypes would be almost identical. However, Englishmen especially after the First World War looked to Germany to see the theory translated into practice. Nude bathing beaches existed in England, but not as part of a movement or an expression of theory. Stephen Spender wrote admiringly about the sun as the primary social force of Germany, which served to heal the wounds left by the First World War. He commented with delight on the open-air swimming pools where boys could sun themselves to deepest mahogany.[57] And Martin Green called his book about young English writers between the two world wars *Children of the Sun*, men sublimating their homoeroticism and even homosexuality into literary sensibility.[58]

English nationalism, when compared to that in Germany, played a minor role in attempting to tame the rediscovery of the body into respectability. The ideal of masculinity taught as a virtue in the great English public schools defined manliness as sexless, passions held in check through self-control over mind and body. Here Evangelical and national influences were mixed; until the Second World

War, the chapel stood close to the center of school life and an English gentleman was automatically a Christian gentleman as well. Moreover, in England there was initially somewhat less emphasis on the outward appearance of the body, at least until the First World War; not looks but proper comportment was what mattered. Admittedly Greek influences were at work in England as in Germany. The London public was amused rather than shocked when in 1822 a monument to the Duke of Wellington, erected in Hyde Park by the women of England, showed that highly respected gentleman as Achilles. The same was true after the First World War when a large statue of a nude youth was erected on the Greek island of Skyros over the tomb of Rupert Brooke.[59]

The rediscovery of the human body influenced literary perceptions, and served as an outlet for the individual's revolt against society. While the English protest against current respectabilities was highly personal, it was still kept within bounds. Male beauty was supposedly deprived of its sensuousness by integrating it with nature, and only with the onset of war would such beauty become a definite part of the English national stereotype.

By contrast, nudity attained much of its strength in Germany through the projection of male beauty as the national stereotype. We shall see how National Socialism was preoccupied with the nude human body, while simultaneously trying to maintain respectability.[60] Nationalism provided an ideal well suited for stripping sexuality from that rediscovery of the human body that had accompanied the *fin-de-siècle* revolt against conventional manners and morals. Its function of keeping intact the distinctions between the normal and abnormal, health and sickness, had not changed.

The dynamic of modern nationalism was built upon the ideal of manliness. Nationalism also put forward a feminine ideal, but it was largely passive, symbolizing the immutable forces which the nation reflected. As a living organism, filled with energy, nationalism tended to encourage male bonding, the *Männerbund*, which by its very nature presented a danger to that respectability the nation was supposed to preserve. Such bonding had been reinvigorated by the rediscovery of the human body at the *fin de siècle*. The male eros tended to haunt modern nationalism.

We have analyzed the ideal of manliness as a vital component of nationalism and respectability alike. It served as an energizing principle and as a standard of beauty transcending both sexuality and sensuousness. But the ideal had to be transferred from the individual to society and the state in order to support nationalism and respectability. Modern German nationalism saw itself as largely based upon a community of men; personal relationships among men therefore became a vital concern. The history of friendship was at the core of these relationships, defining the camaraderie of the *Männerbund*—an association based upon affinity rather than upon the demands of a higher authority such as the state. We have already referred to such *Männerbunde*, from the volunteers who rushed to the colors in war to the Gymnasts or early supporters of the youth movement. The ideal of friendship informed them all. But beyond the specific projection of manliness, the changing concepts of friendship can tell us much about the course of personal relationships and their connection with nationalism and respectability. The interplay between friendship and nationalism in particular serves to demonstrate just how much space the individual retained within society and the state for the appropriation of his own free choice and self-expression.

## CHAPTER 4

# Friendship and Nationalism

## I

The history of sexuality cannot be separated from the history of personal relationships, and especially that of friendship. The ways in which men and women related to one another, how men related to men, and women to women, not only served to define their sexuality but was subject once again to the pressures of nationalism and respectability. National institutions, Rousseau wrote, give form to the genius, the character, the tastes, and the customs of a people, and he meant this praise to include taste in choosing one's friends.

During the Enlightenment, emphasis was placed upon both individualism and the autonomy of personal relationships. Eventually, however, nationalism and respectability worked to restrict such autonomy; men and women should not be allowed to choose freely who their friends should be, just as they must not be allowed to follow their own sexual instincts. Standards must be set and fulfilled. Indeed, the very fabric of society seemed at stake. Alfred Cobban has told us that as the nation came to encompass both culture and politics, it became the sole proprietor of human rights, and the individual and his rights began to fade away.[1] The French Revolution marked the transformation of the nation from a focus of often divided loyalty to an all-embracing principle, and the wars of the French Revolution accelerated this process in western and central Europe. As we saw earlier, in these wars nationalism made its alliance with the quest for moral renewal, broadening its base and appeal.

We shall be concerned with male friendships here, leaving an analysis of friendships between women to the next chapter. Male friendships had played an important role in the life of the cultural élite during the eighteenth century, but they increasingly became a social and political force during the nineteenth and twentieth centuries. Nationalism had a special affinity for male society, and together with the concept of respectability legitimized the dominance of men over women. Male friendship faced that homoeroticism always close to the surface of nationalism. Here we must emphasize once again the distinction between homoeroticism and homosexuality. There were those, especially in England, who saw in sexual relations between men the logical consummation of friendship; but they were a tiny minority.[2] Eroticism was difficult to banish from the ideal of friendship. More often than not, it was combined with a quest for sexual purity. Homoeroticism might encourage platonic love, while homosexuality was perceived as exemplifying the baser instincts of men. Nevertheless, the line between homoeroticism and homosexuality was never firmly drawn, and homoeroticism was for the most part conceived as a danger and a challenge to accepted norms.

It was in Germany that the ideals of personal friendship were most clearly articulated, perhaps because such bonds among Germans could serve in part as a surrogate for lost national unity and aid in the attempt to find it again. As we shall see, the cult of friendship in Germany was for the most part linked to a lively patriotism. During the French Revolution, Germany was praised as providing an example of long-lasting friendships.[3] The eighteenth century saw a veritable cult of German male friendships based upon the "highest kind of equality": mutual independence of will. This ideal of friendship stressed both the personal independence of each separate friend and the interpenetration of their diverse personalities. Friendship was thought to exemplify the ideal of equality so important to the Enlightenment. There must be equality in the practice of humanity and justice among men, so Diderot's famous *Encyclopedia* tells us,[4] while the English *Spectator* saw friends as furthering each other's happiness on the basis of mutual respect and admiration.[5] The very word "brother" used among friends excluded any thought of domination.

The eighteenth-century cult of friendship in Germany had little in common with those earlier groups of writers and poets that had existed ever since the Renaissance. They had included all

manner of intellectuals—humanist theologians, government offi-
cials, as well as writers—who met together to read each other's
work and clarify their thoughts. The circle around Simon Dach in
seventeenth-century Königsberg, for example, wrote poetry for
each other, especially on commemorative occasions, and supported
one another in times of trouble.[6]
These earlier friends lacked the intimacy and sentimentality of
the eighteenth-century cult of friendship, whose gestures of affection seem to us exaggerated and who wrote poetry not just on commemorative occasions, but to each other at every opportunity—love
poetry filled with bathos. Yet unlike the later nineteenth-century
perception of friendship, no suspicion of homoeroticism accompanied their embraces, kisses, and gestures of affection. This sentimentality owed something to the emotional atmosphere of Pietism,
but also to the longing for companionship as a kind of substitute
religion for the cold deism of the Enlightenment or what were already regarded as the superstitions of Christianity. The novelist
Christian Fürchtegott Gellert, in his *Life of the Swedish Countess
of G.*\* (1747–48), defined friendship as sentimental and yet free
from eroticism. The return of a long-lost male friend brings joy to
the count and his countess as all three embrace each other. Gellert
comments that such friendship brings heavenly joy, and through
one glance, one kiss, conjures up a world of feeling without causing
confusion.[7] Friends embracing and kissing each other do not com-
municate desire; on the contrary, they show that they are capable
of keeping their passions under control.
During the eighteenth century an effort was made to distinguish
love as part of friendship among men from love between men and
women. Friendship among men was thought superior to heterosexual love because it was based upon reason rather than the senses.
Friendships among women were not taken seriously; it was men
who defined the norms of society. The new and popular science of
phrenology reflected general opinion when it sought proof through
the study of the brain that women made friends only among men
and never with other women.[8] Male friendships were perceived as
controlling passion, but in the eighteenth century their benefits
could be transferred to friendships between men and women as
well. In one novel published in 1747 the hero comes to experience
true affection toward the woman he loves only when she renounces
all sexuality and becomes a nun.[9] Rousseau's *Nouvelle Heloïse*

(1761) urged men and women to transform their love into friendship. Schlegel's *Lucinde* (1799) took up the same theme: relations between men as well as between men and women must be based upon friendship rather than sexual desire. The novels of Samuel Richardson with their warning against passion in love and marriage—his belief that marriage was based upon friendship rather than sensuality—exercised a strong influence here.[10]

Woman was thus stripped of her sexuality and integrated into the world of men. However, in the eighteenth century such integration led to a greater equality between men and women and not, as it would later, to the subordination of women. Those nineteenth-century women who mimicked the masculine world would have been accepted among the intellectual élite of the eighteenth century, but were now looked upon with suspicion. The manly girl or tomboy, whom we shall meet again, swiftly regained her feminity, and woman as a symbol of man's ideal of respectability or the object of his desire took her place.[11]

These examples should suffice to indicate how in the eighteenth century the ideal of friendship as symbolizing personal relationships attempted to strip itself of sexuality; how it sought to control the passions—and this in spite of the exaggerated gestures and sentimental poems that served to express the love of friends for one another. The danger of male eroticism played its part in the attempt to transcend sensuality. The cult of friendship in Germany was articulated through groups rather than individuals. The so-called *Freundschaftsbünde* were communities of affinity whose members were bound to each other through friendship, not so different from the later bonding of the German Youth Movement discussed in the last chapter. Yet for the most part members of the *Freundschaftsbünde* were married, and their poems expressed the love of women as much as the love of their friends. For example, while the poet Ludwig Gleim (1719–1803) was mildly scolded for kissing his friends on every occasion, his fantasies were firmly heterosexual.[12] The *Bund* of male friends seemed to dominate the lives of its members, sometimes even sealed through an oath of friendship sworn beneath "sacred oaks."[13]

Such *Bünde* fulfilled an integrative function in their admixture of romanticism and rationality. They were communities of affinity outside the social structures of family and estates, crucial in helping to build bourgeois self-consciousness and respectability. The cult of friendship in the eighteenth century presupposed the control of sexual passions and a commitment to German patriotism. Here nationalism and respectability were joined, except that patriotism did not dominate individual sentiment. The integral nationalism of the nineteenth century was merely latent in eighteenth-century patriotism. Even as the poet Ludwig Gleim claimed that the "temple of friendship" was the sole force that gave life meaning, he was writing solders' songs and praising love of the fatherland.[14] The members of the *Göttinger Hain*—one of the most celebrated *Freundschaftsbünde*—for all their idealization of personal friendship, also tried to resurrect ancient German customs. Such groups of friends saw no contradiction between respect for individuality and praise for the nation.

National unity did not as yet claim exclusive loyalty, superseding other associations among men. The state was subordinated to individual freedom. Thomas Abt, in his *Vom Tode für das Vaterland* (*Death for the Fatherland*, 1761), wrote that he was willing to sacrifice his life for that nation he had chosen of his own free will because it provided the most freedom for the individual citizen.[15] Clearly, Abt's praise of Prussia was not based upon a national mystique that transcended the individual and his circle of friends, pressing him into its service. His refusal to distinguish between the soldier and the citizen was typical of his attitude toward the individual and the state. Citizenship took priority: "*Alles ist bürger* (Everyone is a citizen)."[16] Yet the Enlightenment was apt to undermine its own ideals of friendship and individuality. The dispute as to whether men should direct their loyalties and their sense of belonging to small or larger groups was important in preparing the way for the eventual domination of nationalism and respectability over autonomous personal relationships—a domination that would succeed in controlling and redirecting many human passions, including men's sexuality.

## II

For the eighteenth-century philosopher and popularizer Christian Garve, the *Freundschaftsbünde* were no longer sufficient to provide shelter, though he still attempted to find a balance between the personal and the national. The love of the fatherland, he remarked in 1795, must be based upon sentiments similar to those of love of family and friends. Presumably none of these sentiments would predominate. But even while making this analogy, he condemns a "restrictive patriotism" narrowly focused upon the place of one's birth, the province to which one belongs, and those people among whom one has lived. Intimacy was still "precious," but at the same time Garve called on his readers to sacrifice the advantages of a small, manageable bourgeois society for the sake of a nation in which men could be equal one to another.[17] The fact that Garve urged Brandenburgers or Silesians to become Prussians was based upon the Enlightenment ideals of reason and human perfection, to which all men must aspire.[18] Here there can be no differences of purpose or outlook. Thus, the larger unit of the nation was preferable to provincial or local loyalties as an aid to universal perfection. Such arguments did not support the later integral nationalism of the nineteenth century; rather, individual differences were leveled in the name of a common humanity, even though Garve wanted to retain in some fashion the more limited bonds among men.

The nation was no end in itself but merely a step toward a shared humanity, a world citizenship. Typically enough, a sermon preached in 1801 on the occasion of the birthday of King Frederick William II of Prussia asserted that love of fatherland was necessary as a preparation for the love of all mankind.[19] This was a sentiment that would become rarer with the passage of time. The philosopher Moses Mendelssohn summarized what he saw happening during his life. Reviewing a book on national pride in 1761, he wrote that the pride of a nation, like that of an individual, rests upon self-love; however, national pride concentrates upon the superior qualities of our ancestors and fellow citizens, "rather than upon our own search for perfection."[20] The co-existence of patriotism and individualism, though challenged, was very much alive when Mendelssohn wrote his review, and forces other than the Enlightenment, despite its paradoxical attitude, were instrumental in assuring the victory of the nation over the citizen and his freedom to choose country and friends.

Here Pietism and the wars of national liberation together with the demands of mass politics and the beginnings of industrialization played a crucial role. Wars of national liberation, central to the life of any nation, created lasting precedents in Germany. Napoleon, who had defeated Prussia and Austria at the Battle of Austerlitz in 1805, began a dazzling series of military victories that put Germany at his feet. Napoleon's retreat from Moscow gave the signal for the insurrection of the German people led by Prussia in 1813. What Prussia gained by its crushing victory over the French at Leipzig that same year, it was destined to lose again at the Congress of Vienna in 1814, when the old regime triumphed over the wish for national unity. The wars of liberation, which had been prepared during the Napoleonic occupation, provided a shared experience for many Germans scattered among a multitude of states. They fostered a commitment and an enthusiasm which gave direction to many a seemingly purposeless life.

The enthusiasm of the wars of liberation, their myths and symbols, were to fire future generations, the more so as these wars were lost. Max von Schenkendorf set the tone in one of the wars' most famous songs: This was a "German Easter," in which the struggle of man to regain his nation was more important than his individuality.[21] When Theodor Körner sang: "Up and away to a joyful wedding (*So geht's zum lust'gen Hochzeitsfest*)," his ardor was not directed at any specific individual but at that collectivity of "German brothers," the fatherland.[22] The supremacy of the fatherland over the individual subordinated personal desires to the collective consciousness—the Volk, the "people," rather than to the state as symbolized by the dynasty. While kings and queens did not by and large want to open windows into men's souls (as Queen Elizabeth I of England once said), the modern state did set moral goals for its subjects. In return, it required much the same kind of commitment that monks and nuns had made to their Church. Indeed, the constant analogies between national and religious worship, death on the battlefield and Christian sacrifice, were supposed to exhort individuals to let the nation direct their passions and desires, to practice abnegation and self-control.[23] And sexuality (as we have seen) was considered an integral part of the passions the nation must be allowed to absorb and control.

Körner's "Appeal" of 1813 called the wars of liberation a holy crusade, which would restore the justice, morals, virtue, faith, and conscience destroyed by the tyrants of old. Von Schenkendorf's "Song of War" (*Landsturm Lied*) of the same date perceived the flags of the armies as symbolizing humility, friendliness—and self-discipline.[24] Moral rigor thus became part of the quest for national identity. The fatherland was internalized, absorbed into the German soul, preparing to take charge of the passions. Strong hearts glowed for all that was holy, to cite Körner once again; the fatherland was the vessel of God, the intermediary between man and the Christian universe.[25] This process of internalization was encouraged by Pietism, the emphasis upon the inner religious spirit that was said to have found its outward expression in the fatherland. Julius Möser wrote in 1774: "He who does not love the fatherland which he can see, how can he love the heavenly Jerusalem which he docs not see?"[26] Friedrich Carl von Moser linked true piety to the sanctification of that individual who dedicated himself to truth and the fatherland. Both religious truth and the fatherland informed the world of "brothers" and "sisters" that made up the pietistic conventicles and determined who one's companions should be. The circle of friends must subordinate themselves to a system of belief that circumscribed their freedom of movement.

Pietism managed to forge a union between religion and patriotism which sanctified personal relationships by depriving them of autonomy of purpose. It narrowed the horizon, as Robert Minder has shown. Many of those who built German idealism, writers and philosophers at the turn of the nineteenth century, were raised in a Lutheran parsonage. There the importance of the spirit was emphasized, the necessity of discipline in a common cause seen as given for all time. Authority was not to be questioned.[27]

In fact, Pietism and the wars of liberation reinforced a revolutionary tradition that had already penetrated deeply into Germany. Although Germany never experienced its own version of an English or French revolution, nevertheless it had espoused a unique revolutionary ideal ever since the Middle Ages. The apocalyptical view of history gave hope that a new dawn was about to break, that the scourges which preceded the rule of God would be overcome and in this way the passage of time abolished. Paracelsus and Jakob Böhme were the principal prophets of the "underground revolution." It was this apocalyptical tradition that inspired Wilhelm Weitling and his Communist League at mid-nineteenth century, just as Ernst Bloch attempted to harness the "underground revolution" to the left in his *Thomas Müntzer* (1921) after the First World War.[28]

Yet this revolution paradoxically strengthened the right by the way in which it supported German unity. The divine unity of God and nature, central to the apocalyptical vision, was exemplified by the ideal of the Volk as an ever-present utopia. A Germanic continuity was said to exist, which would break through in the end, make time stand still, and abolish death. This Germanic revolution lay in wait, side by side with the effects of Pietism and the lost wars of national liberation. Certainly romanticism was important here, and so were the political and economic factors that first retarded and then accelerated Germany's social and industrial development. German national consciousness turned upon itself; the link between patriotism and the autonomy of personal relationships was about to be broken. The battle would remain undecided until well after the First World War, but Germany now possessed a national dynamic that boded ill for the older idea of citizenship. Where in the eighteenth century friendship had been a place of refuge for the individual,[29] now the national ideal tended to become a haven from the pressures of society. The nation was no longer content to walk arm in arm with the circle of friends, a primus inter pares, a congenial shelter of divergent loyalties.

At the same time that the ideal of the nation was attempting to destroy the autonomy of personal relationships, the cult of friendship came under attack from another direction as well. The embraces and kisses among friends, their love of poetry, were regarded with increasing suspicion. The onslaught of respectability made itself felt and the distinction between friendship and sensuality now became of crucial importance. Kisses and embraces among men must be "manly" and any analogy to the attraction between the sexes avoided. The career of the playwright Heinrich von Kleist (1772–1811) provides an appalling example of the felt necessity to destroy any sexual feelings that might accompany friendship, the more so as homoerotic feelings were often close beneath the surface, a specter to be fought at all costs. There is little doubt about Kleist's homoerotic leanings; as he wrote to a friend, ". . . you have restored the age of the Greeks in my heart. I could have slept with you, dearest boy."[30] But at the same time, Kleist never tired of repeating that only the practice of virtue led to happiness. Moreover, he was engaged to be married, although his relationships with women were always cool and free of that rapturous sentimentality he heaped upon his male friends.[31] Kleist was apt to apply sexual vocabulary to male friendships, yet he fought his homoerotic leanings. Perhaps he was barely conscious of the real nature of his feelings. His constant fears about the consequences of masturbation illustrate vividly the general acceptance of Tissot's theory that this secret vice led to insanity.[32] Possibly Kleist blamed his unsteadiness and his inability to concentrate upon this habit, acquired in early youth: but his barely suppressed homoeroticism surely played a role in his unhappiness and depression. Kleist's suicide in his early thirties cannot be blamed solely upon his sexual frustration. He wanted all or nothing, and the personal and artistic humiliations of the last year of his life must have had an effect upon his decision.[33]

But of greater significance for our argument than the felt need for sexual sublimation, especially for those who rushed to the colors in the wars of liberation, was the strong desire to sacrifice oneself on behalf of a noble cause. Kleist himself sought to sacrifice his life for an end that transcended personal considerations, and such a death seemed to him the most significant affirmation of life. Kleist would have agreed with the slogan much used in the wars of liberation and during the First World War that only a sacrificial death in war could make anything worthwhile and give meaning to an empty life.[34] Kleist was frustrated in his bid to die for Germany, yet he wanted to give his suicide a larger meaning by joining his death to that of a friend who had come to the end of her patience with life. He finally found such a companion in Henriette Vogel, who was suffering from a terminal illness. Kleist's tragic career illustrates the perils of friendship but also the urge to join a higher cause, to transcend one's own life and to sublimate personal relationships.

Yet his suffering is of even wider significance, illustrating the felt need to separate friendship from sexuality, indeed, from individuality. Nationalism and respectability shared these goals, and signs of friendship that had formerly been taken for granted came under increasing suspicion. For example, after the first two decades of the nineteenth century, the portraits that depicted male friends became vague and shallow—often they are not shown as a group, or as holding hands, or making some gesture of friendship, but as a gathering of individuals.[35] Julius Schnorr's *David and Jonathan* (1853) shows the two men holding hands and Jonathan leaning on David's shoulder. But the body contact, slight as it is, appears even less erotic because of the sentimental atmosphere of the painting. The figures of friends have become spiritualized, and in Caspar David Friedrich's *Two Men on the Moon* (ca. 1820) one cannot even see their faces. The sentimentality of eighteenth-century friendship was going out of fashion as friendship became an act of almost religious chastity and dedication. The group of German painters known as the Nazarenes who settled in an abandoned Roman monastery in 1810 was such a *Freundschaftsbund*, whose aim was to revive religious painting. (We shall return to this group of friends in the next chapter.)

The attempt to exorcise the erotic elements from friendship never ceased in the nineteenth century. By the end of the century the poet Carl Gutzkow yearned for that love he could no longer find in marriage but wanted to find among friends. Yet he hoped that his friends would avoid sentimentality in favor of a "warm feeling of manhood."[36] Around the same time the sexologist Iwan Bloch lamented the neglect of friendship among men, and wished that "men could talk about love for each other without coming under the suspicion of homosexuality."[37] At the beginning of the twentieth century Alexander von Gleichen-Russwurm wrote that the Greek philosophers, for all their admiration of youth, had condemned sensuousness as upsetting man's mental and spiritual balance. Friendship was a masculine, firm, and restful ideal. The concept of masculinity came to stand for the ability to transcend the passions, including preoccupation with sexuality. The more masculine a philosophy, he continued, the greater its emphasis upon friendship; the more female, the greater the reliance upon feeling.[38]

The attempt to free friendship of any sensuousness through the use of concepts of manhood would continue; to be manly meant keeping control over the passions. Even close friends must keep their distance. It was during the *fin de siècle* that intense friendships among women, which had been largely ignored or thought harmless, came under suspicion of lesbianism. Whereas even Samuel Richardson had thought nothing of letting the virtuous Pamela share a bed with her woman servant, and male students in eighteenth-century Oxford often shared a bed with each other, this custom was now considered suspicious and inappropriate.[39]

As respectability began closing in, the male national stereotype projected a latent sensuousness supposedly restrained by his virility and symbolic function. The ideal German—whether as warrior, Greek god, or young Siegfried—was often pictured in the nude. This stereotype exemplified the increasing importance of outward appearance, of male beauty, at the precise time when gestures of intimacy among men were being condemned. Whereas the looks and appearance of a friend's body and face had played little role in the eighteenth-century cult of friendship and its terms of affection, they now began to assume increasing importance. We are entering an ever more visually oriented age, exemplified not only by national symbols but also by the effects of sciences like physiognomy and anthropology with their classifications of men according to ideals of classical beauty.[40]

Political symbolism had become of crucial importance as the masses sought to participate in the political process. The Greek revival of the eighteenth century determined the standards of beauty and ugliness. So-called good looks, the classical figure, displaced the warm heart and clear reason, which had no need of outward bodily signs. Ludwig Gleim and his circle knew nothing of the *Symbolism of the Human Form* (to quote the title of Carl Gustav Carus's book of 1853). Yet such symbolism became a sign of national identity. The poet Friedrich Gottlieb Klopstock stressed manly beauty as a characteristic of his German heroes,[41] and the Gymnasts founded at the time of the wars of liberation showed the national stereotype in the making. This manly beauty through its classical harmony and proportions communicated a restfulness to soothe the passions, while at the same time it managed also to project virility. By the beginning of the twentieth century the German Children's Protection League would be proclaiming that "a splendid physique is rarely accompanied by vicious traits."[42] Personal identity was not merely defined by belonging to the nation, but the national ideal of human beauty was reflected in an individual's appearance. Personal relationships were controlled both in body and mind.

The small circle of friends had made way for the more militant *Bund*. Personal relationships in turn became part of other larger and more active concerns. Individuality was projected from man onto the nation: the world was made up of nations, each with its own individuality, which must be respected. Every Volk was equal, each had its place in the sun, and the domination of one nation over others was rejected. This was the principal theory of German nationalism during the first half of the nineteenth century, though it remained alive even later in spite of growing emphasis upon domination and aggression. Within the nation itself, equality was supposed to reign—the nation as a community of affinity, a so-called natural union among men. Yet this community was formed by the nation and believed that the truth for which the nation stood should not bend to accommodate personal differences. The exercise of free will which Gleim had thought of as constituting the essence of friendship, and which for Abt had been an integral part of patriotism, was thus gradually transferred from the individual to the nation. The word *Bund* was now used for the most part not to refer to a group of friends but to those united in the service of national renewal. *Bund* originally meant a fenced-in piece of land, but now this barrier became ever more daunting, made of barbed wire, and entry was granted only to those who shared the myths, symbols, and looks of the nation.[43]

At the beginning of the nineteenth century smaller units were dissolving into larger associations. Many of these associations continued the eighteenth-century tradition, which equated patriotism with individualism and even world citizenship; others were patriotic societies according to the English model, working for the good of the community.[44] The French occupation of Prussia and the wars of liberation meant that the *Bund* became more aggressive as it began to perceive nationalism as a new religion which must direct all attitudes toward life. The Gymnasts (1810), fraternities (1811), or Arndt's "German Association" (1814) were alike devoted to the "seizure of heart and mind." Friedrich Ludwig Jahn, who founded both the Gymnasts and the fraternity movement as instruments in the struggle for German unity, wrote that men must belong to one fatherland even as they belonged to one household, and have one true love in their lives.[45] His *Deutsches Volkstum* (1817) linked nationalism and bourgeois ideals, family life and faithfulness in marriage. Indeed, the Gymnasts while training for battle were supposed to avoid the so-called sins of youth, such as laziness, lustfulness, and uncontrolled sexual passion.

The *Bund* which Jahn or Arndt advocated directed individual aspirations toward the ideal of the Volk, while the concept of beauty was that of the national stereotype. This stereotype bore the marks of its origins during the wars of liberation together with that of the Greek revival mentioned earlier. The cult of masculinity—the male body hard and lithe, poised for battle—made its bid to replace the cult of friendship. Unity of body and spirit was vital here, as indeed it was for the Gymnasts whose bodily contours were made visible by the uniform Jahn designed for them.[46] The national stereotype, its ideal of male beauty, while restraining the passions, simultaneously symbolized an aggressive masculinity—the evolution of the ideal of the *Bund* from friendship to nationalism.

Manliness linked to beauty of form had been anticipated by eighteenth-century anthropologists like Christian Meiners, who attempted to prove the superiority of Caucasians over blacks by praising their beauty of form, sense of order and moderation. These ideals were said to be central in the battle against egotism, lack of shame, and that sensuousness thought to characterize blacks.[47] Manliness was a part of beauty of form, meaning the Greek model of manly beauty, order, and moderation, but symbolizing courage and love of freedom as well. The phrenologists and physiognomists held similar ideas. These new sciences of the eighteenth century advocated an ideal of manliness based not only on Greek concepts of beauty but also upon those virtues of order and moderation, courage in the face of adversity, which were so highly prized in that period, being closely tied to the triumph of the new morality.

Friedrich Gottlieb Klopstock became one of the chief propagandists of German nationalism, and he can serve to summarize the transition from the eighteenth-century cult of friendship to ideals of nationalism and manliness. At first Klopstock had attempted to overcome his loneliness through the cult of friendship. His famous ode, *Wingolf* (1747), celebrates the reunion of friends, each with his own peculiarities and individuality. But Klopstock constantly extends this circle until it becomes a holy élite of "Germanic bards," as he calls them.[48] Thus Klopstock must have been ambivalent when he wrote to Ludwig Gleim in 1750 that nothing in the world surpassed personal friendship.[49] Friendship without having either to command or obey informed Gleim's own world. But for Klopstock such friendship was constantly transcended until it was put into the service of the nation. His play *Die Hermanns Schlacht* (1769), the battle in which Arminius defeats the Roman Legions, substitutes the myth of the hero for the circle of friends. Whereas in *Wingolf* the Germanic bards had sung of friendship, now the young warriors exclaim: We can no longer tolerate the bards, let us go down and fight! The ancient custom of friends fighting and dying side by side in battle is condemned. All must be subordinated to the fatherland, which is "greater than mother, wife and bride, greater than a son in the prime of life. . . ."[50] Manliness here meant knowing how to die for the fatherland, while Gleim, despite his soldiers' songs, had urged warriors to substitute friends and wine for joy in battle.[51]

Yet the ideals of the Enlightenment had not vanished; they were simply assimilated into Klopstock's nationalism. The struggle for German unity, he asserted, was a fight for natural rights. These rights retained their eighteenth-century content—they were based upon the demands of reason and the love for humanity. But unlike Gleim's enlightenment these ideals were dominated by the rough noise of battle, the exclusiveness of the Volk and its blood.[52]

The change is obvious here and it was J. G. Fichte, philosopher-turned-patriot, who expressed it clearly in his *Speeches to the German Nation*, 1808. Man cannot love himself, or anything outside himself, unless such love is part of a system of belief. True love is never fixed upon the transitory but must rest in what is unchanging and eternal.[53] Here individual relationships are dissolved into the nation, a reflection of the cosmos itself, just as manliness is lifted from the individual sphere to that of national service. The evolution of friendship and nationalism in Germany led to the subordination of one over the other.

Those who rejected the German nationalism that derived from the wars of liberation were not affected by its victory, and neither were a number of liberals or socialists. Obviously for many, friendships were always autonomous. But we are concerned with analyzing the collaboration between nationalism and respectability, the part of both in defining and controlling normal and so-called abnormal sexuality. Nationalism in absorbing the ideal of friendship was able to strengthen itself, to collaborate still more effectively with bourgeois society in order to support ideas of respectability, to control a "nervous" age and to contain sexual passions. The nation must transcend sexuality even as friendship must be stripped of eroticism. The love between male friends should not be projected upon each other but upon the nation; in this way, homoerotic temptation would be overcome. The national stereotype symbolized such conquest, drawing unto itself homoerotic desires, only to transcend such passions.

# III

Although we are concentrating upon Germany, the history of friendship in England by comparison brings into still sharper relief the relationship between nationalism and respectability on the one hand, and that autonomy of personal relationships symbolized by friendship on the other. Respectability had found a home in both England and Germany, but despite important similarities, their nationalisms differed in many respects. England had long been united; it did not have to concentrate its energies upon the struggle for national unity. Thus the homoeroticism latent within idealized friendship was less well controlled in England than in Germany. While Germans had experienced the *Bund* of males, the English ruling classes spent their formative years in an autonomous male society in which access to women was the exception rather than the rule. Most upper-class Englishmen experienced intimate male friendships at boarding school and at Oxford or Cambridge. Such an educational system did not exist in Germany, where neither school nor university boarded students, cutting them off from the outside world. German education on the whole was designed to shape and discipline a man through his learning, however brutally enforced. The typical English public school, on the other hand, was meant to provide a microcosm of state and society, to build the character of those who were destined to rule.[54] Whereas in our discussion of friendship and nationality in Germany we remained largely with adults, concentrating on the struggle for national unity, in England we must start with the education of youths as the factor that helped shape ideas of friendship and male society.

The vision of a small group of friends who had found each other in the medieval setting of ancient schools or amid the spires of Oxford and Cambridge remained alive for many an Englishman long after he had finished his education. Although for some this friendship led to the lifelong practice of homosexuality, for most it was an important stage in their otherwise heterosexual behavior, and throughout their lives, they were apt to retain their circle of friends from school and university.[55] This unique and prolonged experience was shaped by the reform of the public schools in the first half of the nineteenth century. The reforms were based upon English evangelism, the religious revival that had such an important effect upon manners and morals. Here, too, the differences between England and Germany were important, not just in the atmosphere through which the English ruling class passed, but in the differences between German Pietism and English Evangelicalism, which in turn influenced the public schools and indeed the entire attitude toward the nation.

The Evangelical tradition had remained alive in England, awaiting use by those who wanted to reform school and society in the nineteenth century. Where in Germany Lutheran Pietism through its inward emphasis encouraged a passive attitude toward authority, in England evangelism generated its own dynamic through an active Christianity. The difference lay between retreat in the face of the world and active involvement. The Lutheran family which dominated the youth of so many Germans withdrew from public concerns, whereas the "Christian gentlemen" formed by the English school and university as the ruling class were supposed to set an active example in public life. Evangelism had a direct effect upon upper-class education—that closed male society through which these young men passed.

"Godliness and good learning"[56] were the principles by which Thomas Arnold sought to reform the public schools in the first half of the nineteenth century. They had been nurseries of vice; now they must nourish Christian gentlemen. This was to be accomplished through exhortation in chapel, rigorous discipline, and a firm control over manners and morals. These reformed schools have been called "sexual concentration camps,"[57] and not entirely without reason. The masters conducted an uncompromising crusade against masturbation, and the fear of homosexuality was always present. W. E. Benson, the headmaster of Wellington, spent hours stringing barbed wire along dormitory cubicles, and in most schools boys were prevented from being alone with one another.[58] Frederic W. Farrar, in the most celebrated book about English public schools, *Eric, or Little by Little* (1858), shows how Eric gradually gives in to temptation and vice. First he learns to use profanity, then smoking, and subsequently drinking and stealing. However, in the end he resists further temptations and atones through a premature death. At a sermon shortly afterwards a master tells the boys that he had mourned for Eric when he went astray, but does not mourn him now that he has died penitent and happy. The dreams of ambition have vanished and the fires of passion have been quenched. Death was a congenial solution to the temptations of vice. Farrar merely alludes to masturbation and homosexuality in oblique terms; such matters were best left to medical texts.

A recent historian of the public schools has summed up in excellent fashion their preoccupation with sexual purity: being manly meant to crush sin, but the worst sin was sex; therefore being manly meant curbing all sex.[59] Michael Campbell in *Lord Dismiss Us*, a remarkable modern schoolboy memoir, has his headmaster say that young people develop feelings before they develop moral sense, and that it was the duty of the school to assure the parents that a sense of morality would develop and run parallel.[60] This meant that within this "emotional hothouse" (as Campbell describes the friendships between boys), all tenderness was turned into shame.[61] The school produced homosexually experienced boys who were riddled with guilt as they tried to form friendships.

For those who reflected the official position of society and the public schools, the ideal was one of boyhood destined to greatness. It was Reginald Farrar, writing about his father's youth in the 1840s, who defined what such a Christian gentleman should be—that gentleman who was to rule the country and set an example for the Empire and all Englishmen. He should have eager, well-opened eyes, clean-cut features, and fine wavy hair (here the general stereotype was very similar to that current in Germany). But above all, he should be "a boy of stainless and virginal purity, who took for his motto the text: 'Keep innocency and do the thing that is right, for that shall bring a man peace at last.'"[62] Respectability and looks were conjoined in the public school, which was regarded by Arnold and others as the microcosm of the state.

Self-control was thought crucial to the making of the English ruling class, which must learn how both to obey and to command. The sixth form (the last before university) ruled the school and enforced discipline, while the entering boys had to "fag" for the sixth-formers—acting as their servants, at their beck and call. Self-control was an integral part of leadership. Charles Kingsley in his novel of Empire, *Westward Ho!* (1855), called upon man to be "bold against himself," to conquer his own fancies and lusts in the name of duty, "For he who cannot rule himself, how can he rule his crew and his fortunes?"[63] Discipline and self-control were supposed to produce that ideal type of schoolboy described by Reginald Farrar. Such discipline and control were reinforced by loyalty to the group, starting with the house at school in which boys lived and on whose teams they played against other houses, continuing with the Cambridge or Oxford colleges to the governing of the nation. Group loyalty was supposed to form a cohesive ruling class. In fact, it produced a new élite not only in government but also among intellectuals, writers, and poets. The ideal of friendship became a part of that reliance upon each other taught at school, to be practiced throughout one's life. Arthur, the hero of *Tom Brown's School Days* (1857), asserts that the true British boy does not play games for his own sake, but so that his side may win.[64]

Equipped with such education, former public schoolboys were tested by wielding power not only at home but also in the Empire. Indeed, many of the heroes of schoolboy stories go off to join their regiments in India. The reality of the Empire proved congenial to the practice of self-control, discipline, and group loyalty, and also as an outlet for sexual frustrations. Ronald Hyam has shown the role that sexual energies played in the dynamics of the British Empire, and to what extent the Empire proved an outlet for unresolved sexual tensions.[65] The Empire was an exceedingly masculine affair. Many famous proconsuls—Charles Gordon, Cecil Rhodes, and H. H. Kitchener among them—were bachelors who continued to live in the same male society abroad as they had at school, still striving to exemplify the virtues of the Christian gentleman. Robin Maugham has given an imaginative reconstruction of how on the night that he faced death at the hands of rebels in Khartoum, General Charles Gordon called on God to give him strength in order to resist sexual temptation in the shape of a young soldier.[66] Such rulers of Empire were engaged in fervent male friendships. To be sure, many (perhaps most) consoled themselves in the company of native women; still, male friendships played an important role in governing the Empire.

Rudyard Kipling wrote to a friend in Johannesburg that "the spectacle of your house full of clean young white men cheered me as much as anything."[67] Kipling himself did not have much talent for friendship, but here were young men who had been whipped into shape by that discipline in which he fervently believed.[68] Such a stereotype, a combination of good looks and virtue, roused the admiration of many of the men like Cecil Rhodes, Charles Gordon, or Alfred Lord Milner who so successfully built and maintained the Empire. Homoeroticism did play an important role in such admiration and group loyalty, however sublimated to the concepts of duty and virtue. The Empire provided a congenial setting in which nationalism and respectability could find full play.

Yet in England itself, and no doubt in much of the Empire as well, male friendship was never deprived of autonomy of purpose, redirected, and absorbed into a higher ideal as it was in Germany, and therefore homoeroticism was more difficult to keep in check. Virtue was always intertwined with vice. The ideal of the public school we have discussed must be pitted against this reality. Cyril Connolly, in one of the best public school autobiographies, set in Eton during the First World War, writes that while homosexuality "was the Forbidden tree around which our Eden dizzily revolved," the end product of public school education was, more often than not, that "familiar type, the English male virgin."[69] The poet and classical scholar A. E. Housman, himself a homosexual, looking back at Oxford toward the same time, wrote that the university was "shot through with rapturous undertones in an age torn between puritanism and the libidinous liberties of ancient Greece."[70]

This was a man's world, whose ideals were spread far and wide through boys' weeklies and popular adventure stories. Here the heroes were not quite without sex;[71] for example, whenever John Buchan wanted to characterize his villains, he threw doubt upon their so-called masculinity. Thus the German Baron von Stumm in *Greenmantle* (1916), who attempts to foil the hero at every turn, has a "perverted taste" for "soft delicate things," and his homosexuality is hinted at as part of the German's bluff and brutal personality. The women in Buchan's or Sapper's stories are really men. For Buchan, the very word "sportsman" has no feminine gender even when applied with approval to a clean-cut girl.[72] The kind of nationalism which for so many boys meant public service at home or in the Empire, in the world of schoolboy adventure meant torturing a "dago" bartender in Valparaiso or hanging a Jewish jewel thief because he had tried to paw a British girl.[73] Just so, in the boys' weeklies and nineteenth-century comic strips the villains were Italians or Portuguese who behaved in a most "unmanly" fashion.[74] The southerner was the villain, lacking that self-control which was basic to all the other virtues of masculinity. In Germany, a writer like Thomas Mann expressed the identical attitude by regarding those who lived in southern Europe as endowed with a sensuousness dangerous to the Puritan North.

Masculine virtues were crucial to upper-class education—toughness, spartan living, and fair play; doing one's duty. Manly behavior meant being part of the team, loyalty to group and country. As one critic points out, "Buchan and Sapper were not strong on love. They wrote of friendship."[75] Women were marginal, and although they entered Oxford and Cambridge in 1919, they were confined to separate colleges just as they had been to separate public schools (coeducation began to make inroads after the First World War, but it never triumphed in such schools until recent times).

Similar ideas of masculinity, though they did not dominate, were a small part of French education. Still, the school directed by a religious order that Henry de Montherlant described so graphically in Les Garçons (The Boys, 1969) as it existed before World War I was not unlike the English public school. Here too protection of younger by older pupils was the rule, and led to adolescent passion. But this particular school was liberal, even at the beginning of the twentieth century. Masturbators were not hunted down; instead, the Father Superior made fun of a large book written by a priest which posited the prevention of masturbation as the chief task of religion.[76] Nor did the Father Superior take umbrage at the close friendship between two boys, though he exhorted them to purity.[77] The English headmaster was on constant alert against both masturbation and friendships between boys too close for comfort. Montherlant himself was influenced by this male society and its homoeroticism, and he was to be obsessed by the search for masculinity for the rest of his life. Many other Frenchmen may have reacted in a similar manner, though the English male society remained unique in its exclusiveness.

Similar ideas of masculinity dominated most European countries, inculcated by education, strengthened by the constant fear that the weakening of sex roles might destroy the ordered society of the middle classes. It is typical that the famed German sexologist Krafft-Ebing should in 1877 have attempted to strip the androgyne of a bisexuality he himself could not face. Androgynes, so he held, whatever their biological construction, had so-called female characteristics. They were "big children," who could not handle money or undertake social responsibility, but loved toiletries and knickknacks. Androgynes, like women, had no learning and no powers of perseverance.[78] Krafft-Ebing's belief that the ideal of manliness must not be diluted by a confusion of sexes was widely shared. This male society in which so many of the English élite were at home determined the evolution of friendship in England. Homosexuality was regarded by some—a very few—as the logical culmination of friendship. This held true for Oscar Wilde and his circle, just as somewhat later, in 1904, Lowes Dickinson put friendship first in his search for the meaning of good, and such friendship was in large measure homosexual.[79] After the First World War, for Wystan Auden and Christopher Isherwood going to bed together was a logical climax to their friendship,[80] while in postwar Berlin, the name "Friendship" was often used to disguise homosexual or lesbian clubs and journals. These are random examples, and it is impossible to say how typical they were, but for some men homosexual experience was certainly an integral part of the ideal of friendship. A few went further. When Edward Carpenter, following the example of Walt Whitman, wrote about freedom and democracy based upon brotherly and comradely love, the love of one's own sex was important as a possible bond among brothers. He seemed to have hoped that his Cambridge friends would form the nucleus of a new society. Shame of body had no place in Carpenter's utopia, and neither did the suppression of sexual instinct.[81]

In Germany, similar ideas of homosexuality as the basis of a better society can be found at the turn of the century within the German Youth Movement. Hans Blüher's *The Role of the Erotic in the Male Community*, based as we have seen on his perception of the youth movement, praised the homosexual as the most socially creative individual, who since he did not have to direct his sexual energies toward his family, could use them to cement communal ties.[82] Blüher was more exclusive than Carpenter, who had never made homosexual relationships basic to this new society. He was also much more militant—his *Bund* was nationalist and anti-Semitic, the very opposite of Carpenter's idealistic socialism. The linkage between nationalism and homosexuality was important here; we saw how in Germany nationalism on the one hand attempted to transcend sexuality by drawing it into its orbit, but how, on the other, this very attempt at transcendence did at times encourage homoerotic attitudes among the *Bund* of men. Those who in Germany saw the *Bund* as the origin of all true states often invoked the power of eros, the dedicated love between men.[83] But they were also quick to separate such a love from homosexuality, and here Blüher, though indifferent to the consummation of such sexuality, was an exception rather than the rule. Moreover, in Germany there was never that easy recognition of homosexuality as an eccentricity that must be accepted among some of one's friends which characterized, for example, the members of the Bloomsbury group.

Yet in England, as in Germany, the laws against homosexuality were stiffened toward the end of the nineteenth century. If Germany had its Krupp scandal (1902) and Harden–Moltke–Eulenburg scandal (1906), in which aristocrats and members of the emperor's court were accused of homosexuality, England had its Cleveland Street scandal and Oscar Wilde trials. The Cleveland Street scandal of 1889–90 involved prominent aristocrats, a homosexual brothel, and possibly the son of the Prince of Wales. This in turn encouraged the trials of Oscar Wilde because prominent persons had been named and the accusation of a cover-up was feared by the government.[84] After the Wilde trials, homosexuality, national degeneration, and the abnormal were closely linked, and anyone seen with long hair, a monocle, and fancy clothes might hear passers-by call out, "Hello, Oscar."[85] Edward Carpenter commented: "a few more cases like Oscar Wilde's and we should find the freedom of comradeship now possible seriously impaired to the permanent detriment of the race."[86]

It was partly as a consequence of the Wilde trials that two intimate friends, John Gray and André Raffalovich, sought refuge in Catholicism, one as a clergyman, the other living nearby, their relationship remaining close but formal. Both were literary men, providing one of the many links between homoerotic literary culture and Roman as well as Anglo-Catholic Christianity. There were others as well who shared André Raffalovich's contention that Catholic Christianity provided the best support for pure and chaste friendship.[87] The individualism which had allowed friendship in England to retain so much of its autonomy of purpose was in danger. Respectability always threatened to reassert its hold. But for all that, it lacked the support of an integral nationalism.

Despite the manifold differences between England and Germany, the triumph of respectability was common to both, and so was the ideal of manliness and even the national stereotype. There is little to choose between Reginald Farrar's ideal schoolboy and the ideal German. Both were part of the quest for respectability, and both through their looks exemplified the distinction between normal and abnormal thought essential to the functioning of society. The link between sodomy and national catastrophe remained alive, and so did fears about degeneration and a declining birth rate. Certainly in England, as in Germany, feelings of national superiority were above all directed against those who, so it was said, failed to control their emotions. Comic books and boys' papers in England, novels in Germany, berated the swarthy Spaniard, Portuguese, Italian, or Jew for their misguided passions. Here nationalism in both countries strengthened its alliance with virtue and righteousness by pointing to supposedly inferior peoples whose very appearance provided a contrast to the strong but calm, sensuous but pure, stereotype.[88]

Both the differences and similarities we have discussed were important in the control of sexuality, the strength or weakness of the alliance between nationalism and respectability. The history of friendship provides an example of the relative effectiveness of the process of transcendence in Germany and England. But it also emphasizes the preference for male society in the nineteenth and twentieth centuries, whether as a *Bund* of friends dedicated to a common cause, as the origin of all states, or simply as a circle of friends based on nothing more significant than personal choice. The importance of such male friendships as a social and political force cannot be overrated. They provided a home and a shelter for modern man. Yet for all their latent homoeroticism, such Germans and Englishmen were for the most part heterosexuals, good husbands and family men, even if among the English ruling class and among some German homosexuals temptation was less easily suppressed. The eroticism inherent in male friendship did not exclude sexual normalcy.

Both nationalism and respectability defined the role of women, too, and the different ways in which these roles were defined has a direct bearing upon the definitions of normality and abnormality in bourgeois society.

CHAPTER 5

# What Kind of Woman?

## I

Nationalism, which co-opted the male search for friendship and community, went on in the first decades of the nineteenth century to assimilate new ideals of womanhood. It reinforced them by fashioning female symbols of the nation, such as Germania, Britannia, and Marianne. These images embodied both respectability and the collective sense of national purpose. Romantic art was called into service in order to give visual and literary dimensions to the new themes. Nationalism—and the society that identified with it— used the example of the chaste and modest woman to demonstrate its own virtuous aims. In the process, it fortified bourgeois ideals of respectability that penetrated all classes of society during the nineteenth century.

If woman was idealized, she was at the same time put firmly into her place. Those who did not live up to the ideal were perceived as a menace to society and the nation, threatening the established order they were intended to uphold. Hence the deep hatred for women as revolutionary figures, almost surpassing the disdain which established society reserved for male revolutionaries. Woman as a symbol of liberty and revolution, "Marianne into battle," contradicted the "feminine" values of respectability and rootedness, and was quickly domesticated or dethroned.

In the ever more sharply defined distinction between men and women, for example, androgyny, once praised as a symbol of unity, became abhorrent. Lesbianism also was particularly difficult to face. As an expression of female sexuality, it was ignored through most of the nineteenth century. This was not merely a "love that dared not speak its name"—it did not even have a name. By the start of the twentieth century the hatred reserved for lesbians seemed, if possible, even deeper than that directed toward male homosexuals. Nevertheless, most lesbians shunned the defiant posture of the decadents. For the most part, as we shall see, they rested their defense on a plea that fundamentally accepted the standards and judgments of society. Even feminists allied themselves with respectability. Yet within an ever more restrictive perception of the role of women, there were times when she could still symbolize liberty.

The French Revolution popularized Marianne as a female symbol of liberty. While revolutionary imagery at times pictured her as solemn, seated and clothed in chaste garments, for the most part she appeared to be young, active, and scantily clad. She would typically wear a low-cut gown and expose her legs below the knees. As Revolution settled down into Republic and then into Empire, the sedate and fully clothed figure prevailed over her tomboy rival.[1] True, woman as a symbol of revolutionary liberty was not so easily buried; she was resurrected once again during the 1830 Revolution in Eugène Delacroix's *Liberty Leading the People at the Barricades* (see plate 5). Lead she does, holding a tattered flag, and most indecently clothed. But as Marianne became established as a national symbol, the nation clipped her revolutionary wings. In 1848 the newly proclaimed Second Republic opened a competition to determine just how it should represent itself allegorically.[2] As a result, though surrounded by the revolutionary symbols of liberty, equality, and fraternity, it was decided that Marianne should be seated in order to convey a feeling of stability (see plate 6).[3] Even when Gustav Doré in 1870 portrayed the female Republic leading a citizens' army in imitation of Delacroix's pose, she was fully clothed.[4] On the political left, lithographs and prints showing a scantily clad Marianne continued to circulate as a metaphor for revolution detached from any specific event.[5] But the revolutionary could not compete with the respectable Marianne.

The female symbol of France was fully clothed, yet eventually nudity itself could be tamed into respectability and lose its sensuousness. The nude males who came to symbolize Germany's virility and manliness illustrate this process, and so do the naked females who often represented the ideal of woman under National

Socialism. Such nudes with their almost transparent, smooth bodies were frozen into position, remote and godlike, quite unlike Delacroix's moving, gesticulating, and very human Marianne. The tradition of Greek sculpture played no great role in French national imagery.

Even in her infancy during the Revolution, Marianne showed signs that she could be tamed, assimilated to the ideal of woman so different from that of man. The Jacobin Goddess of Reason as a direct precedent and inspiration for Marianne provides a good example of this process. To portray Reason as a goddess, through statues and dramas, was a marked departure from viewing woman as a weak, illogical creature who had to be led by men. Yet contemporaries noted that the goddess usually engaged the loyalty of the crowd through her female sexual charm rather than her "masculine" wisdom, whether she was half dressed or whether, like Robespierre's statue of the Goddess of Reason in the Tuileries, she exposed both massive breasts to suckle the populace with wine. In the provinces, festivals sometimes seem to have resembled beauty contests in which the goddess was chosen from among the most beautiful girls in each town.[6] The Goddess of Reason was said to incarnate an ancient Roman deity, though in a more solemn vein her statue was a substitute for that of the Virgin Mary in some French churches, including the Cathedral of Notre Dame. Nevertheless beauty and female passion always played a part in her appeal. Woman thus remained a creature of passion, even if the passion was in the service of a noble cause.

There were men who were shocked to see reason presented in a female form. Only masculinity, they maintained, could provide the energy and strength to throw off the shackles of superstition.[7] In Gotthold Lessing's famous verse drama Nathan der Weise (Nathan the Wise, 1779), that summa of the Enlightenment, reason and superstition are almost equally distributed among men and women, but with the possible exception of the sultan's sister, it is the men who exemplify true wisdom. At nearly the same time Emmanuel Schikaneder's libretto for Mozart's Magic Flute left no doubt that for the Freemasons, whose ceremonies he describes, men exemplified reason. Women must avoid the example of the troublesome Queen of the Night and abandon any claims to leadership and independence.

The traditional attributes of feminity were restored to Marianne, until she no longer jolted men and women into thinking of revolution. Marianne into battle had become Marianne for the nation. When Heinrich Heine saw Delacroix's painting at the Paris exhibition of 1831, he could still exult in this "Venus of the street," this whore who symbolized the will of an untamed people.[8] But soon even nudity was depoliticized. Venus became a goddess of beauty and pleasure, as she had been during the *ancien régime.*[9] Woman remained passionate, but no longer in the noble cause of revolution. Her task once more was to dedicate her passion, beauty, and nudity to preserving the established order. Marianne herself as a national symbol was no longer a passionate young woman but the mother of her people.

Neither England nor Germany experienced the Roman revival that had influenced French revolutionary art. The Greek tradition which held sway in those two countries knew only a fully clad Athena. More important, both nations had fought wars against the French Revolution, and had concluded that "virtue and vice had changed sides" in that immoral nation.[10] Such reactions to the Revolution reinforced the moral rigor of German Pietism and English Evangelicalism. Woman must be chaste and modest, exemplifying, as Samuel Richardson tells us, bridal purity in all her thoughts and actions.[11]

In Germany, even "Revolution" never resembled Delacroix's fury. She was apt to appear as a young blond girl in a white dress. At the beginning of the twentieth century one socialist lamented that the German workers' movement persisted in using a blond young lady to symbolize revolution.[12] The revolutionary tomboy had been tamed into respectability along with the workers' movement itself.

Unlike Marianne, Germania's origins did not stem from revolution. In this, she was a woman with a future, for her type was one that all nationalists would come to cherish, whether in the shape of Marianne, Britannia, or such regional symbols as Bavaria. For the European middle classes, these female national symbols protected the normal in society, the health of the nation. Germania herself probably exercised no direct influence upon national symbols outside Germany, but the parallels are striking, and significant in the more general history of nationalism and its function in controlling the role of the sexes within society.

In ancient Rome, Germania was depicted as a grieving prisoner; but under the German emperors she became a regal figure equipped with crown, sword, and shield. And such she would remain into the present—a medieval figure in the modern age. Admittedly, during the trials and tribulations of the Thirty Years' War she was known by some as *Germania degenerans*, but during the wars of national liberation she became the object of a veritable cult.[13] Germania's role was quite different from Marianne's. Far from being a leader, she was not actively involved in battle. She was likened to the bride who awaits her bridegroom—a united Germany— or perceived as the anxious mother of her people, whose "pure heart" was not unlike that which beat in Cinderella's breast. "Germania Victorious" bore no resemblance to Delacroix's liberty; she was the sedate symbol of a struggling nation. To be sure, the Wilhelminian Germania would later don helmet and armor. Even so, she rarely acted as the aggressor, but rather as the protector of family and state, making the necessary sacrifice, doing her duty (see plate 8).[14]

In the early nineteenth century the German image of woman was heavily influenced by a Catholic religious revival. A group of German artists who settled in Rome in 1810 tried to revive German art on the basis of traditional religious painting. They called themselves the Guild of St. Luke, after the evangelist who had been the patron saint of medieval artists. But the Romans dubbed them the Nazarenes because of their monastic life and the Christian themes of their paintings, inspired to a large extent by Raphael's religious imagery. They were remarkably successful, coming to occupy influential positions in Austria and German academies of art even while their paintings were being reproduced for popular consumption.[15]

The Nazarenes influenced popular art precisely at the time of the romantic religious revival. Moreover, they combined Christian and Germanic themes, as in Philipp Veit's *The Introduction of Art into Germany Through Christianity* (1834–36). They catered to the growing German national consciousness at a critical juncture, and through their paintings gave a welcome religious dimension to the national revival. The sentimentality of nineteenth-century religious and national art in Germany—sickly Christs and Raphael-like Madonnas painted against a Germanic landscape—owed much to the work of the Nazarenes. These artists influenced the way Germania looked as well. Philipp Veit's dream-like *Germania*, painted in 1835, sits under an oak tree dressed in imperial robes, her sword resting on her knee and an imperial crown beside her (see plate 7).[16] Veit's *Germania* hung over the president's chair at the Frankfurt Parliament of 1848 as the assembly debated how a united Germany might be governed.[17]

Germania's career as a national symbol found its parallel in a living model, Queen Luise of Prussia, the symbol of chaste womanhood in the war against immoral France. The queen, wife of King Frederick William II, had fled Prussia in 1806 before the advancing French, to return once more just before her untimely death in 1810. She was actively involved in political efforts to alleviate Prussia'a plight. This "ornament of German women" became a kind of living Germania, whose influence as a national symbol was real though difficult to trace. A veritable cult grew up around the dead queen, in which her patriotism and piety were identified with so-called traditional feminine virtues. She was depicted surrounded by flowers in bloom, as in the monument to her erected in 1880 in Berlin's principal park, the Tiergarten. This active woman was transfigured into an angel, in life as in death, gaining that immutability so essential for any national symbol.[18]

Queen Luise's death mask was sculpted to resemble that of the Virgin Mary (see plate 4) and by the end of the nineteenth century the young queen, with Prince William in her arms, had been fashioned into the so-called Prussian Madonna (see plate 3). Almost immediately the queen on her deathbed, with a Madonna-like face and holding a crucifix in her hand, appeared on many coins and miniature paintings.[19] Gottfried Schadow, the director of the Prussian Academy of Art who sculpted a famous bust of the queen, was close to the Nazarenes.[20] The conscious creation of this national Christian myth was to retain its popularity for over a century.

During the wars of liberation the queen became a symbol of Prussia's resurrection. There was a continuing demand for a living royal symbol that in true Nazarene fashion fused Catholic religious imagery (the hope for the future which the Virgin Mary had always represented) with love for the nation. Germania could not reflect the Christian tradition nearly so directly. Thus the pious Protestant queen was transformed into a Catholic image, sweet and sentimental as popularized by the Nazarenes—an image that conferred immutability even in Protestant Prussia.[21] As the patron saint of Prussia, Queen Luise was supposed to have won the wars of liberation. On the eve of the Battle of Sedan her son, now king of Prussia and soon to be Germany's first emperor, prayed at her grave in order to call down her blessing upon the Prussian army.[22]

The cult of the dead queen was a striking example of the contemporary sentimental cult of the dead, which proved as popular in Wilhelminian Germany as it was in Victorian England. When the monument was erected to the queen in the Tiergarten, her face was once more modeled after the Madonna. As a sign of her abiding popularity, this monument was erected by popular subscription. In the New Year of 1899 the *Berliner Illustrierte*, a very popular paper, asked its readers to name the most important women of the nineteenth century. Queen Luise took first place, followed by Queen Victoria.[23] As we shall see, the Nazis also turned to the queen during the Second World War as an example of how women should act when the nation's honor was at stake.[24]

The queen's artlessness and chastity, indeed her very holiness, were linked to her family life (see plate 2). Even on her deathbed, she was no longer surrounded by the royal court, as had been the custom, but only by her husband and children.[25] Moreover, one of the most popular prints of the royal family, made in 1796, showed the king and queen and their children enjoying an evening together in true bourgeois fashion, in an atmosphere of comfort and harmony.[26] This embourgeoisement of the royal family was typical of the kind of triumph the middle classes achieved, not through power or even influence, but through their lifestyle; and family life was a central component of respectability. In spite of her political involvement, Queen Luise was said to have found fulfillment in marriage and her domestic tasks. Friedrich Schleiermacher, preaching at her death, told his congregation that despite her political courage, Luise never overstepped the line that divided men from women.[27] In the midst of the wars of liberation, nationalism and respectability were thus linked, and the restricted, passive role of women legitimized.

This symbolism of family life or of Germania's medieval setting was a far cry from the street urchin who stands next to Delacroix's Marianne, the archetype of the Parisian *gamin* bursting with enthusiasm for the Revolution. Ferdinand Freiligrath, who had at one time praised the Revolution, returned to the familiar theme of woman as national symbol when in one of his poems he crowned

1. *The Consequences of Masturbation*, a painting that was created for R. L. Rozier's book *Des Habitudes Secrets, ou de l'onanisme chez les femmes* (*The Secret Vice, or Women's Masturbation*, 1822), and was also reproduced in the German medical literature.

2. This picture of Queen Luise surrounded by her children (1808) was often reproduced on postcards and in lithographs. The domestic and romantic idyll is strongly reminiscent of Charlotte surrounded by children in Goethe's *The Sorrows of Young Werther* (1774).

3. Fritz Schaper first cast his figure of Queen Luise and the future Emperor William I in bronze (1897), before it was sculpted larger than life in marble and exhibited in Berlin (1901).

4. This bust of Queen Luise (1810) was stylized by Gottfried Schadow as the head of a Madonna. Schadow worked from a model of Queen Luise's death mask by L. Buchhorn.

5. Eugène Delacroix painted perhaps one of the most famous pictures (1830) of woman as a revolutionary leader.

6. The Republic by Léon Alexandre Delhomme, placed in the University of the Sorbonne in the 1890s, symbolizes a sedate figure in contrast to Delacroix's Liberty. The tiny Athenae point to her role as protector of the nation, while the horn of plenty identifies the goddess of prosperity.

7. This famous Germania by the Nazarene painter Philipp Veit (1835) hung behind the president's chair at the Frankfurt Parliament as it debated German unity in 1848. Sitting under an oak tree, the imperial crown at her feet, she seems a medieval figure.

8. This Germania on the postcard *The German Woman at War* retains her passive image as a national symbol.

9. The figure on top of Menter's *Monument to the Fallen* in the First World War at the University of Bonn illustrates the use of nude symbols, while his "manly pose" should be contrasted with that of Germania.

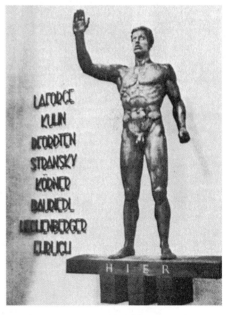

10. War memorials played a representative role in Nazi sculpture. Wilhelm Meller's *Monument to the Fallen of the Nazi Movement* (1940) stood at the Ordensburg Vogelsand, an elite boarding school for future Nazi leaders. Meller had already created earlier monuments to the fallen of the First World War in the 1920s, documenting the continuity of this symbolism.

11. Georg Kolbe's *War Memorial at Stralsund* (1935) is a good example of sculpture crucial to the self-representation of the Third Reich, continuing earlier images of heroic youth.

Deutſche Zeitſchrift
für das Menſchentum unſrer Zeit

Herausgegeben von

Hermann Popert

12. The journal, *Der Vortrupp*, closely linked to the German Youth Movement, was subtitled *Bi-monthly Journal of the Germanic Spirit of Our Time (Halbmonats-schrift für das Deutschtum unserer Zeit)*, which suited this cover better than the subtitle adopted after the First World War, *German Journal for Contemporary Mankind*. It attempted to regenerate German Youth by stressing patriotism, teetotalism and sexual abstinence before marriage.

13. *The Evolution of a Young Member of the Youth Movement from His Entry into the Movement to the Final Stages of His Infection by Homosexuality*. A Nazi attack on the former youth movement as part of a report in 1941 on criminality and dangers to youth.

14. Ernst Seeger's *Comrades in Sport* (*Sportkameraden*, 1939), approximates the contours of the female athlete to those of the male.

15. This photograph entitled *Active Nudity* is taken from a book called *The Victory of Bodily Joy* (*Der Sieg der Körperfreude*, 1940). The Nazis banned nudism, but permitted photographs showing the nude body in motion and at sport.

16. Ludwig Fahrenkrog's *The Sacred Hour* (1912) shows how nudism, the life-reform movement, and nature worship could be combined into a new Germanic religion.

17. Paul Matthias Padua's *The Führer Speaks* (1937) renders devotion to Hitler an integral part of exemplary family life.

18. This photograph of Stefan George illustrates his Goethe-like pose and deliberately cultivated remoteness.

19. Adolf Ziegler's *Fire, Water and Earth* (1937) is part of a panel entitled *The Four Seasons* that hung over the fireplace in Hitler's official Munich apartment.

20. Wilhelm Hempfing's painting of a German girl was considered representational art, as against Adolf Ziegler's nudes.

Germania with a replica of the unfinished Cologne Cathedral as a reminder to all Germans to complete the process of national unification.[28]

Regional symbols such as the Bavaria in Munich also looked to the past. She was graced with a bearskin and a wreath of oak leaves, Germanic symbols, it was said, of all that was lofty, sublime, holy, and strong. Like Germania, she was passive, in contrast to the aggressive monument of Arminius who stood, sword raised, in the Teutoburger Forest. "What does Germania represent?" asked the art historian Cornelius Gurlitt at the end of the nineteenth century. "Deprived of certain explanatory symbols, she is a rather stout female undistinguishable from a Bavaria, a Württembergia, or an Austria"[29]—and, we might add, indistinguishable in character from Queen Luise.

All these national and regional symbols helped to fix woman in her place, further strengthening the distinction between the sexes, and thus between the normal and abnormal as perceived by bourgeois society. Just as it was said at the beginning of the nineteenth century that for a woman, "establishment of order and quiet in a man's family was a better means to keep a husband than good looks,"[30] so women as national symbols exemplified order and restfulness. Woman was the embodiment of respectability; even as defender and protector of her people she was assimilated to her traditional role as woman and mother, the custodian of tradition, who kept nostalgia alive in the active world of men.

In England, Britannia was a much less important figure than either Marianne or Germania in France and Germany. John Bull was a far more popular symbol—good-natured, solid, full of confidence and energy. Precisely when Britannia made her first appearance in modern times is uncertain, but it was sometime during the reign of King Charles II in the late seventeenth century, when she turned up on the halfpenny and the penny, where she remained for over a hundred years.[31] Just as Germania was awakened to new life during the German wars of national liberation, so Britannia gained new popularity in Britain's wars against the French Revolution and Napoleon. James Thomson's "Rule Britannia," first published in 1740 as a protest against the interruption of British trade by Spain, was republished in 1793 by order of the patriotic Loyal Associations, as Britons vowed never to be slaves.[32] Britannia was the foe of Jacobins and tyrants like Napoleon, and a symbol of freedom—in this respect more akin to Marianne than to Germania, who never called for war against tyranny. James Gough's poem "Britannia" (1767) made her a symbol of industry and frugality as well, in contrast to wanton and luxurious France, "where vice usurping reigns." His Britannia aggressively smites the French, but in the last resort she represents not war or military action, but English virtue fighting against vice.[33] Here Britannia resembles Germania, helping to regenerate national morals for the war against France. England and Germany had just passed through a "second Reformation" of Evangelicalism and Pietism, respectively. France was Catholic as well as revolutionary, a lethal combination, as Protestants thought.

In early appearances Britannia sometimes carried a spear along with her shield, but she was generally portrayed with trident and shield, symbolizing not so much the whole nation as its naval power: "Britannia rules the waves." She ruled without force. Despite Gough's poem, she was no more aggressive than Germania, and was usually seated, a figure of quiet strength. She had a classical quality, removed from time and place, unlike John Bull who was usually pictured in modern Victorian dress.

Like all symbols, the female embodiments of the nation stood for eternal forces. They looked backward in their ancient armor and medieval dress. Woman as a preindustrial symbol suggested innocence and chastity, a kind of moral rigor directed against modernity—the pastoral and eternal set against the big city as the nursery of vice.

Feminine virtues held society to its moral goals, while man was the soldier, the heroic figure who translated theory into practice. Because nudity and heroism were linked in Germany through the Greek tradition, the symbolic German warriors (unlike Germania) were usually depicted either half or fully naked. The bas-relief on the Bismarck Monument near Munich built in 1899 on the Starnberger See (Lake Starnberg) in Bavaria highlights the contrast between male and female iconography. There woman symbolized the enjoyment of peace achieved by male warriors.[34] It is surely significant that a nation that prized its army and navy considered women unsuited to share the so-called military virtues of enthusiasm, loyalty, and strength. But nationalism did erect for woman a pedestal all her own. This is the Walküre leading the fallen to Valhalla, the Germania which in a poster of 1914 floats in a cloud of light high above the troops facing the enemy.[35] Was Germania, then, the successor of Walküre, the virgin experienced in battle? Though such origin was claimed for her by Meyer's popular encyclopedia in 1890, together with the qualities of an all-seeing mother,[36] in reality Germania as mother and patron saint was never aggressive or masculine, even when dressed in armor.

Where woman was concerned, the Romantic movement helped undermine the emancipatory ideals of the Enlightenment, acting in conjunction with the division of labor in bourgeois society. Following the romantic tendency to perceive the unknown and the eternal in actual objects, Schlegel or Novalis would see the eroticism of a beautiful woman as an outward sign of an invisible godhead, of the harmony between the world and the stars. These secrets had to be unraveled;[37] it was necessary to look behind the curtain even as the play unfolded at the front of the stage. Such idealism encouraged a symbolic outlook upon the world, and woman was central in this scheme. She exemplified the romantic utopia just as she represented the national ideal, both reaching out and interacting with each other. It was precisely this idealization of woman that led to her de-emancipation in the first half of the nineteenth century, as she lost those small gains she had made during the Enlightenment.

Women became part of the flower symbolism so dear to the Romantics, for whom flowers represented a pure, intense love that appealed not to the baser passions but to the higher instincts.[38] The blue flower, a creation of the German poet Novalis, became the symbol of nineteenth-century romantic utopia. The blue flower of Novalis's dream was the symbol of salvation, always dissolving in all its mysterious beauty, forever escaping man's reach. But when its petals opened, they revealed the "heavenly face" of Mathilde, the future wife of Novalis's hero Heinrich von Ofterdingen (in the novel of the same name published in 1802), a woman of beauty and natural charm. Blue was the color of the Virgin Mary's mantle, of the sky and of water. The lady of the blue flower pointed to eternity, to immutabilities far removed from the present. A romantic utopia reinforced the idealized and preindustrial image of the nation, as women in medieval or classical dress turned their backs on the present.

Flowers were the sounds made by nature's soul, "a green carpet of love" shrouded in secret, as Novalis put it.[39] Roses in particular symbolized virginity. In paintings by the Nazarenes, whose idealized women looked like Raphael Madonnas, the Virgin Mary is showered with roses. Queen Luise of Prussia was sometimes called the *Königsrose*, or King rose.[40] These romanticized women were supposedly robbed of their sensuality. It was typical that the Nazarenes condemned nudity in art. They might paint a nude male saint, but his body was understated and ethereal; women were always clothed. Philipp Veit, for example, hid his disdain for the human body behind the garments that adorned his figures. Even an admiring critic, writing at the beginning of the twentieth century, had to admit this, although he compensated by praising Veit's mastery in rendering the surfaces and folds of the garments.[41]

But the Nazarene ideal of woman was not confined to Germany. Raphael's Madonnas were a metaphor for virginal purity in England as well, where a Madonna hairstyle was in vogue during the early nineteenth century.[42] The Nazarenes influenced some of the midcentury Pre-Raphaelites in their vision of woman and their attempt to reinvigorate national culture through religious imagery. They too perceived woman as a Madonna within an aesthetic church.[43] The rose—here of course an "English rose"—was a symbol of all a woman should be, pure, chaste, and tender.

Thus the national and moral revival in England and Germany found artistic expression in an increasingly visual age. Woman could represent a healthy world partly because she was still so detached from the real world, making time stand still in a nervous age. As the poets of the German wars of liberation sang of national unity and the restoration of Germanic morality to combat the immoral French, woman symbolized a nation not yet corrupted by the modern age.

# II

The wars of liberation facilitated the fusion of nationalism and feminine respectability in Germany. But they also strengthened the ideal of masculinity as embodied in the "Free Corps" volunteers who rushed to the colors, in organizations like the Gymnasts, and the fraternity movement. The division between the sexes was sharpened and their respective roles more clearly defined. It almost seems as if women were transformed into static, immutable symbols in order to command the admiration of truly masculine men.

"God made women weak," says Rebecca in *Ivanhoe*, "and trusted their defence to men's generosity."[44]

Men not only defended and protected women; they co-opted those few women who dared to trespass on their territory. The young volunteer who turns out to be a girl provided a popular theme for literature and legend from the wars of liberation to the twentieth century. The male warrior was flattered that some women should find his example seductive and irresistible. Even though these women had stepped down from their pedestals instead of waiting there for the outcome of the battle, this was not necessarily seen as blurring the distinction between the sexes. For example, one book called *The German Heroines in the War Years 1807–1815* (1912) documents the continued interest in this disguise. It was not concerned with army nurses, as one might think, but managed to find no less than seventeen girls who had disguised themselves as boys in order to fight in the wars of national liberation. These strong, determined women were simply called "masculine" when they demonstrated "male" qualities of heroism and a resolve to do battle.[45] In any case, such women were few, the exceptions that proved the rule. In the happy ending, their true sex was always discovered and they were sent home to resume their assigned roles without complaint. We find such patriotic soldier girls in both France and Germany during the wars of the French Revolution and the Napoleonic era. The pure feminine ideal, however, remained anti-heroic.[46] When German womanhood was praised in retrospect for its patriotism during the Napoleonic wars, the telling images used were the priestess of the battlefield, the maiden with the shield, the spirit that awaits a masculine leader—no relation to the soldier girl fighting with gun and cannon in a modern army.[47]

Activism in sports was also thought to be a masculine preserve. Those women who measured up were evaluated in masculine terms. In Germany and England an athletic heroine was often called a "boyish" or even "a thoroughly wholesome, manly" girl.[48] After the First World War, when men like Henry de Montherlant in France looked to sports to keep alive the challenge and masculinity of war, women with boyish figures became popular.[49]

But the masculine co-opting of women was not strong enough to restore the difference in the roles assigned to men and women, for men were always uneasy about women who crossed over into the world of masculinity. These were thought to be "modern women" of an independent cast of mind. At least in fiction and legend, the threat posed by such women was banished and the traditional division between the sexes triumphed. The cavalry man in the wars of liberation was discovered to be a woman, who then left the army for her traditional role; and sportswomen sooner or later revealed their feminine preference for home and motherhood. In real life, however, it proved more difficult to banish the threat of women trespassing upon masculine preserves and thus challenging the ideal of respectability.

Whatever the dispensation for athletic types or soldier girls (who might, after all, serve as erotic stimulation), "masculine" women would be condemned as abnormal when they appeared to mimic the dress and comportment of men without displaying the heroic spirit supposedly concomitant with masculinity. And when, as in the case of lesbians, there was no happy ending in sight in which the old gender roles could be resumed, such masculine women were seen as threatening society.

The girlish man, sensitive and naive, also had his vogue.[50] A certain femininity crept into descriptions of "flaming youth" at the *fin de siècle* and blossomed in the First World War literature of the trenches. Rupert Brooke, that symbol of English youth who died during the First World War, was such a man—intensely masculine, yet tender and vulnerable to life. The image of soldiers bathing nude behind the front—innocent, graceful, and vulnerable—captured the imagination in both England and Germany. But while these soldiers' bathing poems, as we have seen, had had their predecessors in English homoerotic poetry, they were only metaphors for innocence, for "youth unscathed."[51] To describe a man as having feminine qualities in such a context did not, for the most part, refer to homosexuality. In any case, the boyish woman was more important and her image more widespread than that of the effeminate boy.

These isolated examples of ambivalent approval for the bridging of gender roles were overshadowed by a lasting preoccupation with the androgyne or, as it was sometimes called, the hermaphrodite. The fate of the androgyne, as we mentioned earlier, demonstrates the vital role of gender distinctions in ordering a world which seemed on the brink of chaos, but which nationalism with its emphasis upon respectability was attempting to preserve.

In early nineteenth-century symbolism the androgyne was a

union of spirit and matter, standing for brotherhood and the fundamental goodness and purity of mankind.[52] In those early days of the Romantic movement, it was still an abstract ideal unconnected with any tangible reality. Novalis, for example, regarded the androgyne as a symbol of harmony. It reflected the poet's conviction that the real world was worthless; he preferred to withdraw into the world of the mind, his dream world where the blue flower reigned.[53] Writers like Friedrich Schiller and Wilhelm von Humboldt drew the idealized androgynes in their writings after J. J. Winckelmann's pattern of Greek beauty, the most exalted mankind had known, so they believed. The soft, rounded limbs and slanting hips of Winckelmann's Greek youths seemed to them to combine masculinity and femininity.[54] Winckelmann's homosexuality was ignored as his androgynous ideal of beauty was accepted, though eventually his Greek ideal lost its soft contours and became firmly linked to masculinity.

Earlier centuries had been more ambivalent in their attitudes toward hermaphrodism. For example, G. de Foigny in his *Aventures de Jacques Sadeur* (1629) peopled his Australian utopia with hermaphrodites. They go naked, yet have no sex or desire, love one another truly, but not one person more than another. In the end, Foigny's hero who lives among them turns out to be a man, endowed with all the urges proper to his sex. Hermaphrodism was a deception, fiction devoid of content. Foigny's utopia attempted to normalize hermaphrodites, to divide them into boys and girls. Later, there were those during the eighteenth century who believed that the failure of hermaphrodites to reproduce themselves identified them as monsters.[55] This attitude rather than the admiration of the early Romantics won out in the end. As the pace of industrialization, urbanization, and communication accelerated, keeping order became more important than mystical unity. The unambiguous gender ideals of nationalism had to come to the rescue, lest the vision of passions unleashed should destroy the middle-class society.

The androgyne as utopian ideal was replaced by a quite different, frighteningly real image. The new fear of androgyny was projected onto woman, and by mid-nineteenth century the androgyne as an aggressive and almost masculine *femme fatale* had become a familiar figure in popular literature. Mario Praz has described such beautiful but cruel women as depicted in the popular second-rate literature of the time. Endowed with "male" characteristics, they were tough, domineering, and changeable.[56] Men's sexual fears, reflecting the frustrations that accompanied respectability, were projected upon the androgyne. Gautier in 1845 wrote of Cleopatra, his *femme fatale*, that "sexual cannibalism is her monopoly."[57] She kills her male lovers, including one young man who falls in love with her precisely because she is unattainable.

By the *fin de siècle* the androgyne was perceived as a monster of sexual and moral ambiguity,[58] often identified with other "outsiders" such as masochists, sadists, homosexuals, and lesbians. Eventually even Magnus Hirschfeld, the sexologist who defended male homosexuals, lesbians, and transvestites, condemned the androgyne for its supposed lack of harmony.[59] Greeks and Romans had thought androgynes beautiful, but modern scientists could no longer agree. They were now perceived as misshapen freaks. True, there were those who tried to revive the older image of the androgyne as a symbol of perfect harmony in order to defend homosexuals; for them, the tender youth with girlish body and male genitals provided a corrective to aggressively masculine symbols of power.[60] But in general the distinction between normal and abnormal held, and the androgyne as a biological monster was allowed no happy ending. Respectability had to be fortified to resist the onslaught of those who were rediscovering their bodies and attacking dominant manners and morals.

In England, Aubrey Beardsley at that time used the "wild and abnormal sensuality"[61] of androgynes to taunt established society. When Beardsley came to illustrate Oscar Wilde's *Salomé* in 1894, he pictured that cruel woman as both an androgyne and a *femme fatale*. Dancing with the severed head of John the Baptist, who had spurned her, kissing his lifeless lips, Salomé triumphed over conventional ideals of femininity and rejoiced in those of a monstrous man/woman. The threat symbolized by the androgyne grew still more serious as sexologists learned that male and female sexuality were not totally distinct, and that every individual contained elements of both. Science itself seemed to magnify men's worst fears about their masculinity.

## III

The fall of the androgyne coincided with a new attitude toward lesbianism at the very end of the nineteenth century. It was now seen as a sickness not unlike male homosexuality, and thus as a menace to gender distinctions. During most of the century intimacy among women had generally been free of the suspicions attached to close relationships among men. Voltaire had written that same-sex attraction was much stronger among men than among women.[62] Yet Diderot's *La Religieuse* (*The Nun*), published in 1796, portrayed an evil lesbian Mother Superior who attempts to seduce the innocent heroine. The novel's thrust is anti-religious rather than anti-lesbian, but the lesbian stereotype of mental and moral instability is present nonetheless. However, physical intimacy between women was a legitimate theme of nineteenth-century art. Courbet's *Sleep* (1866), in which two women fondle each other's breasts, was only one of his lesbian scenes. Many of these scenes were given mythological camouflage, and other painters explained similar works in allegorical terms to make them acceptable.[63] But these sensuously painted women were plainly intended to arouse male sexual desire; they bore no relation to the threateningly "masculine" *femme fatale.* Potboiling lithographs in France made lesbianism as explicit as heterosexual pornography, while in England Thomas Rowlandson's *The Female Couple Taken by Surprise* (1803), for example, left little to the male imagination.[64]

Such use of lesbianism, though continuing in the age of photography, became less acceptable once Carl Westphal's seminal study in 1869 of the "congenital invert" forced women's friendships into medically defined categories of normal and abnormal behavior. A woman who dressed like a man could now find herself in an insane asylum.[65] The medical profession, so we hear in 1895, believed that virile men who had sex with female androgynes were prone to paresis, a form of paralysis they classified as insanity, although it actually stems from syphilis.[66] The familiar chain of vice and disease already associated with other so-called sexual abnormalities was now applied to lesbianism as well. Thus an amendment to the German criminal code proposed, but not passed, in 1909 would for the first time have punished both homosexual and lesbian acts.[67]

Lesbians, like homosexuals, menaced the division between the sexes and thus struck at the very roots of society. Indeed, lesbians threatened society, if possible, to an even greater degree than homosexuals, given women's role as patron saints and mothers of the family and the nation. Motherhood was central to the image of women who, like the Madonna, were supposed to be chaste, yet mothers. Fatherhood, however, was not as important in the image of man, even though the father as head of the bourgeois family was also idealized. The ideal male, based upon the image of Greek youth, was part of the community of men, the *Männerbund*, discussed in the last chapter. Interestingly enough, Krafft-Ebing never showed any compassion toward lesbians (who, he thought, possessed a male soul in a female body) in the way that he did, late in his life, toward male homosexuals. This was all the more serious if we remember that Krafft-Ebing in common with many of his colleagues in the medical profession believed that sexual anomalies determined a person's ethical, aesthetic, and social development.[68]

At the end of the nineteenth century, respectability sought to tighten its hold over women. It is no coincidence that such a tightening took place when the movement for women's rights was getting started and male homosexuals as well as lesbians began to emerge from the shadows and cautiously attempt to affirm their own identities.

Lesbian characters in pre–1870 European fiction had not appeared particularly evil. Only after that date were they turned into moral and medical problems.[69] For example, in Balzac's *Girl with the Golden Eyes* (1835) lesbianism is not actually approved of, but the phenomenon is seen merely as one more ingredient in the cruelty, stupidity, and license of Paris life.[70] The lesbian stereotype in those days was often far more appealing than that of homosexual men. Gautier portrayed his Mlle de Maupin (1835), who has a man's soul in a woman's body, and who has sex with both women and men, as tall, wide-shouldered, slim-hipped, and endowed with perfect grace and great skill in riding and fencing. She had nothing in common with her fatigued, sickly, red-eyed male homosexual counterpart. While the type exemplified by Mlle de Maupin would still make an appearance in *fin-de-siècle* literature, she was by then overshadowed by more blatantly masculine lesbians.[71] Such women did not flatter male society as the girl soldier had done; they menaced it instead. Lesbian characters in the past had often been presented as bisexual. Now they tended to be heterosexually frigid. Moreover, like their homosexual counterparts, they exemplified sexual excess, a loss of control over the passions.[72]

When some lesbians spoke up in their own defense, they did not directly challenge bourgeois perceptions but tried instead to find their own place in existing society. Like male homosexuals—indeed, like other minorities such as the Jews—they attempted to escape their negative stereotype by accepting the standards and judgments of the establishment. Male superiority was usually accepted by lesbians as they sought to use their putative masculinity in their own defense—"What women who think in purely female terms have such energy, drive, and clarity of will [as lesbians]?"[73] This sounds like Friedländer's defense of male homosexuals as redblooded men and his claim that they make the best soldiers.

Another lesbian argument, playing on the bourgeois horror of sexual excess, held that lesbians exemplified pure and noble friendship devoid of sexual feeling.[74] The claim could be effective. Even Wilhelm Hammer, a doctor at the start of the twentieth century who considered the women's emancipation movement unhealthy and unnatural and condemned lesbianism,[75] believed that love between partners of the same sex was more stable than love between men and women.[76] This distinction between sex and love, so crucial to the ideal of male friendship as well, was an article of faith in the ideology of nationalism and respectability. The distinction was at work in the idealization of middle-class women and the projection of erotic feeling upon the prostitute.[77]

Pushing the point even further, by repudiating that imputation of masculinity which others had bent to their own advantage, some lesbians contrasted their own supposed feminine purity with the gross masculinity of the dominant society. Lesbians did, they admitted, have sexual relations with one another, but not in an unclean, excessively passionate heterosexual manner. Renée Vivienne, perhaps one of the most important lesbian writers of the early twentieth century, condemned heterosexual intercourse as a tool used by men to oppress women. Sexual purity is one of the aspects of beauty whose worship pervades her work. Pregnancy is seen as deforming the "slim, sexless body."[78] Much later, in *The Pure and the Impure* (1932), Colette was to write about Renée Vivienne's "very natural platonic tendencies."[79] However, the stormy love affair with Nataly Barney, which played a role in Vivienne's suicide, puts such purity in doubt, unless all lesbian love was said to be pure.

# IV

Renée Vivienne's writings, influenced by Baudelaire, breathe an atmosphere of decadence. Hers was indeed what Flaubert described as "the disintegration produced in men's souls by this daily more frantic exaggeration of the life of consciousness."[80] This reads like condemnation rather than assimilation to the existing order. Many articulate lesbians and homosexuals accepted the decadence of the *fin de siècle*, in contrast to those who had defended themselves by accepting the norms of society discussed earlier. Colette described the lesbian circles in which Vivienne moved as being addicted to late hours, darkened rooms, gambling, and a sensuous indolence.[81] This posture of decadence took the bourgeois stereotypes of normality and abnormality and turned them upside down. Aubrey Beardsley in *The Mirror of Love* (1895) catalogued all those sexual perversions he believed had informed the history of middle-class marriage; as for him, he sought solace in the company of the despised androgynes.[82] Established norms were inverted, as virtue became merely a restraint to be broken.

Decadence as a path to lesbian and homosexual self-acceptance did not prove as important in Germany as in France and England, although Otto von Harnack, to his astonishment, heard the word given a positive connotation in 1913.[83] Much of German lesbian fiction, for example, preferred to come to terms with lesbianism through the old emphasis on mental purity rather than the physical. Yet even there decadent themes worked their way into some lesbian literature.[84]

The phenomenon of decadence coincided with the turn-of-the-century revolt of bourgeois youth and the rediscovery of the human body. But the German youth and life-reform movements rejected decadence as they sought out their own kind of manliness, honesty, and simplicity, returning to the fold through a "true" nationalism. The challenge of decadence itself was more difficult for nationalism to co-opt. The avant garde threatened not merely to upset the accustomed order of things but actually to blur the line between the sexes as well. Nationalism co-opted the exaltation of youth from the start, but the *fin-de-siècle* decadents went on worshipping adolescence and celebrating their revolt of youth. Writers like Alfred Jarry in France in his *Ubu Roi* (1896) looked at the world through the eyes of schoolboys, expressing their own longing for sexual liberation by projecting it onto adolescent anxiety. Boarding school love affairs among members of the same sex became common fare in English and German literature, presented sympathetically as an aspect of puberty.[85] Yet sympathy was usually paired with tragedy: lesbian and male homosexual love often ended in suicide. The theme of early death, the image of sensitive youth crushed by the crude taste and behavior of its elders, was part of the decadent sensibility. So was the theme of exhaustion—a result of the constant quest for stimulation, the internalization of the frantic pace of modern life. The themes of the decadents met the despair many homosexuals and lesbians must have felt, and their need to escape by reaching out to any heterosexual group that might accept them as equals.

For most people, the word "decadence" continued to conjure up the fall of civilizations and nations. Had not the Roman Empire ceased to exist because of the softness, hedonism, and debauchery of its citizens?[86] Decadents, however fascinating they might be, were seen as unpatriotic, weakening the nation and depriving it of healthy sons and daughters. Even most homosexuals and lesbians preferred to seek entry into respectable society by emphasizing their masculinity or femininity and deemphasizing their passion. Those few who proudly accepted the accusation of decadence usually tried to steer clear of bourgeois society by combining their worship of beauty with a refusal to grow up, a clinging to adolescence. This phenomenon can be found among some of the leaders of the German Youth Movement, but even more frequently among homosexual scions of the English upper class after the First World War.

It would seem that more lesbians than male homosexuals adopted decadence, perhaps because the males found it easier to project a convincing masculinity as society demanded. The proud female decadents served to reinforce popular perception of lesbians as denizens of an exotic world festering beneath the surface of the metropolis, a perception that co-existed with the image of the lesbian as a woman in masculine clothes, a male soul in a female body. The counter-image of decadence may have thus actually strengthened traditional attitudes toward gender differentiation.

## V

The feminist movement which began at the turn of the twentieth century had far more potential for bringing about sexual as well as political emancipation than did the small group of decadents. And indeed there were some in the movement who did favor the legitimization of forms of sexuality outside the family structure. But most feminists were conservative when it came to sex.

Political rights were divorced from sexual freedom. In both England and Germany, an alliance between feminists and puritans stifled any chance for a change in traditional attitudes. This strategic alliance allowed the movement to stay within the bounds of respectability, while building up a certain kind of female self-respect. "We believe it to be our duty," explained Minna Cauer, a leader of the more radical feminist movement in Germany in 1896, "to educate state and society so that recognition of our equal rights is not only seen as a necessity, but also as desirable for the maintenance of order, manners and morality."[87] Cauer could have cited the example of the many English feminist leaders who joined the National Vigilance Association, the group that succeeded in banning Iwan Bloch's learned *Sexual Life of Our Times*.[88] Feminism and purity were linked to national preparedness as well. Feminists joined others in blaming falling birth rates on the supposed weakness of the contemporary family, undermined by prostitution, adultery, and pornography.[89]

The feminist movement was taking much the same posture as other "outsiders" such as lesbians and homosexuals. To be sure, some accepted the decadent movement and made the most of it, but others defended bourgeois respectability as essential to the welfare of women, the race, or nation. For example, Adolf Brand, the editor of *Der Eigene*, disapproved of the permissiveness of the Weimar Republic, as we have mentioned earlier, because it hindered Germany's moral rebirth after the war.[90] Some of those seen as destructive of all norms by society embraced precisely the manners and morals they were supposed to undermine, and rejected that tolerance which seemed to grant them freedom.

In England and Germany, the feminist commitment to respectability was encouraged by the reaction to the treatment accorded to prostitutes. In particular, the official requirement that they undergo humiliating genital examinations (carried out by men) in the name of hygiene was thought to degrade all women. It gave official sanction to the double standard, since men were never required to undergo similar examinations for venereal disease. Feminists considered the abolition movements against enforced physical inspection in Germany and England as struggles for women's dignity and rights. To them, the treatment and exploitation of prostitutes became symbolic of male attitudes toward women. Thus it was logical for them to go beyond the mere abolition of inspections and crusade against prostitution itself. Once abolition was achieved, the feminist context of the repeal movement dissipated while the crusade for social purity forged ahead.[91] The transition from the advocacy of women's rights to a crusade against all forms of vice helped reconcile the feminist movement with both respectability and nationalism. Once again the outsiders were co-opted, lending new strength to the dominant norms. Such crusades legitimized the interference by the state and nation in the private lives of individuals and strengthened their dominance over all personal relationships.

The majority of those in the German feminist movement adopted the prevailing stereotype of femininity. Society, they said, needed women's "peculiar gifts," "something of their pure love." As custodians of morality, women were responsible for education and helping the poor.[92] Women's suffrage would open public life to "maternal influences," not to female politicians.[93] The effort to remain above politics was important to the majority of women in the movement, and talk about political parties was brushed aside with the assertion that the nation came first.[94]

Significantly, women who were themselves emancipated did their best to head off any assault upon respectability by reaffirming the traditional female role. Writers, even political liberals like the novelist Marlitt, whose books penetrated all classes of the population at the *fin de siècle*, advocated a retreat into the warm shelter of bourgeois life "where everything has its place." The very well-being of the nation depended on a settled family life, the "noble German family life," in Marlitt's words, in which woman played her traditional role.[95] Nataly von Eschstruth, another popular writer, tells us that happiness means withdrawal from the world into the bosom of the family, a fact "the nineteenth century does not seem to understand."[96] These women insisted that they were defending "old-fashioned virtue" even as they called for tolerance and understanding among different peoples and nations. Tolerance, it seems, ended where respectability began.

Such women writers wove the cloth of their dreams out of bourgeois family life, respectability, and nationalism. Cinderella rose in the world through her "pure heart." She did not earn her money, as business was despised; she married into it, since riches were not.

The modern knight still defended his princess. This dream world remained an integral part of German popular literature well into the twentieth century. Hedwig Courths-Mahler continued the Marlitt tradition after the First World War, becoming one of the most popular German writers of all time—some 30 million copies of her books were sold between 1910 and 1941.[97] Her love stories emphasized firm family ties and urged women to show "quiet, dignified restraint." She herself showed great courage in refusing to cooperate with the Third Reich (the Nazis did not dare ban her books), but when any of her heroines has the choice between pursuing a profession and being a housewife, she does not hesitate: the "sweet little tinkerbell" finds fulfillment in marriage.[98] Nationalism is muted in these best sellers, serving as a means of anchoring and supporting respectability. Frequently, as in many of Courths-Mahler's love stories, it provides the setting: a medieval town, a specifically German wood or castle.[99] Here nationalism serves not to glorify all that is German but rather to support the proper attitudes toward life.

Romanticism had become neo-romanticism by the end of the nineteenth century, and in the process it lost its rebellious edge. What remained was an escape from reality into a dream world where time stood still, a world that pointed back to the past rather than forward to the future. Just as the face of Mathilde had appeared when Novalis's blue flower opened, so woman stood near the center of this new dream, symbolizing a lost world of beauty, chastity, and old-fashioned virtue. She was the Madonna of Nazarene paintings, imitated throughout the century, and the Cinderella of popular literature as well.

The female national symbol reflected this dream, just as the nation itself reflected the image of a healthy and happy world. No defense of "abnormality," no decadence could make inroads upon the myths and symbols which kept this dream alive. The majority of the feminist movement in Germany and elsewhere accepted the dream and tried to adjust to its appeal. The de-emancipation of women which superseded their slight emancipation during the Enlightenment was to triumph at least until the First World War. The nation tried to remove middle-class woman from active life outside the home and keep her from facing a turbulent age. That was man's role—he was destined to be the dragon slayer, the defender of the faith. The glorification of virility and the society of males accompanied the idealization of women. Theodor Körner's poetic promise to his embattled countrymen during the wars of liberation that they would recapture the manners, morals, faith, and conscience of old had been redeemed.[100] The myth of national purity was to gain a new lease on life as the so-called generation of 1914 stormed into battle.

## CHAPTER 6

# War, Youth, and Beauty

The Great War recharged those currents that have occupied us so far, and served as their conduit into the postwar world. They had started to meet resistance; but in the trauma of war, nationalism strengthened its cult of youth, the sense of male beauty, and camaraderie—its stereotype of manliness. Any threatening sensual and homoerotic implications were supposedly stripped away.

War was an invitation to manliness. Christopher Isherwood wrote during the late 1920s that English writers were suffering from a sense of shame that they had missed the war.[1] It had been, they thought, a test of courage, maturity, and prowess that posed the question, "Are you really a man?"[2] George Orwell wrote that his generation had become conscious of the vastness of the experience they had missed—"You felt yourself a little less than a man because you had missed it."[3] Young Germans of that era were also obsessed with having missed the opportunity to prove their manhood. They pored over popular books of war photographs that managed to show the battles without realistic dead or wounded. These volumes taught postwar youth that the war had fashioned an austere, strong-willed German who had retained faith in himself and in his country's future even after defeat.[4] Women were idealized in books and pictures during and after the war as the "good spirits" guarding the home front or nursing the wounded (see plate 8). But in accounts of wartime experience they could also act as the prostitute who satisfied the soldier's sexual needs before sending him back to the comradeship of the trenches.[5]

To be sure, after it was over many rejected the war and declined its invitation to manliness—more so in victorious England than in defeated Germany. But even many among the English literary élite who did so, like the Sitwells, came to admire fascism. Christopher Isherwood wrote that he himself might have become a fascist had the opportunity presented itself.[6] In reaction against the war, the decadence which had characterized the *fin de siècle* did gather renewed vigor in some circles. But the preoccupation with masculinity, having passed through the cameraderie of the trenchcs, surged into the postwar world, and while it might be rejected, it could never be ignored.

We must distinguish the myth of the war experience from the reality of the war as millions of soldiers experienced it. What these soldiers actually felt in the trenches or in battle cannot be recaptured; there were no polls to probe their true feelings. In France, a few studies appeared about the meaning of comradeship during the war, but they were based upon a minuscule sample. Only a relatively small group of soldiers articulated their feelings about the meaning of war. Most of these were writers, volunteers of the generation of 1914 who had rushed into battle. It is doubtful that the majority of the population welcomed the war. The most detailed study, which comes to us from France, seems to show that they did not.[7] A kind of resignation in the face of the inevitable governed the response of many Italians toward the outbreak of war.[8] But even if the nationalism associated with the generation of 1914 pertained mainly to university youth and a segment of the middle class,[9] it possessed an élan that allowed it to override the negative, resigned attitude of perhaps the majority of the population.

The myth of the war experience created by these volunteers, most of them officers, imposed itself on much of the postwar world. It is not hard to see why. Bill Gamage, a historian, after examining thousands of letters from soldiers, in his book *The Broken Years*, summarized the contradictory attitudes that made the myth attractive, the conflict for veterans who wanted to forget the horrors of the war but knew that the experience was the high point of their lives.[10] The myth managed to obliterate the horror and heightened the glory; the dead and wounded faded away before the exaltation of young manhood steeled in the trenches.

A variety of motivations were at work as the generation of 1914 rushed to the colors at the outbreak of the war, but the quest for masculinity cut across them all. "The overly clever, precocious lad had no soul. But then the first of August [the outbreak of war] pointed the way to an acceptance of . . . life's vastness and power."[11] The volunteers felt that by "casting off the artificiality of civilization" and becoming "simple and natural," they would reaffirm their manhood. Withdrawing from a corrupt world, they would create a new and virile universe, in which man was conscious of his strength.[12] This was immediately translated into medical language: robust health was to replace the sickness of a weak, effeminate, and over-refined society. The generation of 1914 shared in the anti-bourgeois revolt so strong at the *fin de siècle*, the revolt of the children of the middle class against their parents' society. Yet now the idealized alternative was not decadence but virility.

The war fulfilled the search for the exceptional in life, for adventure. It freed man from the restrictions and responsibilities of bourgeois society. Friedrich Schiller's song "Only the Soldier Is Free" was still popular in Germany during the First World War, while in England Douglas Reed wrote that "I had no idea what war meant. To me it spelled freedom."[13]

Rupert Brooke summed up what the war meant to so many articulate and educated youth, not merely in England, when he likened the volunteer to a swimmer "into cleanliness leaping," escaping from a world "grown old and weary." This is the flight from modernity which Eric Leed rightly characterized as typical of the generation of 1914, its celebration of primitive strength and manliness.[14] Such an escape also meant a return to arcadia, to unspoilt nature. Brooke's metaphor of the swimmer is reminiscent once again of the soldiers' bathing poems. Brooke himself was described in such terms: "A young Apollo, golden haired, stands dreaming on the verge of strife, / Magnificently unprepared for the long littleness of life."[15] Except that life in the war was no longer little, but filled with meaning. In Germany, too, the soldiers' bathing poem was a metaphor for cleanliness as contrasted to the corruption of society, an exaltation of male beauty and vulnerability.

When the war brought the erotic element in manliness and male friendship close to the surface, it became ever more urgent to strip that element away. Here Rupert Brooke can serve as an example once more. Even before the war, he had sought to overcome the erotic impulse by repudiating love in favor of friendship without lust; for him, "cleanliness" meant "cleansed of sexuality." Brooke had a puritanical suspicion of physical love[16] combined with the fear that others might think him homosexual. For young men like Brooke, war idealized the masculine into an absolute principle transcending the so-called baser instincts. In Germany, the fact that the first volunteers were blessed in church sanctioned the feeling of transcendence: "Now we are made sacred."[17]

The national cause was supposed to absorb man's sexual drive and his eroticism. Ernst Jünger left his dugout whenever soldiers began to talk about sex, for national unity and sacrifice must not be sullied. War, so we hear, is an antidote to egotism.[18] Private fantasy and passion were not to be tolerated. The inscription on the wooden cross which marked the front-line grave of Walter Flex, the German war hero, imparts the same lesson: "He who takes an oath of loyalty to the Prussian flag no longer possesses anything he can call his own."[19] Nineteenth-century thinkers like Hegel had asserted that man gains consciousness of his own nature only when he appropriates all that is his. Now the nation had appropriated man and given his life meaning and direction. Wilfred Owen was not the only Englishman to write about "chaste love" during the war. For homosexuals like Owen, the sacrifice of personality was a defense against the label of "abnormality" that might raise questions about his masculinity and soldierly bearing. The war, then, was regarded by many volunteers as an instrument of personal and national regeneration, transcending the sexual instinct and exalting the instinct for aggression and battle. It mattered little to the myth of the war experience that reality was different, for the songs soldiers sang marching to the front were often obscene; bawdy texts sung, as in England to the tunes of familiar Protestant hymns.[20]

For all that, a new type of man was said to have emerged from the war experience, self-confident, joyful in sacrifice, and personally pure. Walter Flex in Germany and Rupert Brooke in England symbolized this new man—who was really none other than the old national stereotype rejuvenated by war. The two writers were indispensable in weaving the myth, however much their actual personalities differed from this ideal. Brooke's poetry was easily remembered and quotable, and so were the short, pithy, and emotional stories of Walter Flex. Both men abhorred the city and loved the countryside, thus conforming to the preindustrial self-image of the nation. Typically, Flex came from the ranks of the German Youth Movement. He was a living link between its search for the genuine Volk and the war experience. Flex's *Wanderer Between*

*Two Worlds* of 1917 and Brooke's sonnets of 1914 projected all that youth was now supposed to represent—not the rebel of the *fin de siècle*, but an example of devotion to the fatherland, of reverence for the national past and for unspoilt nature, personal beauty, and sexual purity.

Flex's friend Wurche, the hero of *The Wanderer Between Two Worlds*, exemplified such youth, we are told. His motto "Remain pure and become mature," taken from the youth movement, implied moral cleanliness. "Himself clean in soul and body," so Flex wrote of Wurche, "he educated his troops to find joy in cleanliness, smartness and order." As for Flex, by his very presence he stopped soldiers from telling dirty jokes.[21] There is no evidence that Flex shared Brooke's neurotic attitude toward physical love or that he was troubled by suspicions of homosexuality. Nevertheless, for him too, sexual purity as a prerequisite for mental cleanliness was an integral part of the sacrifice demanded by war.

Wurche symbolized a "joyous restfulness," identical with that symmetry of body and spirit Winston Churchill had stressed in his obituary for Rupert Brooke. Brooke, so Edward Marsh wrote in his *Memoir*, was restful to be with.[22] Flex and Brooke were no avant-gardists; on the contrary, they were conventional writers whose work was easily understood. Moreover, and not least important, their myth was built at a time when the war was going badly. Brooke's poetry appeared when the feeling of stalemate had replaced belief in a quick victory in England, and Flex's book was published at a time of German reverses on the western front.

For both Wurche and Brooke, physical appearance was said to be a mirror of the spirit. This was essential for the transformation of man into the marble of the national stereotype. The two men came to symbolize traditional national ideals. Their beauty was not new or unprecedented; on the contrary, it was merely a version of the national stereotype we have already met—the young Siegfried, or Greek god, symmetrically formed, restful yet virile, not without eroticism. *The Wanderer Between Two Worlds* is filled with physical descriptions of Wurche: his light eyes, shy smile, lithe body, proud neck, and well-formed chin and mouth. The words "light" and "pure" are constantly applied to his appearance, his voice, and his temperament. Rupert Brooke is almost never referred to without a comment on his appearance; and even if Francis Cornford's "young Apollo, golden haired," was perhaps written with tongue in cheek, Brooke's "sunniness" was stressed by one and all. Edward Marsh's memoir, which did so much to create the legend of Rupert Brooke, went out of its way to describe his harmonious temperament and his beauty. The reality was apparently somewhat different. Virginia Woolf, who rather disliked Brooke, mentioned that he was jealous, moody, and ill-balanced.[23] His rugged good looks had an almost feminine cast in the portrait that accompanied the collected poems of 1915. Yet it is the myth that counts, and here, once more, Brooke and Wurche were alike—their wholesomeness, gaiety, masculinity, and harmonious temperament were reflected in their sunny looks.

These qualities of body and mind were associated in the myth with nature and the metaphor of the genuine, preindustrial past, so important in legitimizing nationalism as an immutable force. Wurche and Flex would spend their leave from the trenches walking together in the woods, or just lying in the grass beside a riverbank. Several lyrical passages are devoted to their bathing. We see the meadow, the sun, the blue sky, and the nude figures of Wurche and other soldiers leaping into the water, their bodies transparent in the sunlight: "The eternal beauty of God and the sun . . . shone as a protective shield over his luminous youth." This vision of Wurche, nude in the midst of radiant nature, beyond the noise of battle, was for Flex the most important experience of his life.[24] Paul Fussell has written that watching naked soldiers bathe became a setpiece in almost every English war memoir, symbolizing both the erotic and the pastoral.[25] In England homoerotic poets had already created the genre, while in Germany the eroticism of the national stereotype nourished by Winckelmann's Greek ideal of masculinity lay close at hand.

Brooke was linked to nature by the metaphor of sunniness, by his supposedly wholesome personality, by his long stay in Tahiti, and by his love of the vicarage at Grantchester with its "most individual and bewildering" garden. His poem "The Old Vicarage of Grantchester" praised the fresh water that embraces the naked flesh of the swimmer, evoking once more that image of cleanliness so central to his work. He was also taken with the symbolism of flowers: "An English unofficial rose."[26] The metaphor of the flower was crucial to German romanticism, as we saw earlier, and equally important in England, especially during the war. Flowers symbolized home and hearth, permanence amid the changing fortunes of war. The Imperial War Graves Commission specifically emphasized the importance of planting English flowers upon English graves in Flanders. The close association between flowers and home—and the full weight of this symbol as a central part of the national image—was summarized in one terse sentence in Sir Frederic Kenyon's report to the Commission (1918), "There is much to be said for the occasional introduction of the English yew (where soil permits) from its associations with our own country churchyards."[27] The England referred to in Rupert Brooke's most famous lines, "some corner of a foreign field / That is for ever England,"[28] was Grantchester, not London or Birmingham. Preindustrial and pastoral symbols prevailed.

When Rupert Brooke died in 1915 on the island of Skyros en route to Gallipoli, Stanley Casson commented that this was apt, for Achilles had spent his boyhood on that Greek island, and its simple, sturdy shepherds provided a pleasant contrast to the banalities of town-living Greeks. When the monument to Brooke was unveiled on the island in 1931, it was said that the bronze figure of a naked youth suited a poet inspired by the image of Homer naked before the sacred sea.[29] Nature, nakedness, and the sea all embody at once the eroticism of the myth and its purity. Cleanliness and sunlight strip nakedness of its sexuality, leaving only the beauty to be admired.

Nakedness also symbolized freedom. T. E. Lawrence, writing about his war experience in the much read *Seven Pillars of Wisdom* (1926), claimed that desert life did not veil man's nature beneath a thick armor of clothing. Naked man in the stark desert lived close to the elemental forces of life—"Man in all things lived candidly with man."[30] Women meant nothing here. Arab youths fulfilled their sexual needs among themselves, using each other's own clean bodies, finding "there hidden in the darkness a sensual coefficient of their passion for liberty."[31] For Lawrence, homosexuality in this context was natural, genuine, and clean, an integral part of the camaraderie of the desert. As an expression of manliness, it was, he believed, part and parcel of the Arab struggle for independence and liberty. The contrast with Europe, where the tradition of respectability demanded that untold energies be spent to control illicit passion, was clearly implied.

Cleanliness here does not exclude lust, nor does nature purge the erotic element from nudity. This was not the sentimental garden of

Grantchester or the sweet, sun-drenched meadows and lakes behind the trenches, but nature in the raw, in tune with man's basic
instincts. Such a definition of nature was not unknown in Germany where during the war the natural was often associated with
the primitive. The novelist Hermann Löns wrote in 1917: "What is
culture, what meaning does civilization have? A thin veneer under-
neath which nature courses, waiting until a crack appears and it
can burst into the open."[32] And Ernst Jünger's description of a storm
trooper, one of those going over the top and into the enemy trenches,
celebrates the primitive emotions: "Rage squeezed bitter tears
from my eyes . . . only the spell of primeval instinct remained."[33]
But in Germany nature in the raw never encroached upon respectability. Passion was stopped short of sexual fulfillment by the individual's dedication to the overriding national cause. Lawrence,
after all, was projecting his sexual fantasies upon the desert and its
exotic people.

The great popularity of *The Seven Pillars of Wisdom* rested largely
on its character as an adventure story played out in the wide-open
desert, so different from the muddy fields of Flanders. Yet Lawrence
was also reflecting the role Arabia had played in the sexual fantasy
of many Englishmen and Europeans. The book was probably read
not so much as history as myth. Lawrence did not really like Arabs,
but in retrospect he placed them in a genre that had always appealed to industrial society—the desert as a metaphor for freedom,
the Arab as the new noble savage whose mores were unconventional but who in his own setting made the abnormal clean. Many
Englishmen and women had fleshed out their fantasy life with
stories from Arabia, seeing in the Arabs the last remnants of both
chivalry and unabashed sexuality. One hundred and fifty years earlier, Edward Gibbon had written in his *Decline and Fall of the Roman Empire* that the Arab enjoyed, in some degree, the benefits of
society without forfeiting the prerogatives of nature.[34] It was said
of David George Hogarth, who served as Lawrence's mentor and
played an important role in extending British interests in the Middle East, that "Arabs appealed to every romantic and lawless instinct in his body."[35] How these fantasies must have refreshed the
respectable Englishman with his corseted emotions and frustrated
sexuality!

Frenchmen could also see the Arabs in this light, while Germans, who had but slight experience of the Arab world, projected

their fantasies upon the American Indians. Karl May (1842–1912), one of the most popular German writers of modern times, contrasted his Indian or German heroes living and hunting on the North American Plains with "the prison civilized man calls his home."[36] The beautiful, virile man of Western national stereotype thus found release from narrow political and moral boundaries at a safe distance from home.

Lawrence's hero, the emir Faisal, exemplified an ideal of male beauty not so different from that of Wurche or Brooke. He was tall and slender as a pillar, graceful and vigorous, with a beautiful gait and a royal dignity of head and shoulders. He was a man of action rather than thought.[37] Though he lacked that restfulness so important to Brooke and Wurche, his moodiness merely showed how free he was of artificiality or the need to disguise his passions. The basic ideals for which Brooke, Wurche, and Faisal stood were similar, including physical beauty and leadership; but the eroticism supposedly transcended in Brooke and Wurche remained out in the open with Faisal and his people. Lawrence's analogy between the desert and freedom pushed the homoerotic implications of the national stereotype to their logical conclusion.

Eroticism remained close to the surface for both the English and German national stereotypes in their emphasis on good looks and the love men bore for each other. Thus, after Donald Hankey tells us in *A Student in Arms* (1916) that his hero is very good-looking, he adds: ". . . we loved him. And there isn't anything stronger than love, when all's said and done."[38] German wartime literature also endowed most of its heroes with good looks and lovable qualities, which were given concrete expression in bronze or marble through the many monuments to the fallen with their statues of naked youth modeled upon Greek examples. The erotic interest was rendered harmless—at least in theory—being subsumed under the immutability of nature, Christianity, and the nation. As war monuments these Greek youths were frozen into position, unchangeable symbols transcending their own nudity (see plates 9 and 11).

That the myth took similar shapes in Germany and England shows that it filled needs common to both countries. But the differences between Flex and Brooke are important as well, especially their contrasting response to the nature of war itself, the actual business of killing. As Flex and Wurche sun themselves in the verdant meadow, Wurche tells Flex of his wish to become a storm trooper in order fully to experience the beauty of battle. He shows Flex his sword: "It is beautiful, my friend, is it not?"[39] Sentimental nature and human cruelty are paired in the beautiful youth, and that even before Germany's defeat. By contrast, Rupert Brooke never exalts the soldier's trade. As we follow Edward Marsh's memoir, Brooke is seen to lack enthusiasm at the start of the war. Only gradually does the patriot emerge, when he looks forward to doing battle at Gallipoli; he never rejoices in the battle itself or praises the "beauty" of war.

Brooke was a member of the English literary élite. Before the war, as a restless youth in rebellion against authority, including that of his mother, he left England to travel through Europe, America, and the South Seas. These facts were never hidden in the fashioning of his myth. Indeed, his relative sophistication, wide travels, and literary tastes added an upper-class dimension to the image, which in England commanded respect. Flex, on the other hand, never questioned authority, nor sought to escape family and friends through travel. It was quite natural for him to become tutor to the children of the Bismarck family. A heaviness hangs over Flex that is absent in Brooke; there is no self-irony here, no momentary lapse from high purpose. These contrasts between Brooke and Flex typify different attitudes widespread in their respective countries, or at least among many of their most representative figures.

The contrast extended to those past traditions each thought meaningful. Brooke was apt to refer to ancient Greece,[40] while Flex leaned on the German Pietist tradition. As a student of theology, Flex could call upon reserves of Christian sentiment to help face the unprecedented experiences of the war. Images of death and resurrection, revelation and sacrifice were frequent. In discussing the war, Flex never tired of joyful references to the martyrdom and resurrection of Christ. Wurche, too, was a student of theology; his beauty and purity of mind are compared to a "religious spring."[41] The New Testament was never far from his side, although neither were Goethe's works or Nietzsche's *Zarathustra*. Flex stood in a tradition popular among German nationalists. As we have seen, earlier poets had likened the wars of liberation to a "German Easter" —"Only that which is timeless has positive value,"[42] and here such timelessness was associated with the strong pietistic tradition. The German nation was the vessel of God. Those who sacrificed their lives in its honor imitated the martyrdom of Christ and were assured of resurrection. As for Goethe and Nietzsche, they were treated as idealistic philosophers reaching out to absolute values beyond the ferment of the contemporary situation.

The idealistic leanings of *The Wanderer Between Two Worlds* are a far cry from Brooke the connoisseur's love for the pagan Greeks, Russian ballet, or avant-garde poetry. Pietism accounts for the unrelenting seriousness of Flex's writings as compared with the lighter tone of much of Brooke's poetry. Two different nationalisms confront us here: the self-assured English variety, resting on a long history of national unity and a far-flung imperial domain, and the nationalism of Germany, newly united and reaching out for its first taste of world power.

Because of the relentless mechanization of war, the interplay between men and machines, a new martial stereotype began to emerge, especially in Germany, that celebrated this mechanization in a departure from the dominant preindustrial imagery. The soldier himself is now described as a machine. Ernst Jünger wrote about a "new race of men," lean and muscular, with faces chiseled in stone. Their language was said to be choppy as the rattle of a machine gun.[43] Such men would not lie in green fields and watch other soldiers bathing, nor would they be at home in the vicarage of Grantchester. They had no need to contemplate immutable nature in order to cope with the hardships of war. Battle was part of their very being. "They carried war in their blood," we read, "like their ancestors the Roman Legions or the German Landsers in the Middle Ages." Such men-machines found their emotional release in battle, drunk on blood and mad with rage. With these soldiers, Jünger believed, manliness surpassed itself.[44]

Such transcendence entailed not the repression of sexuality but its redirection. The storm troopers "burst with male eroticism" as they met the enemy.[45] As Karl Prümm has noted, Jünger used explicit sexual vocabulary to describe battle. The feeling of ecstasy as the bayonet sank into the white flesh of a French or English soldier was likened to an orgasm. When the battle was over, the sober new storm trooper left behind the "disheveled bed" of the trenches.[46] Aggression here is fueled by the libidinal drive; Jünger's storm trooper can satisfy his sexual needs in much the same manner against the enemy in battle or against women when the battle is done.

The writings of Franz Schauwecker show a similar libidinal relationship to war. For both men, war brought release from sexual restraint.[47] This was not fabled Arabia, but nevertheless a world of its own, cut off from traditional Europe. The freedom which the generation of 1914 had sought in war was pushed in unforeseen directions. The quest for moral and personal purity that had inspired so many volunteers became an unleashing of the instincts of a predatory animal. The lust for life was to be satisfied through cruelty in combat. Wurche had revealed a cruel side when praising the beauty of his sword, but he was really more at peace in the benign lap of nature than amid the din of battle. Lawrence's Arabs were noble savages whose sexuality did not have to be stimulated by aggression and cruelty.

Jünger's storm troopers anticipate those soldiers who refused to demobilize after the war, fighting on to protect Germany's eastern frontier. "Soldiers without banners," they called themselves, abandoned, according to their own legend, by one and all. In reality, these "Free Corps" were organized much like a regular army.[48] Nevertheless, the myth of the "Free Corps" satisfied the nostalgic longing for wartime camaraderie in the chaos and disorganization of peace, as well as the persistent quest to escape the fetters of bourgeois society. Eventually, some elements of this myth were attached to the Nazi SS by the foreign volunteers who joined its ranks. They saw themselves as a new race of men above the law and even the nation—an order of chivalry in the service of racial purity and the new Europe.[49] As with Jünger's storm troopers, all those excluded from their masculine band were mere objects; this included women, Jews, and the Slavic peoples. These young men channeled their sexuality into aggression against the enemy, once more saving respectability from a possible threat. For all that, it was youths like Wurche or Brooke who remained national symbols, rather than such a new race of men.

However heroic and exalted, the ideal youths we have discussed were conceived not as individuals but as components of a collective experience. Brooke and Flex never stood apart. They were merely the first among equals in the framework of wartime camaraderie. Jünger's storm troopers projected a collective existence, no matter which individuals were singled out to represent the whole. Here the myth was close to the truth, since most soldiers really did experience some form of camaraderie during the war. It is not surprising that the ideal of camaraderie became one of the most effective components of the myth of the war experience.

"The war," we are told, "restored genuine contact among men. All artificiality and stiffness dropped away."[50] The camaraderie of the trenches gave many a young man his first experience of community, one where each member had to support the others if any were to survive, and where a rough equality existed even between officers and men. The squad at the front has been likened to a miniature welfare state,[51] guaranteeing each member's well-being provided he himself contributed to the well-being of the others. To be sure, there were always outsiders, those who did not pull their weight or who could not share in the rough and ready sense of fellowship. The writer Franz Schauwecker was victimized for being an intellectual and, more significantly, for being slight of build. Despite his own experience, Schauwecker became a powerful advocate of the myth of camaraderie after the war.[52]

In this myth, the comradely relationships at the front exemplified the morally uplifting effects of the war. Through his altruism, by sublimating his personality in that of the group, each man would be cleansed of his baser passions. The selfish sexual drive would be absorbed by concern for the community as a whole. Franco Sapori wrote in one of the first Italian novels about trench warfare (La Trincea, 1917) that he had found the strength to bear his wounds without tears because among comrades even his pain was pure.[53] Especially in Germany, wartime camaraderie was regarded as the cell from which a new nation pure in body and mind might develop, with a more genuine form of democracy than that provided by representative government. In the trenches, so we hear, "equality established itself naturally."[54]

Because the myth of camaraderie was created largely by officers, it contained a goodly dose of sentimentality about the men, for many upper-class soldiers met the so-called lower classes for the first time in the trenches. In fact, "natural equality" did not exclude hierarchy. On the contrary, it presupposed a so-called natural leadership within the cross-class community, to be assumed only by those who had proved themselves in action and possessed manly virtues and masculine good looks. Here too the role of physical appearance in the charisma of leadership contained homoerotic elements difficult to suppress. For example, one Italian soldier wrote that his captain was "young, tall and good to look upon."[55] Good looks and modesty were major factors enabling Wurche to win the hearts of his men.

They also played their part in the close and intimate friendships that often sprang up between fellow officers, for example, between Siegfried Sassoon and Dick Tiltwood—another English double of Wurche's, with his fair hair, firm features, and radiant integrity of expression.[56] Ernst Raymond tells us how the war made his friendship with Edgar Gray Doe into "a beautiful whole."[57] Had it not been for the war, their paths might have diverged after leaving school. Such intimacy played a practical role during the war,[58] often assuming the form of a protector/protected relationship. The radiance of such friendships survived long after in poetry and prose, the more so when one of the friends was killed. For his aging partner, the fallen comrade sometimes became a symbol of his own lost youth.

Even women could not get in the way of camaraderie. War memoirs and novels were filled with episodes in which soldiers met their sweethearts on leave, only to turn back without a second thought when their units came under fire—"Whether or not I receive an order to go back to the front, I belong wherever there are some comrades in danger."[59] Jünger writes that those at the front felt no real passion for their former sweethearts, or for the prostitutes behind the lines.[60] They worried about their inability to form more intense relationships with women, but their surplus energy found a ready outlet in the dangerous life among comrades in the trenches. Just so, in a German right-wing novel published after the war entitled *Die Freundschaft (Friendship)*, one soldier forces his comrade to break his engagement: "a soldier who has a bride, no, no . . . that is an impossibility when he has to fight as much with his soul as with his body; he cannot be tied to a woman." After the war, the two comrades fall in love with the same woman. While one loses out to the other, their own friendship remains unimpaired.[61] One might gather from *Le Reveil des Morts (Summoning the Dead*, 1923) of Roland Dorgelès, one of the most famous French war writers, that the most dangerous enemies were in the rear—not only the war profiteers, but also the women who betrayed their husbands at the front.

In reality, women haunted soldiers' dreams and fantasies, but the myth of camaraderie relegated them to the familiar nineteenth-century categories either as objects of sexual desire or as pure, self-sacrificing Madonnas; in other words, the field prostitute or the battlefield nurse. Sexual fantasies played a large role in wartime propaganda. The rape of women by the enemy was copiously illustrated. There was also a vogue for scatological postcards, uncensored because the fantasies were projected onto the enemy, depicted as covered with excrement, their bodies and even sexual organs exposed.[62]

As the celebration of camaraderie raised the old ideal of the *Männerbund* to new heights, so it revived the fear of male eroticism. Such fear was greater now, when the gestures and emotions of friendship were no longer taken as casually as they had been in the eighteenth century. Indeed, they were definitely regarded as unmanly, and uncomfortably reminiscent of homoerotic and even homosexual feeling.

As the ideal passed into the postwar world, the effort to strip away any trace of eroticism sometimes took on grotesque forms. The popular second-rate novelist Rudolf Herzog in his *Kameraden* (*Comrades*, 1922) has his soldiers give each other a "manly kiss" and goes to great lengths to attach a sweetheart to each of his principal characters. These future wives play no real role in his novel. They are simply props designed to make male friendship respectable.

Studies written under the Third Reich concluded that the trenches had been places where people could find one another, schools of manly deportment. The communal experience was said to have included devotion to honor, duty, and work.[63] Can it be that camaraderie at the battlefront—for years the site of horror, strife, and chaos—was actually seen in the postwar world as an education in respectability, a finishing school for masculine manners and morals?

The ideals of manliness and camaraderie were converted to peacetime uses. Henry de Montherlant, an extreme case, viewed sports as a peacetime continuation of the war, the best surviving test of masculinity. *Les Olympiques* likens the football team to the wartime squad, and contrasts male camaraderie favorably with sexual passion. Montherlant is preoccupied with the spiritually elevating beauty of the male body as exemplified by the Greeks—a beauty that is the prerogative of youth.[64] Montherlant was no nationalist; he did not call for a nation in arms.[65] Rather, the war exemplified the possibility of leading a truly masculine way of life with its heroism and beauty of body. There seems little doubt that Montherlant was a homosexual who did his best to hide that fact and instead sought refuge in an ideal *Männerbund*, whether of the stadium or of battle.[66] Women have no place in this pantheon, except if they are good at sports, in which case they are pictured as male in attitude and appearance, lacking the contours of the female body. Woman as woman is merely the stupid and obedient object of sexual lust. Montherlant was not alone in equating sports and war. In W. II. Auden's early poems, for example, the images of war merge imperceptibly into those of school athletics.[68] The masculine society of the public school blended into the masculinity of war.

The new medium of film gave its own imprimatur to the ideals of manliness, especially in Germany. In the wave of Alpine films immediately following the war, stars like Louis Trenker and Leni Riefenstahl used the strength and beauty of their bodies to conquer mountains. Mountaineering was the sport through which the human body sought to pursue the immutable, to appropriate a "slice of eternity."[69] Here the unspoilt peaks, crystalline air and water, and pure white glaciers symbolized regeneration in the face of Germany's defeat, economic chaos, and revolution. Although the Alpine films had no overt nationalist message, their implication was clear enough: a strong, virile, and morally clean nation could be rebuilt. The popular film *Paths to Strength and Beauty* (1925) had a similar message. In the opening scene, in which scantily clad young men practice athletics in an ancient stadium, the narrator proclaims that "the Greek ideal combined virtue and beauty," while the film makes clear that such virtue and beauty is essential to the strength of the nation. Modern clothes are condemned as tight and clumsy, as the human body is rediscovered once more. The conclusion is predictable. In the past, military exercises were the only means to ensure that sufficient attention was devoted to the body. "Today, it is not military drill but sports that is the nation's strength."

So the war reaffirmed and strengthened the alliance between nationalism and respectability. It further encouraged a male stereotype both sensuous and yet stripped of sexuality, as well as the camaraderie of men as a form of friendship superior to other human relationships. It also brought changes. For example, some young Italians raised the cry for greater sexual emancipation, in-

cluding quicker divorces, equality for women, and even the abolition of marriage.[70] The tolerance for all forms of sexuality in the
Berlin of the Weimar Republic needs no documentation. However,
in England, as in Germany and France, at least some of those who
rejected all war, who supported the left and the anti-fascist struggle
during the 1930s, cherished the ideals of manliness as part of the
myth of the war experience. Men, we hear, can no longer perform
great deeds but they can be tough, stoical, and loyal to one another.[71] The bourgeois order held; indeed, its survival was never in
doubt.

On balance, the ideal of manliness served the right better than
the left, by stressing hierarchy as well as equality, pointing the way
toward personal and national regeneration, and using evocative preindustrial symbols. The working class is missing from this scheme,
transformed into a body of craftsmen or small property holders,
men who could fit into the national hierarchy as easily as they had
accepted the role of foot soldiers in the war. As for the left, it de-
spaired when confronting a myth of the war experience so contrary
to its own pacifism and cosmopolitan leanings;[72] but it had few
hesitations in continuing to accept wholeheartedly the ideal of respectability that still served to define bourgeois society.

Although the right and left shared the ideal of respectability, it
was the right that pushed it to its limits. The undoubted devotion
of the right to the power and strength of the nation served to tighten
the alliance between nationalism and respectability. The menace
to bourgeois society and to the nation seemed to increase after the
war. The transition from war to peace was thought to entail not
only political and social but also great moral danger. Men and
women might seek compensation for the deprivations of wartime
life, whether as a result of the absence of available men for so many
years or because of the possibility that former front-line soldiers
might show their contempt for the home front by attacking the
manners and morals of bourgeois society. Furthermore, the threat
of the Russian Revolution, of Bolshevism, loomed large as an in-
citement to immorality—the French Revolution had been perceived in a similar manner a century earlier, and with equally little
justification. After a brief period of experimentation with sexual
freedom, which might indeed have led to a radical change in morality, Bolshevism became the very model of respectability with a fervor worthy of the European right. Like the French Revolution, the

Russian Revolution symbolized the fears of the respectable classes
—and here reality did not count.

The fight against the so-called rising tide of immorality was
waged in England and throughout Europe after the war. London
was seen as a new Gomorrah by many Englishmen, and most Germans regarded the relative tolerance of the Weimar Republic as a
sign of decadence. But it was only now, during the war and in the
postwar period, that Germany began to follow its own ominous
road to national and moral salvation, to find a "German way" out
of decadence and defeat. All nations had called for national unity
during the war and had been suspicious of anyone who refused to
conform. But in Germany many now began to direct their hostility
against a specific group, the Jewish population, which upheld the
standards of society in an exemplary manner and had shouldered
its part of the burdens of war. Once a speedy victory had eluded the
German high command, the so-called Jewish question was debated
in the German Youth Movement. Still more ominously, in 1916 an
official count was instituted in order to determine how many Jews
were serving at a front and, by implication, how many were shirking their duty. How shocking this singling out was for Jewish soldiers fighting side by side with their Christian comrades can easily
be imagined. The comrade was branded as an outsider; moreover,
the results of the poll were never released, which fed the suspicions
of shirking.[73] Finally, after the war, Jews were not accepted for
membership in the German veterans organization and were forced
to found their own group, quite different from the practice in England or France. This isolation of the Jews was a reflection of fears
of defeat and then of the turbulent transition from war to peace.
Such treatment of the Jews was symptomatic of what was to be the
special German path to salvation in the postwar world, though a
good many Germans looked with suspicion and even hatred upon
the nationalistic right.

In spite of the singular liberality and tolerance of the newly
founded Weimar Republic, the difficult postwar conditions, which
cannot be compared to those of either England or France, played
into the hands of the right rather than the left. The shock of defeat,
of revolution and counterrevolution, seemed to demand a national
and moral revival. Meanwhile, Weimar Berlin challenged the moral
posture of the German right. Through its night life, for example,
homosexuality and lesbianism were highly visible. Homosexual

bars increased from some forty in 1914 to about eighty in 1929. At the same time, those who wanted to pry into the recesses of a hidden female sexuality had the choice of about a dozen lesbian bars and Cook's Tours of Berlin included visits to some of these establishments.[74] The Republic did pass a law against pornography, but it was halfheartedly enforced. The Nazis decided not to repeal it and substituted their own more ruthless methods in order to preserve respectability. It was the visibility rather than the mere existence of a homosexual and lesbian subculture that was important, for London and Paris also contained such a culture, but in Berlin it was more readily inspected, photographed, and written about. Thus, Christopher Isherwood could look upon Berlin as a city where homosexuals might lead a free and fulfilling life. This moral challenge must not be underestimated as providing fuel for the right and eventually for National Socialism; there must have been others besides the mother of Albert Speer who voted for Hitler because the young Nazis marching in the street looked so clean-cut and normal in contrast to Berlin's West End, the setting of many well-to-do Jews and of the homosexual scene.

The German political right called upon racism to shore up a crumbling respectability and at the same time to prepare the nation to revenge defeat. Racism had a long history behind it in which France, rather than Germany, had hitherto played the leading role. But now racism forged ahead in Germany as part of the mass politics practiced by "respectable" nationalist political parties as well as by the extreme political right. This was the essence of Germany's "special path" to recovery from defeat and the dangers of the postwar world. As such, the relationship between racism and sexuality was another, more extreme attempt to divide the normal from the abnormal, to define the nature of the outsider and insider clearly and decisively according to the entire spectrum of moral and physical qualities so often encountered in this book. The alliance between nationalism and respectability now moved toward its culmination as an alliance between nationalism, racism, and respectability.

## CHAPTER 7

# Race and Sexuality:
# The Role of the Outsider

## I

Nationalism together with bourgeois respectability played a crucial role in determining how men and women were perceived by modern society. Racism strengthened both the historical and the visual thrust of nationalism; it emphasized the stereotypes of superior and inferior races, while the distinctive history of each people was said to determine their superiority or inferiority for all time to come. Racism was a heightened nationalism: the differences between peoples were no longer perceived as chance variations, but as immutable, fixed in place. Racism in its various forms did not always follow the same inspiration or lead to the same results, yet it always encouraged nationalism in its tendency to claim absolute dominance. As a form of heightened nationalism, racism supported bourgeois respectability. It emphasized the distinction between vice and virtue, the necessity of a clear line between the normal and abnormal according to the rules society laid down. This racism was at its height in the years between the two world wars, but it had made its influence felt ever since the middle of the nineteenth century.

The association between racism and sexuality was immediate and direct. Racism brought to a climax tendencies that had been inherent in the alliance between nationalism and respectability. From the beginnings of European racism in the eighteenth century, the description of blacks included their supposed inability to control their sexual passions, as anthropologists and those who elabo-

rated national stereotypes transformed the noble savage into a sans-
culotte—without shame, living in a state of chaos, unable to govern
himself. Jews were thought lustful long before Adolf Hitler's decision to join the anti-Semitic movement, taken in Vienna where, as
he tells it, he saw Jews waiting to catch Aryan girls—the icy-cold,
shameless, and businesslike managers of prostitution and white
slavery.[1] The stereotype of the so-called inferior race filled with
lust was a staple of racism, part of the inversion of accepted values
characteristic of the "outsider," who at one and the same time
threatened society and by his very existence confirmed its standards of behavior. Racism branded the outsider, making him inevitably a member of the inferior race, wherever this was possible,
readily recognized as a carrier of infection threatening the health of
society and the nation. Above all racism was a scavenger ideology,
harnessing to its banner the fears and hopes of bourgeois Europe.

Lack of control over their passions characterized all outsiders, although individual racists might vary their description of the inferior race. The black was thought feckless, while the Jew was
without a soul; his morality resided in the lower part of his body, as
a tract of 1892 graphically tells us.[2] The insane, homosexuals, and
habitual criminals shared this lack of control, striking at the very
roots of society. All those who stood outside the respectable norms
of bourgeois society were thus blended—the "accursed race," as
Marcel Proust called Jews and homosexuals,[3] but to which we
must add habitual criminals and the insane.

Racism projected its stereotype upon any who failed to conform
to the proper manners and morals. Sander L. Gilman has put it suc-
cinctly: "the statement that someone 'looks Jewish' or 'looks crazy'
reflects the visual stereotype which culture created for the 'other'
out of an arbitrary complex of features."[4] Stereotyping through
looks was basic to racism, a visually centered ideology. The bodily
and mental features of outsiders reflected the fears of society—restlessness and sloth, mirrored through a "moveable physiognomy."[5]

The police officer F.C.B. Avé-Lallemant, describing the language
and customs of German thieves in Das Deutsche Gaunertum (German Rogues and Vagabonds, 1858), remarked on the fact that pictures of criminals in former times showed widely distorted faces
and physical deformities, when in reality criminals were indistinguishable in appearance from honest folk.[6] He could have made
the identical remark about Jews, the insane, or so-called sexual per-

verts. The outsider, when made to look and behave indecently, became less menacing because he could be more readily recognized and controlled.

Racism emphasized certain distinctions between the normal and the abnormal which we have met before, but which served to nail down still more firmly society's preconceptions and prejudices about looks and behavior. Exhaustion played a large part in this iconography, in contrast to that youthful vigor which society needed and valued so highly. Jews and so-called sexual perverts werc often pictured as fragile, close to death, the victims of premature old age. For example, Jews whether on the German stage or in Balzac's novels, were almost always portrayed as old men, while Schopenhauer asserted that homosexuality was a function of old age—nature's way of preventing the old from conceiving children.[7] This stereotype of old age deprived Jews of a family, at least on the German stage. Only during the nineteenth century did grown sons of Jews make an appearance; children would have radically destroyed the loneliness of the stereotype. Thus the Jew as an old man was denied integration into bourgeois life, while the homosexual's isolation was taken for granted. Oscar Wilde, as usual, got it dead right when he parodied society: "wicked people are always old and ugly."[8]

Masturbation, the foundation of most vice as the nineteenth century saw it, led to hideous deformations of the body and complete exhaustion of the nerves. Bertrand's wax museum in Paris illustrated these preconceptions graphically. Paris schoolchildren guided through in groups stared at the wax figure of a young masturbator in the last stages of agony, but also at those disfigured by venereal disease and a youth who had cut off one of his limbs in a "délire amoureux."[9] All sexual excess led to disfigurement or death. Ambroise Tardieu at mid-nineteenth century pictured homosexuals in a similar manner; their diseased and exhausted bodies gave them away.[10] The outsider had to be clearly recognizable in order to be punished or excluded from society, hence the homosexual was condemned by law (and we remember the importance of forensic medicine in creating his stereotype), the insane committed, and the Jew isolated.

Exhaustion meant nervousness, so Jews, homosexuals, and the insane were pictured in constant motion. The iconography of hysteria popularized by the French psychiatrist Jean-Martin Charcot in the 1880s,[11] with all its contortions and grimaces, determined to a large extent not only how the insane but all those subject to nervousness were supposed to act. The nineteenth-century medical doctrine of the exhaustion of the nervous system supported this iconography as physicians spoke of "railway nerves" and Max Nordau found the causes of degeneration in steam and electricity, which had turned life upside down.[12] Fatigue was both a moral and physical disorder, a sign of weakness and absence of will. It accounted, as the novelist Joris-Karl Huysman wrote at the end of the century, for sensual aberrations produced by exhausted brains.[13] This though Huysman's own anti-heroes of the decadent movement were characterized by their lack of will and rejection of youthful energy. Such portrayals of decadence usually included heightened sensibilities and a nervousness opposed to settled life. The pressures of the industrial age made this decadence ever more dangerous—stability was particularly vital in the midst of rapid change.

Moreover, for many physicians as well as racists, departures from the norm were caused by the surrender to modernity. One so-called sickness was often thought to lead to another—the outsider must be totally diseased. Iwan Bloch believed that the "vibrations of modernity" led to homosexuality, while Albert Moll, another sexologist, held that mental illness was widespread among the parents and kin of homosexuals.[14] Nervousness was often perceived as a specifically Jewish disease, leading to a high rate of insanity among Jews, as anti-Semites like Edouard Drumont claimed. The association of Jews and mental illness was in all probability furthered by another tradition as well that had no tie to the practice of medicine. Even at the height of the Enlightenment, it was said of one Prussian town official who converted from Christianity to Judaism that "in all probability he suffers from mental illness."[15] To leave society voluntarily raised the suspicion of mental illness; to be excluded by birth or by sexual preference implied an unsettled mind. Karl Heinrich Ulrichs, who in 1864 was the first person in Germany publicly to call for an end to the persecution of homosexuals, was declared insane by a Prussian textbook on forensic medicine.[16] Men like Ulrichs were "sexual freaks," often lumped together with vagrants, criminals, and religious cranks, described in books that took the place of the old "cabinet of curiosities." The imputation of insanity was fastened upon such outsiders and racism made good use of it. Racism projected such stereotypes upon the inferior race, and if found among the superior race (after all, most of these outsiders could be Aryans), detected a process of degeneration which had to be stopped at all costs. The home of such "outsiders" was the big city, as we saw earlier in our discussion of homosexuality. By the end of the century the city had become a metaphor for everything unnatural. Popular works during the century like those of Balzac or Eugène Sue had already emphasized the artificiality of the city, its rupture from the genuine forces of life. Balzac wrote about the physical and moral degeneration that took place within its rush and bustle, where nothing was permanent and everything provisional. Small wonder that so many Parisians looked like living corpses (not unlike those in the wax museum), "people dreadful to behold." The American physician John H. Girdner in his *New Yorkitis* (1901) discovered a communicable disease, a special kind of inflammation, as he called it, which resulted from living in the big city. He found symptoms in "nervousness and lack of direction of all muscular movements."[17] Once again medical diagnosis locked a highly subjective image into place and gave it the immutability of science. Here too racism made use of a process we have traced ever since respectability became a matter of health and sickness in the early part of the nineteenth century.

Normality required keeping in touch with the immutable and genuine forces of nature. The quest for rootedness which informed the bourgeoisie set it against its place of origin. Its members feared the impersonal monster they themselves had created: the monumental streets and buildings, the anonymous mass. Thus on one level the bourgeoisie sought to establish historical continuity— city halls were to imitate Gothic cathedrals, private villas, the palaces of the Renaissance. But above all the healing power of nature, symbolizing the genuine and the immutable, could serve to reinforce human control over a world forever on the brink of chaos. Such a use of nature was common in the nineteenth century, and became ever more popular with the speed of industrialization and urbanization—the need of men and women to annex a piece of eternity in order to keep their bearings.

Nationalism, racism, and bourgeois society all sought to base themselves upon nature in order to partake of its immutability. Proust tells the story of how he thought a friend cured of his homosexuality after he had spent a hard day riding, had climbed a mountain, and slept in the snow.[18] Here the healing power of serene nature had supposedly routed nervousness, and youthful energy had overcome exhaustion. Nature knows no vice, and in this context it seems less bizarre to find sexologists discussing among themselves whether or not homosexual animals existed. Such animals would put a blemish on nature, and indeed their existence did provide homosexuals with an argument against respectability.[19]

Conspiracies were supposedly the rule in big cities, linking those hostile to society with their immoral environment. Immorality and conspiracy were closely associated throughout the nineteenth century. During the French Revolution, as we saw, Germans had complained that the French were robbing them of morality, while some English, with greater imagination, held that France sent dancers across the Channel to corrupt the nation with their lewd gestures.[20] Proust called homosexuality a freemasonry more powerful, more extensive, and less suspect than the orthodox one. Just before the First World War, Maximilian Harden described a supposed homosexual conspiracy in the imperial German government in words that could have been taken from any racist tract about the Jews: "Everywhere there are men of this tribe, in courts, in high positions in the army and navy, in ateliers, in the editorial rooms of large newspapers . . . merchants, teachers and even judges. All united against their common enemy."[21] The conspiracy of homosexuals to subvert society ran parallel to the universal world Jewish conspiracy; both Jews and homosexuals were regarded by their enemies as a "state within a state." Racism did not invent conspiracy theories any more than it invented stereotypes. It simply used them as one more factor to lock inferior races and the "racially degenerate" into place.

The subverters of the bourgeois order represented the "anti-type" as against the "ideal-type" of youth, energy, and beauty—the clean-cut German or Englishman. True beauty stood in sharp contrast to the so-called lower passions and material things. An unbridgeable gulf exists, we hear in 1896, between perfect beauty and the desire to perform sexual acts with such beauty.[22] At much the same time Walter Pater was remarking that the very whiteness of Greek sculpture, as Winckelmann had described it, stripped nudity of its sensuousness.[23] Human beauty without sensuousness—such was the basic demand of respectability, just as beauty itself was a sign of moral and spiritual superiority. Nietzsche castigated this respectable concept of bodily beauty as pale and idiotic and called for the worship of the human body in all its sensuousness, with all its desires, wherever they might lead. Yet at the same time he shared one of its fundamental presuppositions when he wrote that it was "sheer insanity to believe that anyone could carry a beautiful soul in a misshapen body."[24] Nietzsche also fell under the spell of Greek sculpture, even if he attempted to transcend the respectable nude through his image of the Superman, whom one artist at the end of the century depicted naked, monumental, with angels' wings and at his feet little dwarfs in academic dress. Here, in spite of Nietzsche's own love of the body, a feeling of chastity was conveyed by the symbols attached to the figure of "Nietzsche, the giant."[25]

The ideal of beauty as symbolizing man's self-control reinforced the purifying gift of nature, whether in the form of national heroes like Walter Flex or Rupert Brooke or in the war memorial of the University of Munich, which was a copy of the sculpture of the youth Doryphorus by the Greek Polycletus. The symbolism of nature as reinforcing the ideal of manliness has been our constant theme. Leni Riefenstahl, much later, once again summed up the relationship between beauty and nature. The second part of her film on the Olympiad of 1936, *Festival of Beauty*, interposed shots of the beauties of nature with shots of the human body.[26] This was the apotheosis of manliness: young, virile, energetic, and chaste. Racism in propagating the Aryan ideal type stood on solid ground, supporting a stereotype basic to the existing order.

Here only the healthy and the normal could be beautiful; they alone could live in harmony with nature. Just as an energetic and vigorous homosexual was beyond imagination, so a beautiful Jew was regarded as a contradiction in terms, even though the beautiful Jewess continued to haunt the imagination—largely because of Scott's *Ivanhoe* and the need for the exotic and mysterious as elements of sexual stimulation. Johann Jakob Schudt in his influential *Jüdische Merkwürdigkeiten* (*Jewish Memorabilia*, 1715) had written that among a hundred Jews not one could be found without some blemish, some ugly feature.[27] This would become one of racism's most often repeated assertions. At Auschwitz, Dr. Josef Mengele carried out examinations upon young Jews who seemed to meet society's standard of human beauty partly in order to discover the ugly feature necessary to racism, and he rejoiced if he saw a clubfoot or suspected hereditary disease.[28] Through racism, the distinction between the normal and abnormal was driven to its logical conclusion. Just as medicine had legitimized standards of respectability from the beginning, so now some physicians sought to support racism. When Dr. P. Möbius proclaimed as an article of racial faith that "the healthy human being is mostly lithe and tall, his face is never ugly,"[29] we recall Oscar Wilde's taunt that the wicked are always ugly. But it was Oscar Wilde who went to prison, and Dr. Möbius, one suspects, who spoke for the image society liked to have of itself.

# II

Yet the homogenization of outsiders was never perfected, despite the similarities we have analyzed. The differences in the way they were viewed by society were to have some consequences once racism gained power in Germany. The distinctions between society's perceptions of the Jew and the homosexual are illustrated in excellent fashion by the accusation of sterility leveled against them both. This was a serious accusation, given the fear of falling birth rates during the nineteenth century. In both cases Jews and homosexuals weakened society and the nation. It was not surprising that homosexuals should be accused of depriving the nation of its future soldiers and workers. Jews were not as a rule accused of being homosexual themselves; instead, they were endowed by their enemies with an uncontrolled sexual drive directed against gentile women. Through their lust they were thought to corrupt the nation's mothers, thus preventing the birth of healthy children. Moreover, Jews were accused of inventing birth control—another means of destroying the Aryan race. The condemnation of contraception by racists was not confined to Germany. Sidney Webb warned that unless the decline of the birth rate was averted, the English nation would fall to the Irish and the Jews.[30]

While rarely accused of being homosexual, Jews were thought to have spread homosexuality in order to attain cultural dominance in Germany. This argument was popularized by the Nazi obsession with decadence as symbolizing abnormal appearance and behavior. But decadence had been equated with degeneration much earlier by physicians like Max Nordau, who characterized modern art as due to shattered nerves or distortion of the eyeballs. Homosexuality, associated in any case with figures like Oscar Wilde or the permissiveness of Weimar Berlin, was easily identified as one of the causes of degeneration. Racism did the rest. For example, *Das Schwarze Korps*, the newspaper of the SS, wrote that "all of those who are different" cannot be creative because they lack all appreciation of nature. Thus Jews and homosexuals were working hand in hand to destroy all that was creative in man and so undermine his virility.[31]

Respectability and creativity were equated here. The outsiders were once more stereotyped, in spite of the fact that specific accusations of sexual perversion were for the most part not directed against the Jews. Of course there were exceptions, and the more enthusiastically exploited for all that, taken as witness for a connection which as a rule proved difficult to make. Magnus Hirschfeld, the sexologist, a Jew, and ever since the beginning of the twentieth century a leading figure of the homosexual emancipation movement, became a constant target of attack. His own name and that of the Institute for Sexual Science (*Institut für Sexualwissenschaft*), which he founded in 1919, were used as metaphors for sexual perversion, symbols of the threat to bourgeois respectability posed by Weimar Berlin. The Institute was concerned with the study of all sexual diseases, eugenics, and marital problems. But most spectacularly it concentrated upon the medical study of homosexuality, as well as hermaphrodism, and in addition functioned as a counseling center for homosexuals. Hirschfeld never publicly admitted to being a homosexual, though he lived with a friend, but it was his putative homosexuality which made Sigmund Freud call him flabby and unappetizing.[32] The truly pioneering work of his Institute was recognized by only a few liberals, while German racists delighted in so easy a target. Besides Hirschfeld, Walther Rathenau, the Jew most prominent in German public life during and immediately after the First World War, was occasionally called a sadist and a homosexual. Yet it is surprising that these accusations occupied such a small and insignificant place in all the abuse directed against him, for Rathenau's sexual preferences were rumored about at the time. Rathenau himself never took a public stand on homosexual rights. His feelings were hidden. He praised blond Germans and sought out young friends for long conversations, but only his passionate and as yet unpublished correspondence with the blond Wilhelm Schwaner, racist and hater of Jews, gives us a tantalizing glimpse into his repressed sexuality.[33]

Still, Jews were not thought to endanger society by their supposed homosexuality but rather by their evil heterosexual drives. Why did racism leave the occasion almost unused to close the circle of vice around the Jews, outsiders accused of every conceivable crime, lacking control over their passions and tainted with insanity? Reality, however tenuous, must inform myth. Jewish family life was greatly admired by many anti-Semites because it was hard to ignore,[34] even when set side by side with the retention by anti-Semites of the old and isolated Jewish stereotype upon the German stage. Adolf Stoecker, one of the most famous anti-Semites in Wilhelminian Germany, conceded that Jewish life was centered upon the family while at the same time attacking the Jews for undermining Christian and Germany morality.[35] Jews, unlike other outsiders such as the insane or homosexuals, to the confusion of racists exemplified many of the virtues the bourgeois were supposed to possess. But while family life was intact among the Jews themselves, it was, so racists asserted, directed against the family life of others. Even though the outsider was a faithful family man, he was still a threat to existing society. The racist distinction between German bourgeoisie and Jewish bourgeoisie solved the problem presented by Jews successfully entering bourgeois life— for homosexuals such a problem never arose in the first place. Yet this was not the principal difference in the perception of Jews and homosexuals, though it was significant in all anti-Semitic and racist literature.

Their respective place in medicine was of special importance in defining the differences between the two kinds of outsiders at a time when, as we saw, physicians were tending to become the guardians of respectability. Jews, like homosexuals, became the topic of medical discussion during the nineteenth century. They were thought subject to mental illness, as we have seen, specifically nervousness and neurasthenia. Jean-Martin Charcot, the famed Paris physician and one of Freud's teachers, held that Jews were prone to such illness due to an inbred weakness of their nervous system, while Krafft-Ebing attributed this loss of nerve to inbreeding, a result of Jewish exclusiveness. Moreover, Krafft-Ebing tells us, these Jewish diseases led to religious fanaticism and an intensified sensuousness.[36]

Thus the excessive sexuality ascribed to Jews found a medical explanation. These physicians, and especially Charcot, also believed that women suffered fits of hysteria because their nervous system was much weaker than that of men. Here learned physicians agreed with Otto Weininger—the self-hating Jew and racist whom we shall meet presently—in projecting female characteristics onto the Jews. Manliness, once again, meant normalcy; it exemplified that self-control and harmony of body and mind which society prized so much. Those not manly must be in some manner diseased.

This medical analysis of the Jews legitimized the Jewish stereotype. Racism made good use of such legitimization through science, proclaiming that the Jews could never be cured because nervousness was an integral part of their race. Krafft-Ebing and Charcot had been careful to qualify their "Jewish disease" as a tendency rather than an absolute, and had maintained that it could be cured. But for racism, a healthy Jew was a contradiction in terms. The outsider must be irrevocably fixed as exemplifying that restlessness, rootlessness, and lack of virility so feared by respectability.

Nevertheless, the medical stereotyping of the Jews was the exception rather than the rule; it was secondary to the many other arguments directed against them. For homosexuals, on the other hand, medical study was of central importance. They became the objects of an analysis from which there was no escape. Homosexuality was above all a disease like other diseases—so ran the common medical wisdom—acquired by masturbation or by infection through bad example (though by the end of the nineteenth century congenital homosexuality was beginning to be recognized). Even so, most homosexuals might be cured, while Jews were beyond redemption. Racists faced the dilemma that most homosexuals were Aryans even if they undermined the health of the nation.

In 1937, *Das Schwarze Korps* asserted that only 2 percent of all homosexuality was congenital; yet in accordance with medical theories which had asserted that homosexuality spread like an infectious disease, that 2 percent could be counted upon to corrupt 2 million Germans. While congenital homosexuals must be exterminated, the vast majority could be cured through hard work. *Das Schwarze Korps* considered them slackers, selfish men who could return to normal if they wished.[37] The treatment of the insane in the nineteenth century was in some ways similar to that of homosexuals, within their respective medical categories. It was thought that establishment of control over the emotions would restore to the insane a normal facial expression as well. The ability to work hard eventually played an important part in saving the mentally ill from Nazi euthanasia.[38] Jews, of course, were considered unproductive, unable to do honest work, and could never be cured.

The Nazis gave homosexuals a chance to reform; but if they refused to do so, or could not comply, they were to be exterminated like the Jews. If a great many homosexuals and a handful of Jews survived in the end, it must not be forgotten that homosexuals proved difficult to recognize despite the efforts of forensic medicine, while most Jews were members of an established religious community which kept membership files. The Nazis did have some fragmentary lists of homosexuals at their disposal through the names of financial supporters printed in Magnus Hirschfeld's *Jahrbuch für Sexualle Zwischenstufen*,.though some of those listed may not have been homosexuals at all. In the last resort, the homogeneous stereotype was more important than the differences.

The grave accusation of confusing genders, directed with a kind of logic against homosexuals, was directed toward the Jews as well. We saw earlier how the division of labor between the sexes proved essential to the maintenance of respectability, and here again racism reinforced what had become commonplace in bourgeois society. It was usual to find racists proclaiming toward the end of the nineteenth century as an article of faith that "the more feminine women are, and the more masculine men, the more intimate the family life, the healthier the society and the state."[39] While some physicians believed that Jews shared with women a tendency to hysteria, as we have seen, it was a racist commonplace that Jews were aggressive toward the female sex, lecherous, and given to corrupting Christian girls. Yet despite such putative masculine aggression, the accusation of confusing genders leveled against the Jews remained intact as well; it was simply lifted from a practical to a theoretical plane. Jews lacked manliness as demonstrated by their nervousness, their failure to control the passions, and their treatment of women as goods to be bought and sold. Jewish materialism, their lack of soul, prevented them from distinguishing between love and lust, beauty and sensuousness. Once again the qualities of manliness coincided with the ideals of bourgeois society; they served to symbolize those manners and morals, that ideal of beauty and energy, that made the difference between the normal and abnormality.

Otto Weininger's *Sex and Character* (1903) was one of the most influential racial tracts of the twentieth century, profoundly affecting the views of Adolf Hitler and many other racists. The characteristics of gender provided its principal argument. Weininger accepted Freud's contention of the bisexuality of children, and went on to argue that every human being contained within him male and female elements. Yet he sharply distinguished between the male and the female and assigned to each quite different characteristics. Women, for him, were totally preoccupied with their sexuality, whereas men knew how to be social, how to fight, how to debate—understood science, commerce, religion, and art.[40] Women never grew to maturity. All their lives, he wrote, they remain restless children. And Jews for him had a preponderance of female qualities, even though they were male in their practice of sex. Weininger's conclusion follows: For true men, sexuality plays a secondary role. The more lofty the morality, the smaller the place that sexuality occupies in human consciousness.[41] Neither women nor Jews possess moral sense; they know only sexual passion.

Weininger removed the qualities of charm, femininity, and motherhood from the image of woman, leaving her a creature composed solely of passion and emotion. Those physicians concerned with female hysteria had not opposed the traditional feminine ideal. Indeed, they wanted to cure women and give them back their own dignity and self-control. But Weininger was a misogynist and a racist, who believed that to be either a Jew or a woman was a physiological state that could not be cured. *Sex and Character* was built upon the clear distinction between men and women—"Whatever intermediate forms of sexuality may exist, in the end a human being is either a man or a woman."[42] Weininger succeeded in transforming the nineteenth-century ideal of woman into an evil force quite foreign to those who had built this image, yet still echoing romantic notions of the *femme fatale*.

Such notions owed nothing to nationalism. Weininger had a low opinion of Bismarck and German unification, and regarded all those who aspired to lead the people as rabblerousers.[43] *Sex and Character* seems rather to reflect the author's fear of his own bisexuality. As every human being contained something of both male and female, he himself might lack masculinity. Nevertheless, the book lent itself easily to co-optation by nationalism, since its supposed psychological insights were dressed in racial garb. The fascination which Weininger's thesis exercised over so many men and women—not all of them nationalists—is startling and depressing. In the first place, the discussion of theories of sexuality was becoming both fashionable and respectable, and those inclined to racism found here a new, up-to-date argument, both scientific and emotional, dealing with basics. Weininger's book, like most racist tracts, was also meant as a criticism of contemporary culture, directed against the anarchy and decadence of his time, and that surely added to its attraction. Finally, his self-hate as a Jew and his suicide immediately after the book was published gave the work a certain notoriety.

Homosexuals were not forgotten in *Sex and Character*, providing further evidence of Weininger's need to defend manliness and its racist virtues against the "unmanly" who had corrupted culture and society. Like women and Jews, homosexuals lacked creativity and appreciation for the genuine in life. They craved "the pose, the audience, the theater," and lived for the fleeting moment, while for the true male, "only timeless objects have value."[44] Homosexuals were thought to live in an artificial world which, like life in the big city, signaled a criminal temperament. "That is why the homosexual is a criminal."[45]

We have seen how such analogies became widespread, part of the stereotyping of all outsiders. History could not be invoked by those wanting to prove the habitual criminality of homosexuals because their spiritual ancestors, the Greeks, had been cleansed and appropriated by respectable society. The homosexuals were deprived of a specific past, but neither could they be accused of having an inherited predilection for criminal acts. Homosexuals, after all, shared the Aryan past, and the views of medical science had to take the place of history.

But the Jews had their own past, and the accusation of criminality against them was much more consistent than that leveled against homosexuals. Here racism could make full use of its appeal to history. Racist theorists turned back to those Jewish gangs of thieves who had worked hand in glove with their German colleagues during most of the eighteenth century. Friedrich Christian Avé-Lallemant in *Das Deutsche Gaunertum* had demonstrated that the vocabulary of the German underworld was filled with Hebrew and Yiddish expressions. Lallemant was no anti-Semite and certainly no racist; he stated explicitly that there were no specific Jewish criminal characteristics.[46] Racists discarded such opinions, however, and used instead the existence of Jewish gangs in the past, and the persistence of Hebrew and Yiddish slang among German criminals, in order to demonstrate that Jews were "born crooks." Some racists, once again making a connection with illicit sexuality, asserted that contemporary pimps communicated through a "Jewish secret language."[47] The final consequence of this linkage between Jews and criminals awaited racism in power. Then those engaged in euthanasia would ask asylums to single out—besides the mentally ill—both Jews and habitual criminals.[48]

Lombrosian psychology, elaborated chiefly during the 1860s, made the accusation of Jewish criminality still more meaningful. Cesare Lombroso had maintained that habitual criminals were easily recognizable through certain bodily deformities; for example, handle-shaped ears, Lombroso tells us, were "found in criminals, savages and apes" and, so racists added, among Jews as well.[49] Racists liked nothing better than to use doctored pictures of Jews in order to demand rhetorically, Do they not look like criminals? The sexual passions with which Jews were endowed were part of their putative criminality. Despite the homosexual scandals at the turn of the century—the Wilde trials and the Cleveland Street scandal in England, and the Eulenburg affair in Germany—homosexuality and criminality never became so closely associated. Both Jews and homosexuals were supposed to conspire against society and both were perceived as enemies of respectability. But the specific accusation of criminality against Jews made their defamation easier. It was an accusation racists did their best to encourage precisely because it could be so effectively exploited.

## III

Lombroso held that as criminality was part of the habitual criminal's physiology and could never be changed, he must be executed. The death of the outsider was never far from the imagination of those inside society. The young masturbator in agony in Bertrand's museum demonstrated the wages of sin, while a fixed and deathlike gloom was said to dominate the facial expression of the insane.[50] All seemed close to death—the Jews prematurely old, the homosexual burned out, exhausted, and the insane steeped in gloom. Just as their life had differed from that of the respectable bourgeois, so their death had to be different, closely related to their rejection of society's norms. The manner in which men and women died was important to a society that had largely lost its traditional moorings and sought reassurance in the face of death.

The nineteenth century, which saw the final formation of bourgeois society, also witnessed the sentimentalization of death in words and pictures. Death no longer had a stern lesson to teach us, as in the Enlightenment, but became personalized in the romantic cult of melancholy.[51] Flowers now became an essential part of funeral rites. Bourgeois death was surrounded by a ritual designed to facilitate the transition from this world to the next. The deathbed scene was romanticized: the dying person lay on his bed in a dimly lit room, surrounded by his family, blessing his children, and asserting that he had accomplished all that could be expected in life and had no regrets.[52] The death of Goethe, as his biographer Emil Ludwig described it in 1922, provides a specific example of how the life of the virtuous man might reach its conclusion: "While he leaned back comfortably in his armchair, his spirit vanished, toward midday, at the hour of his birth."[53] Symmetry and order are preserved in death as in life. The moral was plain—a respectable life led to a tranquil death.

When in 1800/1801 the Institut de France organized a competition in order to find out the most desirable form a funeral might take, most of those who took part were careful to distinguish between funerals for those who had led a virtuous life and for others who had shown criminal tendencies or led a life given to vice. "We are equal by birth but not in the life we lead."[54] Some of the Institut's correspondents suggested that those whom public opinion had judged evil, who refused to conform to the norms of society, must be refused a proper burial.[55] In his reply, Pierre Dolivier, a former priest, suggested impaneling a jury that would pronounce over every dead man whether he had been useful in life. If found wicked, his corpse would be sent off into a common grave, condemned to a quiet burial without ceremony.[56] Dolivier was a philosopher of the Enlightenment who rejected the idea of sin and repentance, but he was not alone in his belief that the wicked should be separate in death as they had separated themselves from society in life.

Racists often used the image of the Jewish cemetery to illustrate the difference between gentile and Jew. For example, Sir John Retcliffe (Hermann Gödsche) in his novel *Biarritz* (1868) tells us that the Jewish cemetery in Prague is informed by a different spirit from Catholic and even Turkish cemeteries. Graves are heaped upon graves, buried in underbrush: at any moment they might spew forth Ahasverus the wandering Jew and send him on his way once more.[57] This cemetery had nothing in common with the orderly Christian examples. Indeed, it was in the Jewish cemetery in Prague that the "elders of Zion" were said to have plotted the enslavement of non-Jewish peoples.

The modern Christian cemetery was a creation of the late eighteenth and early nineteenth centuries, when burial grounds were moved out of the cities. Here a tranquil and undisturbed sleep for the respectable dead was symbolized by the tidy arrangement of lawns, flowers, and graves, while in the untidy Jewish cemeteries restlessness was thought to prevail in death as in life. The Jewish cemetery was symbolic of Jewish death, indeed, of the death of the outsider.

Jews and homosexuals could not die a bourgeois death. They were without soul; their selfishness and restlessness prevented the serenity necessary for a tranquil transition from life to death. Homosexuals lacked that family life essential for the deathbed *mise-en-scène*, while the supposed materialist religion and nervousness of the Jews prevented the romanticizing of their death.

Bourgeois death also provided a contrast to that ebbing of the life-force which the decadents had seen as an expression of artistic sensibilities. Death as a sensuous experience seemed blasphemous to the existing order, typical of the wicked who could not control their sexual feelings. Decadence was associated, in any case, with avant-garde artists and homosexuals. The image of the languid youth dying slowly but beautifully was hardly in tune with normative ideals of manliness. Practitioners of the "solitary vice" (masturbation) were doomed, and homosexuals must die a lonely, ugly death because all beauty was strange to them. Vice must be punished and the outsider separated from the insider in death as in life.

Ahasverus the Jew is condemned to loneliness as well, incapable of proper human relationships, destroying all he touches. Gustav Freytag's *Soll und Haben* (*Debit and Credit*, 1855), one of the most popular German novels, has the Jew Veitel Itzig drown in a dirty river—the reverse of those clean waters which provided a metaphor for moral purity. Edouard Drumont in that breviary of racism *La France Juive* (1886) wrote with satisfaction that sudden death was becoming more frequent among Jews as incidents of suicide were on the rise.[58] The Jew was an outsider for whom there could be no comfort even in death. Johann Jakob Schudt, director of a school in Frankfurt, had set the tone here at the beginning of the eighteenth century by maintaining that Jews were incapable of martyrdom. In the face of death they screamed, cursed, and defended themselves.[59] Fear of death, rather than tranquility and a suitable acceptance, remained an accusation directed against the Jews. Schudt's description was echoed in 1895 by the Italian journalist Paolo Orano, who contrasted the supposed Jewish fear of death, avarice, pacifism, and lack of spirituality to the Christian and Roman spirit.[60] Paolo Orano's *Gli Ebrei in Italia* (*The Jews of Italy*, 1937) signaled the beginning of the hectic anti-Semitic campaign that led to the introduction of the racial laws in fascist Italy.[61]

The outsider's death symbolized his life. All of those taking part in the competition of the Institut de France had asserted that death was an integral part of life as it had been lived.[62] Thus emphasis upon the totality of life was used to widen the gap between the bourgeois and those outside society. Clearly, the manner in which outsiders died was one of the many factors preparing the way for the "destruction of unworthy life" when racism came to power in Nazi Germany. Those whom they attempted to exterminate were precisely those whom bourgeois society had always regarded as threatening, who knew neither how to live nor how to die.

# IV

The ideal of respectability, and the concomitant importance of the division of labor between the sexes, faced awesome challenges during the nineteenth century. The consciousness of change, of the new speed of time, of the possible loss of control over one's life, were basic issues to which racism addressed itself. Through its appeal to history and nature it attempted to make time stand still, to provide men and women not only with a usable racial past but also with a piece of eternity that would give them support. The outsider fulfilled a crucial function as the anti-type—a warning of what the future might hold if society relaxed its controls and abandoned its quest for respectability.

Lack of control over sexual passions was part and parcel of that lack of self-control thought characteristic of the enemies of ordered society. The enemies of society and the inferior race were identical in racist thought, while the superior race possessed the attitudes, manners, and morals of existing society. There was no basic difference in the way in which nationalism and respectability on the one hand, and racism on the other, regarded the outsider, though there was a gap in the degree of tolerance for those who were different. Racism abolished any relative tolerance that might have existed during short periods of the nineteenth and twentieth centuries, while giving a new dimension of immutability to that conformity basic to respectability and the nation. All outsiders were to a large degree rendered homogeneous, but Jews and homosexuals, rather than criminals and the insane, were thought to use their sexuality as an additional weapon against society. Whatever the differences in their stereotype, they shared this special dimension of evil.

The relationship between racism and sexuality must be set in this wider context. Sexuality was not just one more attribute of the racist stereotype, but by its attack upon respectability threatened the very foundations of bourgeois society. Such outsiders were regarded as potential revolutionaries, as frightening as any who mounted the barricades. The attitudes toward the outsider penetrated deeply into the very fabric of society, so that many victims seemed to accept the stereotype of themselves and sought to transcend it by integrating themselves into the existing order. However, such integration meant accepting not only bourgeois lifestyles but also the very stereotyping of the outsider that was themselves. There seemed little escape from this vicious circle. We have seen how homosexuals sought to become insiders by stressing their virility and aptitude for the military profession. Jews in equal measure attempted to emphasize their respectability and patriotism, even if the very effort at transcending outsiderdom gave them a tradition of liberalism and tolerance which in Germany was to last until the very end. There National Socialism put an end to the effort of the outsider to become an insider, while in England the struggle continued. Always the outsider confronted a society dependent upon keeping the division between insider and outsider intact because it was thought as vital to the distinction between what was normal and abnormal as to the division between the sexes.

National Socialism was the climax of that history which has been our concern. It contained all the bits and pieces of the past we have tried to analyze and make coherent: respectability, nationalism, manliness, the ideal of woman, the rediscovery of the human body, and racism. It exemplifies the alliance of nationalism and respectability in all its intimacy and tensions. But as National Socialism was a part of European fascism, its specifics must be discussed within this wider context.

## CHAPTER 8

# Fascism and Sexuality

## I

The attitude of fascism toward sexuality was not one of simple oppression, although all fascism sought to strengthen the distinction between the normal and abnormal and to preserve the division of labor between the sexes. Fascism was opposed to what Ezra Pound called an "indefinite wobble,"[1] whether in social relations, politics, or sexuality. The so-called fascist style demanded a strictness of form which did not allow for ambiguities or vague definitions. Yet it is necessary to distinguish here between fascism as a movement and fascism in power. As a movement struggling for power, fascism contained a dynamic directed against the existing order of things: it wanted to destroy bourgeois society and to preserve it at one and the same time. Here fascism was the heir of the revolt of youth at the end of the nineteenth century—a revolt (as we have seen) directed not against social or economic conditions but against the lifestyle of their elders. Nationalism became a means through which many a youth fulfilled his quest for the "genuine" in contrast to the artificiality of bourgeois life. Nationalism provided a dynamic faith that promised both community and self-fulfillment. Those who joined the youth movement in Germany internalized the national landscape, historical traditions, and customs.

The rediscovery of the human body was part of this quest for the genuine, to free man from his golden cage and lead him back to nature. This rediscovery was tamed, as we have seen, by treating the body as a symbolic form transcending sexuality, exemplifying nature and the nation. Yet the First World War posed a new challenge to respectability. To be sure, the so-called generation of 1914, those who rushed to volunteer, articulated their concern for moral purity as opposed to the wanton decadence of bourgeois society. The danger to respectability came from the reinvigorated cult of youth and beauty, as we saw previously, but it came from another direction as well—from the peculiar nature of the war itself.

The warfare on the western front created a new feeling of community among those who lived in the trenches. Here that community of affinity for which so many had longed in an ever more restrictive society seemed to come alive. This was a community of men, a *Männerbund* that symbolized strength and devotion, within which men could test and prove their manliness. Here was a dynamic which continued into the postwar world when the need for community seemed greater than ever before. Thus immediately after the war, one leader of the German war veterans talked about the creation of an invisible church within which men could find each other through love and faith, with former front-line soldiers as priests and the German forest as the altar.[2] Though exaggerated, this was not an isolated expression as the war experience was transmuted into an abiding nostalgia for comradeship.

The rough and ready manners in use among wartime comrades were part of this ideal and came to symbolize true masculinity in comparison to the weaklings who misruled the nation. Such men demanded a continual struggle for power and showed a certain indifference to the demands of respectability. The new barbarians whom Oswald Spengler glorified immediately after the war, or Jünger's "new race of men," cared little for the conventions of the civilized world and worshipped their own roughly hewn strength.[3] The *Männerbund* was central to the vision of state and society of many a veteran, and they were apt to confuse preoccupation with their own manliness with the strength of the state.

Fascism based itself on the continuity of the war into peacetime and presented itself as a community of men. Its ideal type was the storm trooper in Germany or the Arditi in Italy, soldiers who had led the charge against the enemy. Gabriele D'Annunzio in Italy praised the Arditi, using their emblem, the black torch, as a call to personal and national regeneration.[4] Ernst Jünger's front-line soldiers, hard as steel with eyes grown used to unspeakable horrors,[5] were joined by wartime heroes like Wurche whose youth and beauty were informed by a fighting spirit. Jünger's notion that battle in war was no longer an isolated incident but a "condition of life"[6] found its parallel in the speeches and actions of fascists directed against the internal enemy. We saw earlier how others also wanted to continue the war in peacetime as a further test of their manliness—Henry de Montherlant in France, who saw sport as the equivalent of war in the postwar age, or the films of Louis Trenker and Leni Riefenstahl which, in a Germany stunned by defeat, symbolized conquest and struggle.[7]

The quest for continued war in peacetime waged by such a new race of men might easily leave respectability a casualty on the battlefield. Fascism, in reaching for power, had to be on its guard. It needed these former front-line soldiers in order to wage civil war against parliamentary government, and it sought to represent their ideals and aspirations. But it was also dependent to an ever greater extent upon the support of the bourgeoisie, who wanted to see a restoration of order and morality. The more so as Italian fascism and National Socialism came to emphasize their role as political and parliamentary parties.

The new race of men about whom Jünger wrote were imbued with the ideal of struggle, waging war against all comers, but at the same time disciplined—types rather than individuals. They were locked into place after 1918 as the vanguard of a new anti-bourgeois order. Instead of soldiers, Jünger now called them workers. The "worker" in touch with the elemental forces of death, blood, and soil would take control of technical progress, of the machine, as a means of determining the society of the future. His drive for power, his contempt for the "feminine" effort of bourgeois society to reconcile opposites, rendered the worker the peacetime inheritor of the myth of the war experience—a new aristocracy that would transcend the border between order and anarchy.[8]

If this seems rather a vague blueprint for the nation's future, then the answer must be that Germany had to be transformed into energy-come-alive, that it was the style of life that mattered, and not the quest for security of a decadent bourgeois order. Jünger's worker was supposed to exemplify the apotheosis of manliness. Jünger exemplified attitudes common to many front-line soldiers who had survived the war; similar ones were to be found among the squadristas in Italy and many of the so-called shock troops of other fascist movements. The inherent contradiction between the need for action and the control of discipline bedeviled all of fascism and determined its attitude toward sexuality as well.[9] The transformation of the front-line soldier into a stereotype would facilitate control over morals and manners, because such a stereotype subordinated himself to the discipline of the group. Yet it took time effectively to use and control this new race of men, who while they wanted to integrate themselves into the national community, cared little for conventional manners and morals.

The problem of making such men respectable even while keeping up a political dynamic and permitting acts of violence against the enemy was more easily solved in Italy than Germany. There, some young Italian veterans about to join the fascist movement called for a new activism and at the same time demanded greater sexual freedom.[10] Such demands for sexual freedom were absent from the programs of those veterans who in Germany joined with the radical right. Perhaps it was due to this youthful avant garde, which stood at the origins of Italian fascism, part of its futurist and syndicalist heritage, that Italian fascism provided many more outlets for individual creativity than National Socialism and tended to be less strict in matters of manners and morals. Hitler, unlike Mussolini, could not have afforded to have kept a series of mistresses, however discreetly; this was not a way of proving one's manliness in Germany.

More seriously, the division of labor between the sexes was less rigid in Italy. Women were at times encouraged to enter new, hitherto closed professions. In direct contrast to National Socialism, Italian fascism, even if against its avowed purpose, opened the doors of the university to women, who were permitted to study subjects like physics, chemistry, mathematics, and engineering. During the Second World War the official Nazi women's journal reprinted this list, adding that the acquisition of these skills made it easy to integrate Italian women into the war effort.[11] The magazine failed to comment on the handicaps German women faced when compared to their fascistic sisters. Mussolini as prime minister even attended the meeting in Rome in 1923 of the International Women's Suffrage Alliance.[12]

The liberality of Italian fascism must not be exaggerated; the basic view of woman was more alike than different among the various brands of European fascism. Italian women were still supposed to produce children and prove themselves as wives, mothers, and preservers of family life. Margherita Sarfatti, as Mussolini's long-time journalistic colleague and sometime mistress, wrote that he regarded his wife and children not as equals but as his possessions. And with gentle irony, in the midst of her hero-worshipping biography of the Duce, she tells us that for Mussolini woman has but one task: to be beautiful and give pleasure.[13]

Hitler's and Mussolini's private views of women were similar. While in Germany women had had the vote ever since the First World War, a very limited franchise to vote in local elections was granted in 1925 to Italian women who were self-employed or who were their children's guardians. Significantly, Mussolini himself, if he had had his way, would have withheld the vote from women living in open adultery. (For all his mistresses, he continued to act as the family man.)[14] The fascist criminal code foresaw especially harsh punishment for adultery and for those who lived together without the benefit of marriage. The appearance of respectability was important to Italian fascism as well as to National Socialism— part of the moral regeneration of the nation, but applied less consistently in practice. Italian fascism, with its mixture of chauvinism, futurism, and syndicalism, could tolerate greater cultural variety than National Socialism, based as it was upon a narrow volkish and racist nationalism.[15] Here, as in the arts, Hitler had to bear the burden of an ally who seemed to tolerate and even at times encourage what he himself hated and suppressed. Yet the basic need to maintain respectability was the same, and so was the need to tame the putschist mentality, the rough and ready manners of the squadristas or storm troopers, which helped to initiate these fascist movements.

Despite references to Italian and other European fascist movements, we must for the most part continue to confine ourselves to Germany. That nation has stood in the forefront of our discussion, whereas England now drops away because its own small fascist movement was of little importance. Italy and France will be drawn upon for purposes of comparison—Italy because it was the only other fascism in power, and France because it witnessed fascism at its most intellectual, without governmental responsibility.

Mussolini managed to bring his revolution under control by 1926, proceeding with the embourgoisement of his party by taking direct charge and making effective use of his image as the infallible leader.[16] Hitler accomplished the same goal with his purge of the

S.A. in April 1934. This was intended to please the regular army, which feared the storm troopers as rivals, and to eliminate a potential threat to his own supremacy. But in addition the purge was meant to further the party's image of respectability. The danger to accepted sexual norms inherent in the *Männerbund* played its role here, for Ernst Röhm, the S.A. chief of staff, was a well-known homosexual, as were other top leaders. As late as 1932, Hitler had strongly supported Röhm when he was accused in public of misusing his position as a leader in order to seduce some of his men. Hitler blamed Röhm's homosexuality on his life in the tropics when he had organized the Bolivian army, and asserted that his private life was his own affair as long as he used some discretion. He added typically that Röhm provided an indispensable link with the regular army.[17] (Röhm had been an officer of the general staff, procuring rifles and guns for right-wing organizations after the war, before he went to Bolivia and subsequently returned to head the S.A. He was also a first-rate organizer.)[18] Clearly, tactical considerations rather than moral judgments determined Hitler's attitude toward his homosexual chief of staff.

Even while defending Röhm, the party managed to polish its image as a defender of respectability. Wilhelm Frick, future Nazi Minister of the Interior, then a Nazi Reichstag deputy, introduced a bill in 1930 calling for the castration of homosexuals, "that Jewish pestilence."[19] Defense of respectability was used to stereotype the outsider and to affirm his immorality. This defense was bound to succeed with the party's entry into the political system, its competition for votes, and its opposition to the lax and permissive Weimar Republic. Hitler himself probably cared little for accepted standards of behavior; he fancied himself a bohemian, never kept regular hours of work, and looked back with nostalgia to his life in the trenches. However, like most bohemians, he stopped short of attacking accepted sexual norms. Hitler seems to have feared his own body (he would not even undress before his physicians).[20] Yet, whatever his private feelings, tactics were all that mattered.

Two years after his defense of Röhm, Hitler personally directed the murder of the S.A. chief of staff. The purge of the S.A. was officially justified as a blow against homosexuality. Indeed, Hitler's instructions to Röhm's successor as S.A. chief of staff, which were made public, commanded him to run an organization to which mothers could entrust their sons (thus admitting implicitly, what he had denied two years before, that the sexual comportment of the leader mattered).[21] Here, as in all subsequent decrees concerning morals, the Nazis made use of the phrase "in order not to offend the sensibilities of the people," which had been used both in Wilhelminian and in Weimar Germany to justify legislation against homosexuality and pornography.[22] The period of struggle for power had ended, and with it any ambivalence about the predominance of bourgeois morality. The assertion of respectability went hand in hand with disciplining the storm troops. Front-line soldiers were no longer needed to fight against the Republic; bureaucracy could now take over and deal with what was left of the internal enemy without any risk of losing control.

It was Heinrich Himmler, in particular, who perceived the temptation to homoeroticism and even homosexuality implicit in the *Männerbund*, to which the party remained committed. This was a danger that had to be avoided, and therefore a mythical past was substituted for the actual past of the S.A., and the memory of Röhm and his leadership was blotted out. Thus the S.A., whose appeal depended in large part upon action and not ideology, received a history in which respectability had always triumphed over real or potential dangers. Defending respectability meant posing as advocates of family life against the supposedly decadent Weimar Republic. The autobiographies of members of the S.A., written in the 1930s but describing the original struggle for power, were used to drive home the point. In one, a member of the troop, resting after doing battle with the Communists, asserts that "the family does not concern us, we are National Socialists and our only loyalty belongs to the party." For this remark he is rebuked by his leader: "The family is the most important cell of the state; whoever attacks the family acts against the well-being of the state. National Socialism has restored the family to its rightful place."[23] Just so, another member of the S.A. tells how in bygone days his troop used to discuss on Christmas Eve whether to go and beat up the Communists or celebrate at home with their families. The family Christmas tree won out, symbolic of the spirit that supposedly prevailed among the S.A.[24] In reality it is highly unlikely that such a discussion ever took place at all, for most members of the S.A. were too young to have had families of their own; some were teenagers, others barely out of their teens.

So a mythology was created that was in constant conflict with the demands of the Nazi Party and its symbols, which exalted energy and virility. Arno Breker's classical warriors and sportsmen, brutal in their monumentality, guarded public buildings, while the ritualized mass meetings were, for the most part, free of references to the bliss of family life. Symbols of family life were to be found instead in some of the paintings hung in the various exhibitions of German art; for example, in a famous work by Paul Matthias Padua entitled *The Führer Speaks* (1940), in which a peasant family from baby to grandparents listens with rapt attention to the radio (see plate 17). Here the soil, the family, and the Third Reich find symbolic unity.

Interestingly enough, the virtual abandonment of Germania as a national symbol during the Third Reich, when so many other traditional symbols were given new life, was due to her function as a public symbol without any direct link to bourgeois society. Germania had no family of her own, bore no children to the state, and therefore could not serve as an example German women should follow. Queen Luise of Prussia was resurrected, instead.[25] The theme of the "Prussian Madonna" proved more congenial to the Third Reich than that of a chaste Germania whose family could not be personalized but consisted in the entire nation.[26]

The Nazi attitude toward sexuality, with its emphasis upon the home, the family, restraint, and discipline, is at first glance almost a caricature of bourgeois respectability. Indeed, the leader of the German Evangelical Morality League (*Deutsch-Evangelische Sittlichkeitsbewegung*)—founded in 1885 and inspired by Josephine Butler's English Abolitionist Federation, which was designed above all to fight prostitution—joyously welcomed the Nazi seizure of power as putting an end to the moral chaos of the postwar age. The new Germany would usher in an era of discipline, morality, and Christianity. Other purity crusaders voiced similar hopes for a new Germany now that the backbone of the state had been strengthened.[27] In reality, however, some of the priorities of the Third Reich proved irreconcilable with these ideals. For example, the overriding imperative for women to bear children led to the sanctioning of extramarital relationships. At first illegitimate children were said to suffer from the absence of a father as a person of authority, while infant mortality was believed to be higher among illegitimate than legitimate children. But other voices were heard as well: childless women became hysterial or sick, so an illegitimate child was better than none at all.[28] It was this viewpoint that prevailed during the war, in 1940, when official measures were taken to place illegitimate children on a legal footing with legitimate children. The problem of extramarital relationships and illegitimacy could be solved. But the danger that the patriarch of the family might break loose and withdraw into the society of men was perceived by the Nazis as a much more serious challenge. The *Männerbund* might destroy the family and endanger normal sexuality as well.

Lydia Gottschewski, the leader of the League of German Girls (BDM), and for a short time in 1933 of the Nazi Party women's organization as well,[29] in her *Männerbund und Frauenfrage (Männerbund and the Women's Question, 1934)* attempted to warn of the dangers inherent in this male society. The book is of special significance as she was no friend of women's emancipation, but instead praised Queen Luise of Prussia as a role model for Nazi women.[30] Typically, she affirmed her belief in male supremacy. The *Männerbünde*, she wrote, had created the German state and they must now see to it that their ideals were fulfilled.[31] She then went on to express her reservations about the glorification of such *Bünde* in the Third Reich, which were apt, so she tells us, to advocate spiritual as distinct from bodily love, assigning to women a purely corporeal function and assuming that the tie between men and women was of less value and importance than the community among men.[32] This emphasis on spiritual love designed to maintain the respectability of male friendships within the *Männerbund*, however intimate or passionate, was used by Gottschewski to explain the anti-feminism of the Nazi movement. The identical observation had been made directly after the war by a woman critic of the German Youth Movement: The *Männerbund* leads to the atrophy of female sexuality. The justified struggle against the liberal women's emancipation movement has been transformed, so Gottschewski tells us, into opposition against the female sex as a whole.[33]

These are surely revealing lines when we consider that they were written, not by an opponent of the regime, but by a committed Nazi whose greatest hope was to remain the leader of all German women. Lydia Gottschewski failed in this aim, perhaps because she was too outspoken, or because her prickly personality offended the male hierarchy, which appointed the inoffensive Gertrud Scholtz-

Klink instead. In spite of its affirmation of women's passive role, the book nevertheless contains criticism, however veiled, of the official view that women should be prepared to make every sacrifice, remaining the silent, all-suffering companion of men. Indeed, it points to a certain dissatisfaction among some Nazi women with their status in the Third Reich. After all, as late as 1930 the Nazi women students' organization had found praise for the emancipation movement which, so they wrote, contained eternally valid principles. Such rebellion ended abruptly in 1932 when the fight against this very emancipation movement became the official goal of National Socialist female students.[34]

The confusion that reigned during the first months the Nazis were in power must not be underestimated. At that time all the contradictory trends within the party came to the surface until more often than not Hitler intervened with his directives. Thus, he aborted the enthusiasm of Nazi student youth for Expressionist art and the sports competitions in Berlin between Hitler Youth and right-wing Jewish youth organizations.[35] The confusion about women's role was no exception. In Baden, one party faction called for their withdrawal from the labor market, while others advocated the opposite and even called for women to receive military training.[36] There were women who continued to criticize the male-orientedness of the party, and others, even as party members, who desired a greater measure of female emancipation. The quest for status continued among women in the Third Reich, and we will return to it later, though it never presented a real and present danger like the *Männerbund*. As a matter of fact, Heinrich Himmler shared Lydia Gottschewski's fears about the potential dangers of the *Männerbund*, but for the opposite reasons. He cared little for the spirituality of women, but feared that the *Männerbund* might encourage homosexuality and thus strip women of their corporeal functions, leading to the extinction of the race.[37]

## II

The Nazis advocated a clear and unambiguous division of labor between the sexes. Hitler sought to keep this division intact by applying to it a precept which was to be used throughout the Third Reich: difference of function must be accompanied by equality of status. Thus hierarchy and leadership could be brought into line with that equality that must prevail among all members of the Volk. The inequality of the division of labor between men and women was not considered discriminatory by Hitler himself. Women, he said, were important because of their instinct and feeling, qualities which were often deficient in men, who inclined to trust their reason.[38] Yet such importance was of little consequence when the division of labor had to be upheld: "It is one of the miracles of nature and providence," Hitler told German women, "that a conflict between the sexes . . . is impossible as long as each fulfills the task set to it by nature."[39]

Gunther d'Alquen, the chief editorial writer of Himmler's *Das Schwarze Korps*, held that keeping the division between the sexes intact cleansed art of all that was sick and abnormal. National Socialism, he continued, had put an end to Jewish cultural predominance, saving art from its embrace by homosexuals and "manly women." Thus art was no longer a momentary experience, catering to the lower passions, but a reflection of the immutable and divine order. So-called normal sexual behavior had become a prerequisite for true creativity; indeed, according to d'Alquen, "he who is different" is unable to recognize the laws of nature.[40] Tolerating those who were different would lead to the degeneration of the Volk and the nation. In this way traditional respectabilities and ideals of creativity were claimed by National Socialism as its own invention.

The sexual division of labor was considered part of nature; it had been crucial in maintaining respectability for over a century. The so-called outsiders—Jews, homosexuals, criminals, and the insane—threatened to disrupt the division of labor, joined by the various emancipation movements at the end of the nineteenth century. However, during the Third Reich, while some Nazi women wanted greater recognition of their status, the real danger to this principle of order came from a male dominance that might endanger so-called normal sexual relationships.

The homoeroticism always latent in nationalist symbols and the ideal of masculinity now faced the danger of coming into conflict with respectability. The alliance between nationalism and respectability, in which one had reinforced the other, threatened to break apart. Wilhelm Frick's proposition that all homosexuals should be castrated foreshadowed a policy meant to safeguard respectability and at the same time preserve the image of the Third Reich as a male society. Action was taken immediately after the seizure of power to combat pornography in general and homosexuality in particular. Hitler came to power on January 30, 1933. On February 23 an ordinance was issued which proscribed all pornographic literature, as well as organizations that had defended homosexuals or called for their emancipation.[41] Subsequently, shortly after the Röhm purge, the secret police began to compile lists of all known and suspected homosexuals. The creation in October 1934 of a special team within the criminal police whose task was to fight homosexuality (*Reichszentrale zur bekämpfung der Homosexualität*) made the persecution of homosexuals a priority of the state.[42] The close connection between the persecution of homosexuals and the effort to maintain the sexual division of labor was demonstrated when the same team which combated homosexuals was given the additional task of proceeding against abortions.

Yet the Nazis passed no specific legislation against lesbianism, more evidence that their fear of homosexuality was rooted in the party's structure as a *Männerbund*.[43] Moreover, the leadership probably found it all but impossible to envisage women outside their stereotype. Just as homosexuality confused gender roles, so abortion negated the specific task which nature had assigned women. The duty of the *Reichszentrale* was to keep the division between the sexes intact and persecute all who threatened to disrupt it by blurring the distinction between normal and abnormal sexual behavior.

Heinrich Himmler was the driving force behind the persecution of homosexuals, and more than any other Nazi leader he articulated the sexual policies and fears of the Third Reich. If Hitler clothed himself in respectability mainly to win popular support, Himmler seemed obsessed with the danger of deviant sexuality to the Third Reich. Here his own struggle over his sexuality as a young man is relevant—his effort at "iron" sexual self-control,[44] his prudishness, and his extreme conventionality.[45] Himmler seems to have feared his own sexuality as much as Otto Weininger, and shared the definition of feminity as weak and masculinity as strong and aggressive. Moreover, Himmler apparently regarded sexual differences as mutually exclusive, and whatever psychological interpretations one might give to his own adolescent struggles,[46] a clear division of labor was the essence of middle-class respectability. Eroticism could play no part here, and homosexuality was "an error of degenerate individualism which is contrary to nature."[47] Such viewpoints would not change with the passage of time.

Moreover, quite apart from Himmler's private feelings as the founder and leader of the SS, the fate of Röhm must have served as a warning to the Nazi leadership. Still more important, since the death of Röhm, homosexuality had been kept constantly in the public eye. For once the power of the S.A. had been curbed, it was the turn of the Catholic Church to be brought into line through accusations of homosexuality against priests and monks. Between 1934 and 1937, Germany witnessed the spectacle of public trials of churchmen for crimes against decency, though in the end only some 64 out of the 25,000 priests and members of religious orders in Germany could be convicted even by corrupt courts.[48] In 1938, the same accusation was directed against a former chief of the general staff in order better to control the army.[49] Such accusations proved a powerful political weapon at the same time that they legitimized the new regime as a bastion of respectability.

Himmler had masterminded this use of homosexuality; but for all its political usefulness, he was also convinced of the reality of the threat, and that as leader of the SS, it might infect his own *Männerbund*. He believed that at the Nazis' seizure of power, Germany contained some 2 million organized homosexuals. Small wonder he was alarmed, and though he admitted to no more than one case of homosexuality a month in the SS, he regarded it as an infectious disease that could at any moment spread throughout Germany. Homosexuality, if unchecked, would mean the end of the Germanic race.[50] In the SS and the police, both led by Himmler, it was therefore considered the gravest of crimes. Already in 1937 he had decreed that any member of the SS who had been convicted of homosexuality must be executed. During the war, at Himmler's urging, Hitler issued an ordinance to safeguard "the purity of SS and police." This continued the death penalty for homosexual acts, but, in addition, pushed the definition of homosexuality to new lengths. Caressing, even if fully dressed, was now included in the definition of homosexuality, while men kissing each other faced death. However, until the Second World War no execution for alleged homosexuality took place, in spite of monthly expulsions or retirements of suspected homosexuals. The decree of 1937 was ceremonial rather than practical, once more demonstrating the importance of symbolic gestures for the Nazi movement.[51] The definitions of homosexuality went far beyond the performance of sexual acts. Himmler built upon the ever-widening nineteenth-century definition of homosexuality, which had stressed the contrast between homosexuality and manliness, sickness and health, and thus extended the performance of a sexual act into a judgment upon all aspects of a homosexual's personality. Homosexuality—so a confidential Nazi report on criminality and youth published in 1940 tells us—is inherently asocial. That youth who comes into contact with it not only faces a moral danger but imperils all aspects of his personality (see plate 13).[52] Here was a stereotype which, if it spread, might destroy Germany; homosexuality as an infectious disease had a dynamic all its own. However, Hitler's directive and its broad definition applied only to those formations of the police and SS directly under Himmler's control. Even units serving with the army were exempt.[53] Moreover, no similar order was issued to the Hitler Youth, with its relatively high rate of expulsion for homosexuality.[54] Himmler's obsession demanded specific measures for those units under his own control.

Convictions had been sporadic during the Weimar Republic, but under paragraph 175 of the old criminal code, which required punishment for so-called indecent sexual acts, they increased drastically during the Third Reich. Here too any fondling, even if it was not accompanied by sexual acts, was brought to court as indecent behavior.[55] Yet only Himmler thought that the punishment for homosexual acts should be "the snuffing out of life as if it had never existed."[56]

Himmler explained his views on sexuality to his SS leadership in a long and rambling speech given at Bad Tölz in November 1937. This speech must rank as the most wide-ranging and thorough discussion of sexuality by any National Socialist leader. Himmler starts with an appeal to his leaders to preserve the good name of the SS by expelling even old and valued comrades if they behave rudely or drink too much. Then he goes on to warn them against gossiping about other people's marriages and thus interfering with their private lives.[57] This seems an odd statement for the head of the Gestapo to make, but Himmler was obsessed with the need to produce children regardless of the quality of the marriage itself. He commanded his men to marry, but in the end the production of children by a member of the SS and a woman of impeccable racial credentials was considered more important than any consideration of legitimacy.

Because Himmler felt that homosexuality was acquired through lack of feminine contact, he condoned prostitution. Prostitutes should be treated generously, for otherwise German youth might be drawn into homosexual activity.[58] Here Himmler was in direct conflict with the official policy of the Third Reich, illustrating once more the always latent conflict between respectability and the perceived necessities of the *Männerbund*. With the Nazi seizure of power, any conspicuous behavior likely to promote unchastity was declared an offense. Prostitution was forbidden in the vicinity of public buildings and in dwellings where there were children under eighteen. Moreover, an order was issued against any concentration of prostitution, and houses of prostitution were abolished.[59] Himmler remained undeterred. Driven by his fear of the destructiveness of homosexuality, he asserted that contact with prostitutes was especially important for young people in the cities, since the village happily preserved a healthy attitude toward sexuality. Despite centuries of Christian teaching, Himmler tells us, the village youth still climbs through his girl's window at night and into her bed. This may result in some illegitimate children, but no matter; the ancient custom continues.[60] Prostitutes have a function in preserving normality and must be left alone to fulfill their task, while (as we shall see) male hustlers could be redeemed through reeducation.

At the beginning of his speech Himmler had asked for discretion in private matters of sexuality; yet the tone changes as soon as he comes to discuss homosexuality. Now, suddenly, all matters concerning sex are public and not private, determining the life or death of a people.[61] The reason for this change brings us to the heart of his speech—the definition of the new state. Germany is a masculine state, Himmler tells his audience. There have been matriarchies and Amazon states, but "for centuries, yea, millennia, the Germans . . . have been ruled as a *Männerstaat*" (a state based upon the comradeship of men).[62] The *Männerbund* has become the *Männerstaat*. The ruling class is now a male élite—no longer merely the shock troops of war against internal and external enemies. But this ruling class is in danger of destroying itself through the practice of homosexuality.[63]

How is this destruction accomplished? Himmler repeats the traditional picture of the weak and unmanly homosexual, but emphasizes that for homosexuals, love of the erotic replaces emphasis upon individual ability and accomplishment.[64] Here sexual passions reign with devastating consequence for public policy. Himmler thought of the danger posed by homosexuals in bureaucratic terms. Positions will no longer be distributed according to ability, he continues, but through a network of homosexuals who recognize each other, though they cannot be recognized by normal men. (Thus contradicting the stereotype he has just tried to explain.)[65] The conspiracy of homosexuals must be viewed side by side with the world Jewish conspiracy in which Himmler believed so firmly. Both are bent on destroying the German state and race as the implacable enemies of German virtue and purpose of will.[66]

Himmler feared that with the spread of homosexuality, sexual selection might replace the selection of the fittest. He condemns the presence of women in state service for the same reason; here, too, "no one can claim that their selection is based upon ability." A pretty but incompetent girl, he asserts, will always be preferred over an efficient old hag. For all such misjudgment, the pretty young girl will soon marry and leave the service.[67] There is no such hope for homosexuals, who will stay and take over.

Homosexuals are fixed in place through the use of the medical model so popular in the past. They are said to suffer from a grave psychic illness, though proof of this supposed fact is taken not from medicine but from personal observation. The Jesuit, Himmler tells his leaders, lies and does not believe his lie, whereas the homosexual lies and believes it. Moreover, there is no loyalty between homosexuals, he asserts, somewhat contradicting his own conspiracy theory, for they denounce each other in order to save their own skins.[68] Yet like all who are sick, homosexuals might be cured. Jews are beyond help because they are an inferior race. Male prostitutes, for example, in Himmler's view, might be redeemed through discipline, sport, and work[69]—pursuits supposedly rejected by homosexuals, indeed, by all those who were outside ordered and so-called normal society.

Yet Himmler seems to have changed his mind by the time homosexuals were rounded up systematically and put into concentration camps. There, regardless of how well they worked or how disciplined they were, homosexuals were made to lie with a woman and freed or killed according to their sexual reactions.[70] Himmler's opinion that it was lack of opportunity for sexual contact with women which produced homosexuals seems to have been decisive. Himmler considered homosexuality an illness that poisoned the entire body and mind. If the homosexual could not be cured, he must be killed. The concept of the outsider eaten up as by a cancer, felled by a disease that spared no part of his body and mind, was discussed in the last chapter. It formed the climax to the medical stereotype of the outsider, with all its consequences spelled out. But the way in which Himmler described the death that should await the incurable homosexual pushed to new lengths the process of eliminating the outsider and played its role in the Jewish Holocaust to come. The death of the outsider was used to obliterate his very existence.

In the old days, Himmler continues in his Bad Tölz speech, German homosexuals were drowned in the swamps: "This was no punishment, but simply the extinction (*Auslöschung*) of abnormal life." There was no feeling of hate or revenge on the part of the executioners as the homosexual literally vanished.[71] Here reality and symbolism are made to coincide—the victim sinks of his own weight into the swamp. No human hand helps him die, and his life is snuffed out as if it had never existed at all. Thus nature rectified her own mistakes. Small wonder Himmler laments the fact that in the modern world such methods are no longer possible.[72]

So, the outsider was simply "snuffed out." And if the actual mode of execution could no longer be reproduced, the language remained intact. Jews too were "snuffed out" or "extinguished." The outsider was not merely killed; he was supposed never to have existed at all. The abnormal, that which stood outside or differed from the existing order, was not only eliminated but denied any afterlife in heaven or hell. Previously the outsider had been isolated, expelled, even castrated, but never killed. Only in novels, as we saw, was the death of the outsider usually sudden, unclean, or lonely, so different from the death of the respectable bourgeois.[73]

Yet the fictional death of the outsider discussed in the last chapter in fact foreshadowed the Nazi "snuffing out" of so-called unworthy life. Only here was no gentle sliding over from life to death, but an end that was both lonely and painful. If Freytag's Veitel Itzig had drowned in a dirty river, Himmler wanted the homosexual to drown in a swamp and the Jew to suffocate without human assistance in the gas chamber. To be sure, the killing of hundreds of thousands of human beings could most efficiently be achieved in this fashion. Yet for the outsider himself, such a way of dying must be placed against the background of the comfortable death which was the bourgeois ideal. The "snuffing out of life" was diametrically opposed to death in the service of a noble cause on the battlefield or death as the conclusion of a virtuous life.

Basic to all Himmler's fears, including homosexuality, was the threat that the division of labor between the sexes might be abolished. Thus he takes aim at "manly women" who encourage male homosexuality.[74] Homosexuals in turn are infected with mental illness and conspire against the state. The circle of vice, the enemy of all order, which we have met so often before, is completed in Himmler's mind by the Jews, not in this particular speech but on many other occasions. The division of labor as threatened by all outsiders was basic to the Nazi view of sexuality, built as it was upon bourgeois respectability. The exception, the need for children even if illegitimate, did not affect the division of labor. Woman, after all, was still supposed to fulfill her role as mother. Perhaps it is significant that Himmler in his speech at Bad Töltz mentions woman's charm, dignity, and attractiveness, but not her chastity.[75] He was more outspoken than most Nazi leaders, for among Nazi women's organizations, Queen Luise of Prussia, that paradigm of female chastity, was the chosen model.[76]

# III

The *Männerstaat* symbolized an aggressive nationalism based upon the ideal of masculinity. It would crush all those who threatened respectability and the nation. Yet the threat to respectability inherent in the very existence of the *Männerbund* was not the only cause for alarm. The National Socialist attitude toward the human body also presented a presumptive challenge to respectability. Though it was built upon the rediscovery of the human body at the end of the nineteenth century, with its attempt to transcend sexuality, here physical beauty seemed to predominate. "The body expresses our very being," Baldur von Schirach, the leader of the

Hitler Youth, told the League of German Girls. "The striving for beauty is inborn among the Aryan. For him the eternal godhead is revealed through beautiful human beings. . . ."[77] Greek sculpture seemed best to reveal this beauty, and nude or scantily clad Greek male youths came to symbolize the strength and vigor of the Third Reich. The wholehearted acceptance of this Greek heritage, its annexation as the most appropriate expression of Aryan beauty, meant a certain preoccupation with nudity. How National Socialism reacted in the face of nudity provides one more insight into its attitudes toward sexuality and respectability.

The Nazis condemned nude photographs as corrupting youth;[78] moreover, they forbade nudism immediately after their accession to power. The Prussian Ministry of the Interior, in February 1933, though it welcomed the use of sun, air, and water to improve bodily health, castigated nudism as a dangerous error. It was said to deaden the natural shame in women and to destroy the respect men should show at all times toward the female sex.[79] The division of labor between the sexes seemed endangered by the demystification of women. Suspicion of homosexuality was never far from the Nazi imagination after Röhm's execution. Thus in 1935 the Ministry of the Interior warned that nude bathing by people of the same sex could be considered as the first step in violating paragraph 175, directed against homosexual acts.[80]

The Third Reich sought to strip nudity of its sexuality by drawing a sharp distinction between the private and the representational. For example, some of the former nudist journals were allowed to continue publication, but as body-building magazines, whose pictures emphasized various bodily exercises during which the semi-nude body remained abstract, very much like a sculpture.[81] Pictures of the nude body made hard and healthy through exercise and sport were presented as the proper stereotype. For example, Hans Surén's *Gymnastik der Deutschen* (*German Gymnastics*), which went through several editions during the Third Reich, advocated nearly complete nudity in the pursuit of sport or while roaming through the countryside. But the male body had to be prepared carefully if it was to be on public display: the skin must be hairless, smooth, and bronzed.[82] Surén's idea of a beautiful body was modeled once again upon the Greeks. After all, the present-day Germans and the ancient Greeks were considered the twin pillars of the Aryan race.

Surén continued the impulse of the nudist movement into the Third Reich. The nude physique, he wrote, must be regarded with the same joy as nature itself.[83] The body has become a symbol of Aryan and Greek beauty, abstracted through its texture—a living sculpture rather than a living person. But these remains of the nudist movement were of little importance in comparison with the actual sculptures of the ideal male that decorated (or guarded) official buildings such as Hitler's new Reich Chancellery, or were reproduced in official publications. The Third Reich furthered sculpture as that art form best suited to represent Aryan man.

The Greek youth, an important national symbol in the past, reigned supreme during the Third Reich. Hitler's own taste was influenced by the neo-classical revival of the *fin de siècle*,[84] but in any case National Socialism was careful to annex familiar national symbols and bend them to its purpose. Once again the Greek youth was cleansed in traditional fashion, his sexuality driven out by elements of the symbolic and representational—the hard, almost abstracted body whose polish heightened the feeling of remoteness (see plate 10). Nothing remained of Winckelmann's rounded contours. Instead, that whiteness which Walter Pater had praised as removing the taint of sexuality prevailed.[85] However, the Nazis went still further. Such youths were not merely frozen into position (even if supposedly in motion, as on many war monuments) but rendered deliberately static and monumental as well, like the figures done by Arno Breker or J. Thorack which look like gods, to be worshipped but neither desired nor loved (see plate 11).

Arno Breker's monumental figures such as *The Torch Carrier* and *The Sword Carrier* (1938), which stood in the court of honor of Hitler's Chancellery, were carefully sculpted to fit the architecture of the Third Reich. His inspiration was mostly Greek, but he considered Michelangelo one of his teachers, as well as the *fin-de-siècle* painter Hans von Marés, whose pictures of nude youth have themes not unlike those of boys bathing. Breker himself wrote of his nudes exemplifying the "pure air of instinctive drives," and went on to praise the "revolutionary youth of today, which tears the veil from the body hidden in shame,"[86] and thus permits us to see our origins in Paradise, a world still intact, which has provided artistic inspiration for all ages.[87] Although this comment was made after the Second World War, it fits his work before the war as well—that "ideal nudity" which presents a harmonious figure of man.[88] The nude body is not merely symbolic of true beauty and nature, but also points backward to Paradise as the paradigm of a healthy world before the onset of modernity. This symbolism simultaneously strips nudity of its sexuality and projects upon Germanic man the hope of transcending the present in order to recapture Paradise Lost.

National Socialism took a tradition that had served to give respectability to Greek sculpture in the past and carried it to new heights through its urge for symbolic form. Nudity was lifted into immutability. It became symbolic of both national and bourgeois ideals —a process we have analyzed ever since Winckelmann entered respectable society. Strength and virility were expressed through restraint and the absence of undue passion; "quiet greatness" determined the appearance of the ideal Aryan (in contrast to the nervous Jew or exhausted homosexual). The ideal male exemplified Hitler's statement that with the Nazi seizure of power the nervous nineteenth century had come to an end.[89]

The actions in which such sculpted figures were engaged were also significant. This was clearly expressed by one art critic, who, reviewing a Breker piece showing an older soldier dragging a younger one from the field of battle, wrote that here "eternal beauty was exemplified through a relevant and contemporary subject."[90] The date was 1940, the Second World War was a year old, and Breker's monumental sculpture formed the centerpiece of that year's exhibition of German art. Similarly, Leni Riefenstahl had transposed shots of an idealized athlete with shots of sun-drenched nature in her film of the 1936 Olympic Games. Athletic action is performed by a magnificent body in a beautiful natural setting, both symbolic of the new Germany. Sport was viewed as the equivalent of war in peacetime, just as others had perceived it after the First World War—the best available test of manliness until it could once more be challenged in battle.[91] Many war memorials with their statues of Greek youth constituted a direct precedent for Nazi sculpture (see plate 9), a majority of whose figures were engaged in individual (as opposed to team) sports, testing their manliness as discus throwers, runners, or gymnasts.

By means of all these sculptures National Socialism attempted to harness its symbol of manliness to nationalism and respectability. If it succeeded in its aim—and we shall never know—it was surely not just because of the symbolism itself, but also because such figures pressed in on all sides, deadening the sensibilities.

National regeneration was identified with moral regeneration. In Italy as well, fascism in power meant the active prosecution of deviant sexuality, the enforcement of laws against homosexuality and pornography. Moreover, all fascism used the same male symbolism, witness the figures that surround the Forum Mussolini, the stadium built by the Duce in Rome. The Duce himself liked to parade his own manliness; harvesting stripped to the waist, running with his cabinet, exercising his body. Yet these were macho poses, and did not carry with them, as far as we can tell, the same homoerotic overtones that accompanied the development of the German national stereotype. There are clear indications of a more relaxed atmosphere in sexual matters, in any case typical of a Catholic rather than Protestant nation.

One fascism served as a mirror to other fascisms on questions of sexuality and the community of men. The French fascist intellectuals articulated and sought to practice what had been implicit in the masculinity of modern nationalism. If French fascism attained a higher intellectual standard than fascist movements elsewhere,[92] this was because it had captured the imagination of some of Paris's most talented youth—graduates of élite schools and the Ecole Normale—as well as some of France's most powerful writers. They formed an intellectual coterie bound together in friendships often formed at school and university, or founded in heated discussions while trying to edit a journal.

Friendship and youth were elevated into a cult, an exhilaration, which united these men. When Robert Brasillach at the age of twenty-seven came to write his memoirs, published as *Notre Avant Guerre* (*Our Prewar Years*, 1941), youth and friendship formed the core of his fascism, the quest for a poetry of life. Typically enough, he was impressed by the "rough and ready comradeship" that seemed to prevail among leaders and subordinates in the Third Reich.[93] The Nazis want to create a pure race and a new nation, he wrote; they love to be among immense gatherings of males where the rhythm of armies and crowds beats like one huge heart.[94] The nation as a camaraderie of men was indeed how the Nazi Party conceived of the new Germany. But here in fragmented and feeble Republican France, this was the sole fascist experience that counted.

Was there a physical component to this exaltation of male camaraderie leading to the kind of temptation Heinrich Himmler had feared so much? The link between the physical and the spiritual was strongest in the writings of the fascist intellectual Drieu La Rochelle. As Robert Soucy has shown, Drieu held that the physical body determined the spiritual faculties; that if the body grew slack, so did the soul.[95] This was the gospel of masculinity, which devalued the feminine. Drieu was not alone in his appreciation of the male body. Montherlant, though never overtly a fascist, shared such male values; *Les Olympiques* abounded with images of chaste nude athletes in analogy to the "body of France." The women who enter this world threaten to destroy it.[96]

While the suspicion of homosexuality accompanied Montherlant throughout his life, Drieu was known as a great womanizer. He spent a good deal of his time making love and praising war; both were accompanied by consciousness of the beauty and strength of the male body. The physicality of Drieu was not unlike that of D. H. Lawrence. More to the point, it corresponded to that male stereotype through which fascism expressed its dynamic—it was the written equivalent of the nude statues that guarded Nazi buildings or the Forum Mussolini in Rome; but here the male eros remained intact.

Drieu expressed concisely ideas inherent in the *Männerbund*. "For years after the war," he wrote in 1944, "one might have thought that I was especially interested in women. In fact, I was much more interested in men. For me, the drama of friendship between men is at the heart of politics."[97] Robert Brasillach shared these ideas without their overt physicality. True friendship, he wrote, must be a virile friendship, one which he had felt toward a woman only once in his life.[98] The love stories in his novels usually place the woman in a triangle between two close male friends, reflecting perhaps his own feelings toward Maurice Bardèche, whose sister he married. In *Comme le temps passe* (1937), he wrote an extensive physical description of lovemaking between men and women. Yet in the same book he praises friendship among men—a friendship for which men will leave and betray women.[99]

These fascist intellectuals elevated male friendship and youth above all other principles of life; there can be little doubt about the homoeroticism of their politics and personal relationships. During Brasillach's trial for collaboration with the Germans which ended in his death sentence, some of the most damaging evidence against him was found in the articles in which he expressed his love and admiration for German soldiers. The court went so far as to accuse

Brasillach of advocating "a love which dares not speak its name" in his supposedly salacious remarks. This was a court determined upon the death penalty, and the passages from Brasillach's journalistic writings alleged as proof do not bear out this accusation.[100] Yet Jean Guéhenno, who in the 1930s had coedited the pacifist and left-wing journal *Europe*, asked in his diary why there were so many homosexuals among the Nazi collaborators. Did they think that the new order would legitimize their kind of love? With some insight he added that there were those among them who condemned homosexuality, but who except for the most fleeting sexual satisfaction with women withdrew into the world of men.[101] Drieu himself in his novel *Gilles* (1939) lumped homosexuals together with Jews as creatures of the city, unhealthy and rootless.[102] Nevertheless, French facism almost flaunted homoerotic, if not homosexual, attitudes that other fascisms thought to suppress. Here the consequences Himmler wanted to abort seemed to emerge into the light of day.

Any discussion of fascism and sexuality must always return to the worship of masculinity and to the community of men as the ruling élite. Fascism thus threatened to bring to the surface that homoeroticism which had been a part of modern nationalism from the beginning. This introduced a tension between nationalism and respectability which leaders like Himmler attempted to keep under control, and which menaced the alliance between them when, as in France, there was no strong hand to compel respectability.

# IV

Masculine dominance threatened to smother women. Yet, as we saw, a leader like Lydia Gottschewski could be aware of the danger it posed without meaning to question the place of women in the Third Reich. Even the compliant Gertrud Scholtz-Klink, as leader of the German women's organization complained that highly talented and able women were being denied recognition because of their sex. Women were excluded, or pushed out of most professions, until the needs first of the economy and then of war made it necessary to call them back into the world of men. Even then they were to reenter the professions only temporarily.[103] Economic needs did not decisively affect the Nazi image of woman. Woman was the bearer of children, the helpmate of her husband, and the preserver of family life. Nazi attacks against "young ladies" or "sports girls," and girls who marched with rucksacks on their backs emphasized women as custodians of the old-fashioned virtues as a bulwark against modernity.[104] Like Germania, they looked backward not forward; but like Queen Luise, they did so surrounded by their husbands and children.

Grace and beauty were part of such old-fashioned virtues. Women's bodies, like men's, were important to the Third Reich. The League of German Girls (BDM) enlisted girls between the ages of seventeen and twenty-one for its "Faith and Beauty" group, which attempted to form the body through dance and sport while at the same time encouraging the Nazi faith.[105] The beautiful body as the temple for the proper attitude toward life was an aim applied to both men and women. Moreover, female as well as male bodies were shown naked in sculpture, engaged once again in sport, but also through conventional female themes as well, such as *Surrender* or *The Muse*.[106] These female figures were given the same smooth and almost transparent bodies as male athletes or warriors, and like male youths were frozen into position. Again, the effect of remoteness was to strip the body of its sensuality.

This officially sanctioned sculpture rendered men's and women's bodies to some extent homogeneous, creating a "new German," tall and lithe (to use Hitler's favorite phrase), with graceful gestures and quiet force. The similarities between the male and female ideal types as shown in sculpture are remarkable. To a certain extent the female body is approximated to that of the male, in spite of sculptures in which female breasts and hips dominate (see plate 14). This was partly a consequence of the attempt to desexualize nudity, but also of male domination. Women in men's roles must in some ways become masculine. Women athletes in England were called "sportsmen," and in France Montherlant gave his woman athlete a boyish figure.[107] But here, as with those women who managed to fight in wars, those who exhibited masculine virtues and even approximated masculine bodies must retain their female sexuality.

Joseph Goebbels summarized a female charm whose attributes were more widely accepted because traditional. Girls should be strong, healthy, and good to look at, which meant that there must be no visible muscles on their arms and legs.[108] For all such femininity, the similarity between nude male and female sculpture, as well as the emphasis upon women's sports, seemed to disavow this old-fashioned image. Women's sports were an innovation, especially in the cities where sport had not been considered ladylike, just as membership in the BDM fulfilled the dream of many a girl of freedom from parents and school.

The Nazi attitude toward women, then, was not free from contradictions when it came to representations of the ideal type, just as National Socialism found it difficult to reconcile its population policy or the *Männerbund* with the aim of preserving marriage and family life. Nazi painting, unlike Nazi sculpture, frequently still pictured woman as the Madonna, fully clothed, chaste, blond, at work as housewife and mother (see plate 20). Nevertheless nudes also intruded upon so much chastity: female figures in the tradition of naturalism who failed to exemplify "womanly deportment" by their easy blushes and ample dress. Such nudes, however, were hung side by side with chaste peasant girls or a painting like Herbert Kampf's *My Daughter Eva*, in which a girl's young face was framed by garlands of roses, reminiscent of the Nazarenes.

Pictures like that of Kampf cannot have suited Hitler's own taste. Leopold Ziegler was his favorite painter, and Ziegler's fleshy and full-bosomed nudes left nothing to the imagination (see plate 19). Some of these nudes were hung in the Exhibitions of German Art and in the Führer's private apartments. Hitler's own taste was decisive in his preference for erotic painting, but as the Führer he had to concentrate upon those paintings that represented suitable Germanic stereotypes. The works of Ziegler and his like were not supposed to be symbolic or representational, and in this case Hitler preferred a brutal realism that was neither sentimental nor remote.

Nationalism and respectability were supposed to be the essential ingredients of the new fascist world in the making—nationalism to provide the dynamic for its creation, and respectability to control men's passions. The human body exemplified the strength, vitality, and spiritual qualities of the Volk. Preoccupation with the human body was typical for fascism as a visually centered ideology, an attitude toward life based upon stereotypes. Those who did not correspond to its concept of human beauty became outsiders—degenerates or of inferior race. Here again the outsider was in a medical category, considered sick in both body and mind.[109] Such medical judgment was based upon aesthetic and racial preconceptions. This was true of Himmler's condemnation of homosexuals, already discussed, and of his judgment of the Jews as well.

Typical of such fanaticism, Kurt Klare—a functionary of the Third Reich's medical association, and an early party member—fulminated against the "mechanization of medicine," calling for greater reliance upon human instinct, as well as research into a patient's racial ancestry and family as an integral part of medical diagnosis.[110] The direction medical research should take, he wrote, was more important than whether such research was based upon proof.[111] Given his attitude toward medicine and his National Socialist fervor, it comes as no surprise that Klare called for the "utter cleansing of the Reich of homosexuals," and blamed homosexuality for the dominance which the Christian churches and the ideas of the French Revolution had exercised over the German spirit.[112] A diseased body hides an equally diseased mind. Klare as a doctor was reiterating commonplace notions during the Third Reich, and he reiterated too Heinrich Himmler's defense of the *Männerbund* in his assertion that for normal men, the criminal prosecution of homosexuals in no way endangered true friendship or camaraderie.[113] The solving of the "homosexual question," like the solution to the "Jewish question," was a medical imperative. It should come as no surprise that Klare called for the elimination of unworthy life from the community.[114]

National Socialism heightened and brought to the surface what had only been latent or implied earlier as part of the alliance between nationalism and respectability. Thus the "medicalization" of the outsider had supposedly been based upon medical discovery and observation, although in reality guided all along by attitudes based upon ideals of respectability and the acceptance of stereotypes. Even so, the preoccupation with the human body and with the male community, though present throughout our discussion, led to an exclusiveness that aroused Himmler's fears and suspicions, and whose fuller implications were expressed with the coterie of French fascist intellectuals. Women played an ambiguous role in this male world. They were at one and the same time the bearers of children in the image of the Madonna, and young athletes whose bodies were in some ways assimilated to those of men. The exaggerated respect for masculinity not only forced women into passivity but also gave them bodies that should be sporting and earnest, tough and brave.[115] Here a so-called manly deportment was difficult to reconcile with the professed ideal of femininity. Yet the division of labor had still to be kept intact—and here too National Socialism continued a preoccupation basic to the maintenance of respectability.

These ambiguities and predilections were based upon the Nazi wish to be dynamic and virile but also respectable, to attack the bourgeoisie for their formlessness and hypocrisy while nevertheless maintaining bourgeois values. There was to be no change in manners or morals despite certain attitudes that threatened to undermine respectability. Once again respectability held fast, just as it had managed to overcome the rediscovery of the human body at the turn of the century and the strains upon its fabric imposed by the First World War and its aftermath.

The time of the "onslaught of respectability" was long past. The immutability of modern manners and morals, which had at first served to define and legitimize the middle class, had soon captured all classes of the population. Respectability, taken for granted, now became vital for the very existence of bourgeois society; indeed, it provided an important cohesion for the existing order. The social and economic base of this society has been analyzed many times and its importance is obvious and rightly accepted. But respectability was just as important as far as people's actual perception of their society was concerned, how it enabled them to cope with life. It was part of the appeal of nationalism, and subsequently of racism and fascism, that they promised to support respectability against the chaos of the modern age.

## CHAPTER 9

# Conclusion:
# Everyone's Morality

Respectability still determines the manners and morals of society; the history which has filled these pages is still with us. To be sure, nationalism itself no longer plays an important role in upholding respectability. Most national symbols, like national monuments, seem to have spent their force. Yet the stereotypes remain. Clean-cut Englishmen, Germans, or for that matter Americans, are ideal types whose very appearance reflects their sexual restraint, self-control, and quiet strength. Surely, even today, Rupert Brooke or Walter Flex would be welcome as reflecting the best of his nation's youth. The concept of manliness is still very much with us, and perhaps only now is the traditional image of woman giving way, however uneasily, to a more active ideal than that of patron-saint of the nation and mother of the family. Above all, attitudes toward the human body have not really changed. The shame of nudity, of our bodily functions, is still present, in spite of recurring efforts by new generations to rediscover their own bodies. The analogies between past and present must have struck the reader at every turn, for this is a past that relates to everyone's experience of the present.

Respectability and nationalism established themselves in the late eighteenth and early nineteenth centuries at the identical time when bourgeois society was taking hold. Regardless of how much or how little political power was in the hands of the bourgeoisie, its way of life spread upward to the aristocracy and downward to the lower classes. Even in Germany, where the bourgeoisie was largely excluded from political power throughout the nineteenth century, respectability became the unifying force of society as a whole. The process by which the ideal of respectability spread to all classes of the population has not yet been studied, and neither have the political and social consequences of the general acceptance of bourgeois manners and morals. We have merely pointed to certain examples of the embourgeoisement of German society, such as the Prussian royal family, which at the beginning of the nineteenth century mimicked middle-class *gemütlichkeit*. Queen Luise of Prussia could symbolize simultaneously the nation, motherhood, and a settled family life; even at the time of German unification she refused to yield to Germania, her aristocratic and medieval rival. The male national stereotype was derived from the ideal of Greek sculpture, but this was co-opted by middle-class morality as well. Nudity was presumed to have been stripped of sexuality and the nude youth given the attributes of chastity, self-control, and quiet strength.

Respectability was thought essential for the maintenance of an ordered society. The bourgeoisie had created the age of commerce and industry—and it feared what it had created. Thus descriptions of bourgeois life in Germany in the first half of the nineteenth century idealized a steady, rooted life as the precondition for honest trade. Gustav Freytag's *Debit and Credit* emphasized the contrast between a German merchant house, which was rooted in its small town and therefore honest, and a Jewish merchant house, which was dishonest because the Jews were city people who had no understanding of the settled life of the provinces. Industrialization was accompanied not only by the pastoral, as we saw, but also by a nostalgia for an intimate society that could sustain a manageable world. Such ideals were not confined to more backward Germany, for we find a similar nostalgia in rapidly industrializing England, though directed here not toward the small town but rather toward the refuge to be found in a pastoral life. Respectability met this need for order and security in an ever more disordered world. It provided the middle classes with a solid base from which to make the leap, not into moral purification—this they now possessed—but into the not-so-clean world of debit and credit.

The fulfillment of the need for security and order is a partial explanation of why the manners and morals that grew up well over a hundred years ago have lasted so long. Yet they might not have lasted if nationalism had not helped to maintain respectability. Men and women who rediscovered their bodies saw them taken away again, spiritualized and aestheticized, treated as national symbols of strength and beauty. Nationalism claimed to be unchanging and eternal, and through this claim gave to the middle-class way of life an appearance of immutability. Becoming a part of the nation or of nature provided a "slice of eternity," which gave both sanction to the established order and meaning to individual lives. Such sanctification of the individual and society also pointed toward utopia. By becoming a part of the nation and nature, Paradise Lost might yet be regained.

The healing power of nature lay readily at hand, not just for individuals but for the nation as well. In Germany after the First World War, in the midst of defeat, revolution, and counterrevolution, the wave of popular films showing the human conquest of mountains and glaciers was supposed to heal the wounds of the nation by projecting a vision of accomplishment, strength, and beauty. Nature symbolized a healthy world: "mean and wretched people never climb mountains," as Louis Trenker wrote in his autobiography.[1] The nation was part of nature. Indeed, nature was perceived as the native landscape, its mountains and valleys inspiring the members of one particular nation but alien to all others.[2] Although the feeling about the uniqueness of the native landscape was perhaps strongest in Germany, we find it in other countries like England as well. We have seen how as a result of the rediscovery of the body at the end of the nineteenth century and the influence of the German Youth Movement, the quest for the genuine through the power of nature became a search for the true soul of the nation as well.

We have focused upon nationalism as supporting respectability, and yet religion also fulfilled that function. Respectability had part of its origin in English Evangelicalism and German Pietism, as we saw, and was thus sanctioned as religious truth. Throughout the nineteenth and early twentieth century religion played an important role in supporting respectability, not just Protestantism but Catholicism and Judaism as well. Yet nationalism succeeded in infiltrating religion during the nineteenth century and bending it to its purpose, a process that proceeded with greater rapidity in Protestant than Catholic regions. Moreover, medicine tended to replace religion in defining the boundaries between normality and what society considered abnormal. The modern stereotypes of sexual per-

version had made their first appearance in medical literature and
therefore been secularized from the start. The legislation against
homosexual acts at the end of the nineteenth century no longer appealed to religious sensibilities, or the Bible, but instead to the
damage done by sexual perversion to national health, or to the assumption that the people's sense of justice demanded that homosexuality be seen as a crime.[3]

Population policy was also an important consideration in the
passing of such laws; during the Third Reich, Germany's highest
court justified the stiff penalties for so-called unnatural acts through
the damage they might inflict upon the future growth and strength
of the Volk.[4] What remained in such legislation from older times
was the coupling of homosexual acts with bestiality, and no doubt
a deep-seated general prejudice in the population which enabled
some legislators to pose as personally enlightened but forced to
give in to popular demand. Religion largely maintained its hold
over the population; but a process of secularization had taken
place, especially in attitudes toward sexual morality.

This appeal to the people in the attempt to preserve respectability—the activation of what Rousseau called the general will
—legitimized the norms of society through belief in a national consensus, giving, as it were, support from below, when respectability
was already sanctioned from above by the immutable forces of nature, religion, and the nation. There was, in fact, from the early
nineteenth century onward, general agreement that respectability
must be preserved, so closely had it become associated with the co-
herence of society, and any departure from its norms with chaos,
solitude, even death. This wished-for consensus held for most of
the middle class and in time for the aristocracy as well. But we
have much too little evidence of how it affected the lower classes of
the population. We are without compass in charting the relationship between respectability and the workers' movement, for instance, though in England it has been demonstrated that the moral
rigor of evangelism found some of its most enthusiastic adherents
among the self-educated members of the working class. Moreover,
many working-class children learned proper attitudes and behavior
in Sunday School.[5]

Socialism in England and on the continent seems to have supported rather than attacked respectability. Marx and Engels, while
wanting to replace the patriarchal family structure of their day

with a family based upon love and greater equality, were careful to stay within the boundaries of respectability. For example, they explicitly rejected the anarchist Max Stirner's libertarian sexual morality.[6] One of the first German plays written to be performed in the late 1870s at socialist workers' meetings condemned adultery and idealized a settled family life.[7] Echoing a principal theme of bourgeois morality, August Bebel in his much read *Die Frau und der Sozialismus* (*Women and Socialism*, 1883), while calling for women's equality, nevertheless preserved the distinction between masculine and feminine character intact. Socialism, even while championing the rights of women, would strengthen and not weaken a happy family life. Bebel believed in a sexual life that was neither excessive nor abstinent; the "golden mean" led to happiness.[8]

Socialist attitudes toward homosexuality provide further proof of their conventionality. The editor of the Dutch socialist newspaper expressed a general feeling in his party when he wrote in 1905 that homosexuality was the product of a sick imagination, doubly dangerous because it might infect youth.[9] The important socialist theoretician Eduard Bernstein did have a more enlightened attitude toward so-called sexual perversion. He approached homosexuality historically, as a good Marxist should, and blamed the lack of proper social hygiene in a corrupt bourgeois society for the existence of sexual abnormality. Nevertheless, he saw sexual abnormality as a constant in history;[10] the present definition of normality had existed throughout time.

Karl Marx's contention that all systems of thought are products of the time in which they arose was not consistently applied to bourgeois morality. To be sure, from 1917 onward the Soviet Union experimented with new attitudes toward sexuality. Divorce was made easy, equality of the sexes was encouraged, and public displays of nudity were no longer prosecuted.[11] However, Stalin's triumph meant the return to conventional morality. Analyzing this new triumph of respectability, the journalist Louis Fisher wrote in 1930 that "the Communist Party had no theory of sexual revolution."[12] What was true for the Soviet Union held for all Communist parties in Europe, and the Social Democrats as well. The overthrow of bourgeois society meant the retention of bourgeois morality. Economic, political, and social revolution was not accompanied by sexual revolution. The relationship between respectability and socialism seems to demonstrate how effectively respectability had penetrated all classes of the population. Those considered abnormal by society could expect no help from the proletariat.

It is not surprising, therefore, that left-wing anti-fascists used the accusation of homosexuality against the National Socialists, just as the Nazis themselves prosecuted internal enemies, such as the Catholic Church, for homosexual practice in order to break down any resistance. During the war the same accusation was used against England as well.[13] At the same time anti-fascists attempted to prove that the homosexuality of Ernst Röhm had infected the whole movement. Homosexuals among anti-fascists were made unwelcome—the Communist author Ludwig Renn, for example, faced constant hostility until he became a hero during the Spanish Civil War and so proved himself in the struggle against fascism.[14] Renn's final acceptance is not so different from Marcel Proust's belief that riding and mountain climbing cured sexual perversion. Klaus Mann's novel *Vulcan* (1936), by contrast, shows how a homosexual relationship was accepted as a matter of course among anti-fascist exiles from Nazi Germany. Mann was himself a homosexual who must have known the true situation, but for him the Nazis were the real perverts.[15]

While even socialist revolutionaries took respectability for granted, the appeal of nationalism was also cross-class. Through its claim of encompassing all the people, nationalism aided respectability in establishing a broad consensus. The new religion of nationalism promised to sanctify and give meaning to individual lives regardless of class. The economic and social hierarchy was retained and strengthened, but as members of the new nation everyone had equal status, however humble or poor he might be. Nationalism provided order through a hierarchy of function, but at the same time offered equality of status.

The very strength of respectability and nationalism, their appeal, and the needs they filled, meant that those who stood apart from the norms of society were totally condemned. It was no longer the specific sexual acts alone that were considered abnormal, but the entire physical and mental structure of the person practicing these acts. Such a person was excluded from society and the nation. Solitude was the price exacted for abnormal behavior, and the outsider, as we have seen, was supposed to live a lonely life and die a lonely death. If he attempted to enter society, he had to pay the price of admission. In discussing sexuality and race, we saw that society excluded all who seemed to present a danger to established norms and the national ideal: not only those who directly threatened respectability, but the Jews newly emancipated at the start of the century as well. Jews could in fact enter society without losing their own identity. German Jews, for example, were proud to be both German and Jewish, and until the victory of National Socialism, many Germans accepted that claim. Yet even here, there was a price of admission. As rabbis preached the virtues of self-control, chastity, and manly bearing, Jews were to become "respectable" and abandon any signs of their ghetto past. Ever conscious of the stereotype they shared with other outsiders—nervous, lacking restraint, slaves to the lower passions—Jews were often careful not to act or look "Jewish." Assimilation always included a flight from a former identity.

Homosexuals could not enter society and keep their identity. They had to avoid all suspicion of sexual abnormality, even though such different men as Benedict Friedländer and Magnus Hirschfeld pictured them as highly respectable in comportment. Their plea made little difference, and homosexuals were forced to create a subculture of their own, a space in which they could function. This subculture centered upon bars where both socializing and sexual contact were possible. Hirschfeld, as part of his effort to decriminalize homosexuality, described the Berlin homosexual bars before the First World War as modest and restrained, like many heterosexual establishments, whereas Radclyffe Hall described the lesbian bars in Paris of the 1920s as "tragic and garish."[16] Homosexuals had welcomed the movement called decadence at the end of the nineteenth century, as we saw, because it presented a chance to move out into a larger world. The tradition of artistic decadence lasted into the twentieth century in many more pretentious homosexual and lesbian bars of Berlin or Paris, with their often languid and mysterious atmosphere.[17] Yet from the *fin de siècle* onward, books defending homosexual rights proliferated, and so did movements devoted to that cause. At the same time, sexologists were taking a more compassionate stand toward homosexuals than most of their medical colleagues. And yet even those, like Iwan Bloch, who thought that homosexuals were often endowed with fine mental qualities, asserted that the progress of culture was dependent upon a clear distinction between male and female sexuality. Though the homosexual had the same right to exist as the heterosexual, he was of no consequence for the human species or its culture.[18] While well disposed, such advocates, if they did not exclude the homosexual, pushed him to the margins of society.

In the more tolerant atmosphere of the Weimar Republic, the diet was still unable to muster a clear majority to repeal paragraph 175 of the criminal code (which was not in fact repealed until 1969).[19] The forces of respectability were too strong, the needs it fulfilled in society too pressing, to accept a reversal of sex roles that would put the clear definition of norms in jeopardy. We have had many occasions to mention the important role which the division of labor between the sexes played as part of the more general division of labor in bourgeois society: order must prevail. Nationalism symbolized such order, in part through the image of the virile national hero as against the passive and backward-looking Germania, Britannia, or Queen Luise.

Lesbians were in a still more difficult plight, though they had been ignored by a male-dominated Europe until well after the First World War. Lesbianism was brought to the attention of the general public largely through the scandal caused in Britain by the publication of Radclyffe Hall's The Well of Loneliness (1928). This was not the first lesbian story published, but it received much publicity during the successful attempt to ban it in England (the book was published nonetheless in Paris).[20] Significantly, Hall accepted all of society's lesbian stereotypes. Her hero, Stephen, was said to have a man's soul in a woman's body, which found outward expression through her manly clothes and comportment. Lesbians in the book were endowed with the "terrible nerves of the invert" and haunted eyes. In short, "despised of the world, [they] must despise themselves beyond all hope."[21] While the novel is a plea for compassion for lesbians, male homosexuals get rough treatment, being portrayed as effeminate, with a tendency to hysteria. We could hardly find a better example of the outsider's self-hate.

The German diet debated whether lesbianism should become part of the criminal code banning homosexuality in the same year in which The Well of Loneliness was published in Paris. Yet Christa Winsloe's Mädchen in Uniform (Girls in Uniform), the most famous plea for lesbian liberation in Germany, was straightforward and forceful. Winsloe wrote her story first in 1931 as a play, then as a film script, and finally as a novel with the name of her heroine as the title, Das Mädchen Manuela (The Girl Manuela, 1934). The film played in German cinemas and the book was sold for a brief time, for the German Parliament had not criminalized lesbianism after all.[22] Winsloe's plot is set in a boarding school for the daughters of the Prussian aristocracy. There the girl Manuela falls in love with her teacher, Fräulein von Bernburg, a lesbian, who also loves the girl in return. But Fräulein von Bernburg has suppressed her lesbianism and rejects Manuela's love, driving the young girl to suicide. Manuela, unlike Hall's Stephen, is charming and high-spirited, and the villain is the headmistress, who frightens Fräulein von Bernburg into resisting temptation by reminding her "how the world, our world, judges such girls!"[23] The film, unlike the novel, has a happy ending as Fräulein von Bernburg acknowledges her own lesbianism, challenges the principal's authority, and saves Manuela from suicide. And yet the sound of military bugles as the film concludes points toward a possible final victory of social discipline over love.[24]

Lesbians withdrew into their private clubs and bars. A book by Ruth Roellig on *Berlin's Lesbian Women* (1928) complained that such women showed little esprit de corps and refused to fight for their rights either by joining homosexual organizations or by founding their own.[25] They were fragmented by the pressure of society. But relatively few homosexuals joined their own movements, fearing exposure. The outsider was thus made over into his stereotype. Excluded from society, fragmented, he became as lonely as he was supposed to be; constantly subject to blackmail because of the performance of a criminal sexual act, he had reason to be nervous, to have haunted eyes. Radclyffe Hall and Christa Winsloe were themselves lesbians, and Hall's self-hate was duplicated by the experience of homosexuals who admitted to the stereotype of themselves and then tried to escape, but also by assimilated Jews among whom hatred of their own Jewishness was not unknown.

The Jews were to experience at its most cruel and cynical the power of society and the state to make myth come true, actually to transform those branded as outsiders into their own stereotype. It is possible that the Nazis in the concentration camp attempted to transform homosexuals as well, but they were much more obsessed with the Jewish racial enemy, and it is there that we can most clearly follow this process. The Nazis created conditions in the concentration camps which, in their eyes, made Jews behave according to the racist stereotype. Rudolf Höss, the commandant of Auschwitz, for example, accused the Jews in his camp of acting in a "typically Jewish" way, shirking work, clawing at each other in wild competition for those privileges that would enable them to lead a comfortable, parasitic life.[26] No such life could be lived at Auschwitz. Höss himself had created conditions in which survival was all that mattered. Here, through ruthless and dictatorial power, the attempt was made to reduce men and women to their negative stereotype, and racism attempted to make its own theory come true. This racism found nourishment in the conformity respectability demanded, and claimed as its own the virtues of hard work and a happy family life in contrast to the stereotyped outsider.

There was no inevitable connection between racism and respectability; it lay at hand to be appealed to and manipulated. Yet the general acceptance of respectability as an immutable truth, its close link to nationalism, and the stereotyping and medical legitimizing of the outsider, all made it easier for racism to claim respectability as an attribute of the superior race.

The connection between nationalism and racism was more direct. Nationalism not only helped to maintain respectability and to define its ideal types. It also served to close off all routes of escape from the respectable world. To be indecent and at the same time an enemy of the people was an accusation difficult to counter, and, as we saw, the legislation directed against homosexuality at the end of the nineteenth century appealed for its sanction directly to the people themselves. There was, of course, no reason why one could not be respectable and tolerant at the same time; but in moments of crisis the always latent pressure to conform sprang into frightening action. The fears and preconceptions of Heinrich Himmler pushed conformity to its final conclusion, with the assumption that nature itself supported both heterosexuality and the Germanic race, and therefore homosexuals and Jews must be eliminated as unnatural. The role nationalism and respectability played in the rise of fascism has often been forgotten. It is not easy to confront when such factors have determined so much of our own behavior. Respectability, in particular, has become part of the presupposition upon which most people base their lives.

Yet it would be wrong to judge respectability simply by the use racism or fascism made of it. One must not assess a system of thought and behavior solely by its abuses. Nationalism cannot so easily be absolved, though even here, at least until the First World

War, much of it, whether in Germany or elsewhere in England and Europe, was not aggressive but recognized the right of every nation to its existence and its own culture. Nor must we forget that society needs cohesion—without it, not only dictatorships but parliamentary governments cannot function.

In conclusion we must emphasize what has been implicit throughout this discussion: respectability provided society with an essential cohesion that was as important in the perceptions of men and women as any economic or political interests. What began as bourgeois morality in the eighteenth century, in the end became everyone's morality. Was the price exacted for this morality too high? That depends upon how the conflict between society's felt need for cohesion and tolerance of the outsider can be resolved. Like Germania, respectability seems securely enthroned, however new her garments, permitting some latitude of sexual expression provided that it does not endanger her power and dominance.

# Notes / Index

# Notes

CHAPTER I

1. John Boswell, *Christianity, Social Tolerance and Homosexuality* (Chicago, 1980), passim.

2. André Robert de Merciat, *Le Diable aux Corps* (1797), cited by Marion Luckow, *Die Homosexualität in der Literarischen Tradition* (Stuttgart, 1962), 7.

3. For Sarah Trimmer's justification for "trimming," see the reprint of her *A Comparative View of the New Plan for Education* (London, 1905).

4. E. M. Halliday, "The Man Who Cleaned Up Shakespeare," *Horizon*, Vol. V, No. 1 (September 1962), 70.

5. See Harold Nicolson, *Good Behaviour* (London, 1955), 231–46.

6. Norbert Elias, *The Civilizing Process* (New York, 1978); see also George L. Mosse, "Norbert Elias. The Civilizing Process," *New German Critique*, No. 15 (Fall 1978), 178–83.

7. Thea Booss-Rosenthal, "Die lesbische Liebe im Spiegel des Gesetztes," in P. H. Biederich, *Die Homosexualität* (Regensburg, 1950), 83.

8. *Das Zeitalter des Pietismus*, ed. Martin Schmidt and Wilhelm Jannasch (Bremen, 1965), 108–09.

9. David Newsome, *Godliness and Good Learning* (London, 1961), 198–9.

10. G. S. R. Kitson-Clark, "The Romantic Element 1830–1850," *Studies in Social History*, ed. J. H. Plumb (London, 1955), 231–2.

11. Quoted in Maurice J. Quinlan, *Victorian Prelude, A History of English Manners 1700–1830* (London, 1965), 100.

12. Quoted in Jeffrey Weeks, *Sex, Politics and Society* (London and New York, 1981), 27.

13. Quinlan, *Victorian Prelude*, 76.

14. Theodor Körner, "Aufruf" (1813), *Theodore Körner's Sämtliche Werke in zwei Teilen*, ed. Eugen Wildenow (Leipzig, n.d.), 120.

15. "Die Leipziger Schlacht" (1913), poem 157, *Ernst Mortiz Arndt Sämtliche Werke*, Vol. 4 (Leipzig, n.d.), 83.

16. Quoted in Hermann Wendel, *Danton* (Königstein/Taunus, 1978), 362.

17. Jacob Stockinger, "Homosexuality and the French Enlightenment," *Homosexualities in French Literature*, ed. George Stambolian and Elaine Marx (Ithaca, N.Y., 1979), 161–86.

18. See Crane Brinton, *French Revolutionary Legislation on Illegitimacy, 1789–1804* (Cambridge, Mass., 1936).

19. Sir Walter Scott, *Ivanhoe* (New York, New American Library, 1962), 38.

20. Alice Chandler, *A Dream of Order* (London, 1971), 46–7.

21. Nicolson, *Good Behaviour*, 236.

22. Peter T. Cominos, "Late Victorian Respectability and the Social System," *International Review of Social History*, Vol. 8 (1963), 42.

23. H. Montgomery Hyde, *Oscar Wilde* (New York, 1975), 265.

24. Ford Madox Ford, *The Good Soldier: The Saddest Story Ever Told* (London, 1915), 158.

25. Iwan Bloch, *Die Perversen* (Berlin, n.d.), 28.

26. Richard von Krafft-Ebing, *Psychopathia sexualis* (Stuttgart, 1907), 55.

27. E. Hare, "Masturbatory Insanity: The History of an Idea," *The Journal of Mental Science*, Vol. 108, No. 452 (January 1962), 8.

28. *Ibid.*, 23, n. 11.

29. *Ibid.*, 4.

30. *Die Onanie, Vierzehn Beiträge zu einer Diskussion der "Wiener Psychoanalytischen Vereinigung"* (Wiesbaden, 1912), 2.

31. *Oeuvres Diverses de Bertrand-Rival*, nouvelle edition (Marseilles, 1809), 44.

32. J. F. Bertrand, *Tableaux Historiques et Morales . . .* (Paris, 1799). Pp. 44ff give the history of the museum and discuss visits by schoolchildren and Bertrand's visits to schools; 33ff describe the objects in the museum.

33. *Ibid.* (Paris, 1798; the first edition), 37. Description of figures, 37–40.

34. Theodore Tarczylo, *Sexe et Liberté au Siècle des Lumières* (Paris, 1983), 143ff, 177–81.

35. C. Eynard, *Essai sur la Vie de Tissot* (Lausanne, 1859), 78, 85. Theodore Tarczylo, "Prétons la Main a la Nature, L'Onanisme de Tissot," *Dix-Huitième Siècle*, Vol. 12 (1980), 85.

36. See Dr. Tissot, *L'Onanisme* (Paris, 1980), Article I, "Les Symptomes," 29ff.

37. R. L. Rozier, *Lettres Médicales et Morales* (Paris, 1822), xi.

38. Philip Greven, *The Protestant Temperament, Patterns of Child Rearing, Religious Experience, and the Self in Early America* (New York, 1977), 140.

39. George L. Mosse, "War and the Appropriation of Nature," in *Ger-*

many in the *Age of Total War*, ed. Volker Berghahn and Martin Kitchen (London, 1981), 117.

40. See Richard Jenkyns, *The Victorians and Ancient Greece* (Oxford, 1980), 147.

41. Marc-André Raffalovich, *Uranisme et Unisexualité* (Lyons and Paris, 1896), 184; for Raffalovich, see page 88.

42. Wolfgang Lepmann, *Winckelmann* (Munich, 1982), 152.

43. Friedrich Schiller, *Uber die ästhetische Erziehung des Menschen* (Stuttgart, 1965), 8, 60.

44. *Winckelmann's Werke*, ed. Heinrich Meyer and Johann Schulze (Dresden, 1811), Vol. IV, 37.

45. See Klaus Wolbert, *Die Nackten und die Toten des Dritten Reiches*, (Giessen, 1982), 133–4.

46. Bernhard Ruprecht, "Plastisches Ideal und Symbol im Bilderstreit der Goethezeit," *Probleme der Kunstwissenschaft*, Vol. 1 (Berlin, 1962), 215.

47. *Ibid.*, 203–04, 215.

48. Wolbert, *Die Nackten und die Toten*, 128.

49. See George L. Mosse, *The Nationalization of the Masses* (New York, 1975).

50. Wolbert, *Die Nackten und die Toten*, 142.

51. See page 95.

52. Greven, *The Protestant Temperament*, 140.

53. Magnus Hirschfeld sums up this change in *Sexualwissenschaftlicher Bilderatlas zur Geschlechtskunde* (Berlin, 1930), 484–90; for a larger discussion, see pages 102ff.

54. See pages 144ff.

55. See Randolph Trumbach, *The Rise of the Egalitarian Family* (New York, 1978), 132.

56. Rozier, *Lettres Médicales et Morales*, 62.

57. Paul Kluckhohn, *Die Auffassung der Liebe in der Literatur des 18. Jahrhunderts und in der deutschen Romantik* (Tübingen, 1966), 76–7.

58. J. F. Bertrand-Rival, *Vers sur l'Existence de Dieux* (n.p., 1813).

59. Boswell, *Christianity, Social Tolerance and Homosexuality*, 157.

60. Ingeborg Weber-Kellermann, *Die Deutsche Familie* (Frankfurt-am-Main, 1974), 102.

61. Berthold Auerbach, *Dichter und Kaufmann, ein Lebensgemälde aus der Zeit Moses Mendelssohns*, Vol. I, *Berthold Auerbach's gesammelte Schriften*, Vol. 12 (Stuttgart, 1864), 103. *Dichter und Kaufmann* was first published in 1839.

62. Weeks, *Sex, Politics, and Society*, 83; Helmut Möller, *Die Kleinbürgerliche Familie im 18. Jahrhundert* (Berlin, 1969), 79–81.

63. See Hans-Jürgen Lusebrink, "Les Crimes Sexuelles," *Dix-Huitième Siècle*, Vol. 12 (1980), 202.

64. W. H. Riehl, *Die Familie* (Stuttgart, 1854), 123.

65. Carl Euler, *Friedrich Ludwig Jahn* (Berlin, 1881), 118.

66. Quoted in Kathryn Tidrick, *Heart-Beguiling Araby* (Cambridge, Engl., 1981), 19.

67. Michael Foucault, *The History of Sexuality*, Vol. 1, *An Introduction* (New York, 1980), 15ff.

CHAPTER 2

1. Samuel Richardson, Vol. 1, *Pamela* (London, 1914), 137; Körner, "Männer und Buben" (1813), in *Theodor Körner's Sämtliche Werke in zwei Teilen*, ed. Wildenow, 137.

2. Albert Moll, *Handbuch der Sexualwissenschaften* (Leipzig, 1921), 334ff. He collaborated in this work with Havelock Ellis. Nevertheless, Moll asserted earlier that medical ethics must not endanger the moral norm of society—Moll, *Artzliche Ethik* (Stuttgart, 1902), 230.

3. Havelock Ellis, *Men and Women* (London, 1894), 85ff.

4. Lord Baden-Powell of Gilwell, *Rovering to Success* (London, 1922), 106.

5. Arthur N. Gilbert, "Sexual Deviance and Disaster during the Napoleonic Wars," *Albion*, Vol. 9 (1978), 98–113.

6. Günther Gollner, *Homosexualität, Ideologiekritik und Entmythologisierung einer Gesetzgebung* (Berlin, 1974), 106–19.

7. Graf von Hoensbroech, *Das Papsttum in seiner sozial-kulturellen wirksamkeit*, Vol. 2: *Die Ultramontane Moral* (Leipzig, 1902), 310–12, 325. This is a hostile account and has to be used with caution. Von Hoensbroech was an ex-priest. For a sharp criticism of Hoensbroech, see Josef Mausbach, *Die Katholische Moral und ihre ihre Gegner* (Cologne, 1921; first published 1901), 6.

8. Von Hoenbroech, *Das Papsttum*, 125.

9. Isaiah, II: 25. John Calvin, *The Bible, etc.* (London, 1588), 260.

10. George L. Mosse, *The Holy Pretence* (Oxford, 1957), 51.

11. See *Ibid.*, 95.

12. See, for example, B. Gass, *Geschichte der Christlichen Ethik*, Vol. 2 (Berlin, 1881), 1626.

13. Quoted in Ulrich Linse, "Arbeiterschaft und Geburtenentwicklung im Deutschen Kaiserreich von 1871," *Archiv für Sozialgeschichte*, Band XII (1972), 212–13.

14. Joseph Mausbach, *Kernfragen Christlicher Welt und Lebensanschauung* (M. Gladbach, 1921; first published in 1904), 71.

15. See Jeffrey Weeks, "Movements of Affirmation: Sexual Meanings and Homosexual Identities," *Radical History Review* (Spring/Summer 1979), 166. This process of medicalisation is summed up in excellent manner in Vern L. Bullough, *Sex, Society and History*, (New York, 1976), 161–185.

16, Cited in F. B. Smith, *The People's Health, 1830–1910* (Canberra, Australia, 1979), 121.

17. Quoted in J. E. Rivers, *Proust and the Art of Love* (New York, 1980), 108.

18. For a summary of English legislation, see Jeffrey Weeks, *Coming Out, Homosexual Politics in Britain from the Nineteenth Century to the Present* (London, 1977); F. B. Smith, "Labouchère's Amendment to the Criminal Law Amendment Bill," *Historical Studies* (University of Melbourne), Vol. 10, No. 1 (October 1976). For a good survey of such legislation in Germany, see Biedrich, *Paragraph 175—Die Homosexualität*, and Gollner, *Homosexualität, Ideologiekritik und Entmythologisierung einer Gesetzgebung*.

19. M. Tissot, *L'Onanisme, Discours sur les Maladies produites par la Masturbation* (Lausanne, 1717), 193, 219.

20. See pages 11ff.

21. Johann Valentin Müller, *Entwurf einer gerichtlichen Arzneiwissenschaft* (Frankfurt-am-Main, 1796), reprinted in *Der unterdrückte Sexus*, ed. Joachim S. Hohmann (Lollar/Lahn, 1977), 132, 139.

22. Richard von Krafft-Ebing, *Psychopathia sexualis* (Philadelphia and London, 1892), 190.

23. Johann Valentin Müller, *Entwurf einer gerichtlichen Arzneiwissenschaft*, 136.

24. *Ibid.*, 137.

25. Ambroise Tardieu, *Die Vergehen gegen die Sittlichkeit* (Weimar, 1860), 124, 140ff.

26. Johann Ludwig Caspar, in *Vierteljahrsschrift für gerichtliche und öffentliche Medizin* (1852), reprinted in *Der unterdrückte Sexus*, 73, 63, 64.

27. Möbius in *Jahrbuch für Sexuelle Zwischenstufen*, Vol. IV (1904), 499.

28. See Chapter 7.

29. Hans Dietrich Hellbach, *Die Freundesliebe in der deutschen Literatur* (Leipzig, 1931), 38, 43.

30. Adolf Beyer, *Schiller's Malteser* (Tübingen, 1912), 45, 46, 75.

31. *Fichte's Reden an die deutsche Nation*, Achte Rede (Berlin, 1912), 137.

32. See Chapter 4.

33. Friedrich Schiller, *Über die ästhetische Erziehung des Menschen* (Stuttgart, 1965), 36.

34. See Mosse, *The Nationalization of the Masses*, 22, 23.

35. This is an impression left not only by Brooke's war poetry but also by Edward Marsh's *Memoir*, which accompanied the edition of Brooke's collected poems (1918) and was crucial in creating the myth of Rupert Brooke. For more on this see Chapter 6.

36. Pierre Sipriot, *Montherlant* (Paris, 1975), 62.

37. Robert Brainard Pearsall, *Rupert Brooke, the Man and the Poet* (Amsterdam, 1964), 140.

38. Johann Ludwig Caspar, reprinted in *Der Unterdrückte Sexus*, 59.

39. Alois Geigel, *Das Paradoxon der Venus Urania* (Würzburg, 1869), reprinted in *Der unterdrückte Sexus*, 7.

40. See Gilbert, "Sexual Deviance and Disaster during the Napoleonic Wars," *Albion*, Vol. 9 (1978), 99.

41. See page 167.

42. Magnus Hirschfeld, *Berlin's Drittes Geschlecht* (Berlin and Leipzig, 1904), 37, 41 (quoting from Rudolf Presber's *Feuilleton* "Weltstadttypen").

43. Iwan Bloch, *Das Sexualleben unserer Zeit, in seine Beziehungen zur modernen Kultur* (Berlin, 1906), 384–5.

44. *Ibid.*, 753.

45. Iwan Bloch, *Die Perversen*, (Berlin, n.d.), 26, 37.

46. Quoted in F. B. Smith, *The People's Health*, 300.

47. Interestingly enough, Bloch quotes Edward Carpenter to the effect that self-control is essential for the proper kind of love—*Das Sexualleben unserer Zeit*, 280; for Edward Carpenter, see Chapter 3.

48. Alois Geigel in *Der unterdrückte Sexus*, 7.

49. Benedict Friedländer in *Jahrbuch für sexuelle Zwischenstufen*, Vol. 1 (1905), 463–70; see also James D. Steakley, *The Homosexual Emancipation Movement in Germany* (New York, 1975), 69.

50. Krafft-Ebing, *Psychopathia sexualis* (1892), 6 op. cit. (1898), 186.

51. Bloch, *Das Sexualleben unserer Zeit*, 601, 464, and 468.

52. Tissot, *L'Onanisme*, 66.

53. Cited in *Der Spiegel* (March 12, 1979), 123.

54. See Erwin H. Ackerknecht, *Kurze Geschichte der Psychiatrie* (Stuttgart, 1957), 51, 52. The Morel title is *Traité des Dégénérescences Physiques, Intéllectuelles et Morales de l'Espèce Humaine*.

55. Annemarie Wettley, *Von der "Psychopathia sexualis" zur Sexualwissenschaft* (Stuttgart, 1959), 45–6.

56. Max Nordau, *Degeneration* (New York, 1968), 325.

57. *Ibid.*, 329.

58. *Ibid.*, 18.

59. *Ibid.*, 37, 39, 41, and 541.

60. See Chapter 7.

61. M. Proust, *Remembrance of Things Past*, Vol. 2 (New York, 1932), 14.

62. *Ibid.*, 311.

63. Jean Recanati, *Profils Juifs de Marcel Proust* (Paris, 1979), 119.

64. Eugen Dühren (Iwan Bloch), *Englische Sittengeschichte* (Berlin, 1912; first published in 1903), 14, 24, and 46.

65. Bloch, *Das Sexualleben unserer Zeit*, 541, 543, 591, and 595.

66. Magnus Hirschfeld, "Ursachen und Wesen des Uranismus," *Jahrbuch für Sexuelle Zwischenstufen*, Jahrg. V, Band 1 (1903), 35, 93.

67. Krafft-Ebing, *Psychopathia sexualis* (Philadelphia and London, 1892), 5, 6.

68. Krafft-Ebing reasserted his belief in homosexuality as a sign of degeneration even in the revised *Psychopathia sexualis* of 1903; see Wettley,

*Von der 'Psychopathia sexualis' zur Sexualwissenschaft,* 96, n. 93.
69. *Jahrbuch für sexuelle Zwischenstufen* (1901), 7, 71.
70. See Vincent Brome, *Havelock Ellis, Philosopher of Sex* (London, 1979), passim.
71. Phyllis Grosskurth, *John Addington Symonds* (London, 1964), 191.
72. Frank J. Sulloway, *Freud, Biologist of the Mind* (New York, 1979), Chapter 8.
73. Philip Rieff, *Freud: The Mind of the Moralist* (New York, 1961), 172.
74. Freud's letter to the mother of a son who was a homosexual, April 9, 1935. Sigmund Freud, *Briefe 1873–1939* (Frankfurt-am-Main, 1960), 416.
75. Sigmund Freud, *Sexuality and the Psychology of Love* (New York, 1963), 25.
76. See Steakley, *The Homosexual Emancipation Movement in Germany,* Chapter 20. James Steakley is now writing what promises to be the definitive biography of Magnus Hirschfeld. The ideas of sexologists legitimizing homosexuality came to England with the founding of the British Society for the Study of Sex-Psychology in 1913. The society was founded after Edward Carpenter had sponsored lectures and an exhibit by Magnus Hirschfeld at the International Medical Congress in London the same year. See Lawrence Housman, "A Peaceful Penetrator," in *Edward Carpenter, an Appreciation,* ed. Gilbert Beith (New York, 1973; first published in 1931), 110–11.
77. See, for example, Iwan Bloch's list of famous and intellectually distinguished homosexuals, which includes only King Henry III of France and King Frederick the Great of Prussia as politically active or military men in a list of fifteen homosexuals—*Das Sexualleben unserer Zeit,* 560–61.
78. Wettley, *Von der "Psychopathia sexualis" zur Sexualwissenschaft,* 63, 64.
79. See Hirschfeld, *Berlins Drittes Geschlecht,* 37, 41.
80. André Gide, *Corydon, Oeuvres Complètes,* Vol. IX (Paris, n.d.), 203.
81. Marion Luckow, *Die Homosexualität in der Literarischen Tradition* (Stuttgart, 1962), 57.
82. *Jahrbuch für Sexuelle Zwischenstufen* (1905), 563–70.
83. Benedict Friedländer cited by Karl Franz von Leexow, *Armee und Homosexualität* (Leipzig, 1908), 5, 61–3. He charged that all effeminate homosexuals had gathered not in his own, but in Hirschfeld's organization devoted to the furtherance of homosexual rights. Benedict Friedländer, *Die Liebe Platons im Lichte der Modernen Biologie* (Treptow, 1909), 203–4.
84. Emil Szittya, *Das Kuriositäten-Kabinet* (Konstanz, 1923), 60–1.
85. Marx Nordau quoted in *Die Körperliche Renaissance der Juden,* Festschrift zum 10 Jährigen bestehen des "Bar Kochba" Berlin (Berlin, May 1909), 12; Max Nordau, "Jüdische Turner," *Jüdische Monatshefte für Turnen und Sport,* XIV, Heft 6 (August–September 1913), 173–4.
86. For a discussion of this issue, see George L. Mosse, *Toward the Final Solution* (New York, 1978), 122–7.
87. *Der Eigene, Ein Blatt für männliche Kultur,* with concluding re-

marks, by Joachim S. Hohmann (Frankfurt and Berlin, 1981), 331.
    88. *Der Eigene*, 183–4. The original page is reproduced, but no volume or date is given.
    89. Friedländer shared these ideas; see Harry Oosterhuis, "Homosocial Resistance to Hirschfeld's Homosexual Putsch: The Gemeinschaft der Eigenen, 1899–1914," *Among Men, Among Women*, Gay Studies and Women's Studies, University of Amsterdam Conference, June 22–26, 1983, 305–14.
    90. *Der Eigene*, 365.
    91. Adolf Brand, "Freundesliebe als Kulturfaktor," *Der Eigene*, Jahrg. 13, No. 1 (July 15, 1930), n.p.
    92. *Der Eigene*, 338.
    93. See Chapter 8.
    94. Bryan Farwell, *Burton, A Biography of Sir Richard Frances Burton* (London, 1963), 378.
    95. See pages 120–122.
    96. A. J. Langguth, *Saki: A Life of Hector Hugh Munroe* (New York, 1981), 258, 83.
    97. *Teleny, or the Reverse of the Medal* (London, 1893), 96. On the history of the making of this book see the introduction by Winston Leyland to a new edition of *Teleny, A Novel Attributed to Oscar Wilde*, ed. Winston Leyland (San Francisco, 1984), 5–19.
    98. *Ibid.*, 11, 23.
    99. Luckow, *Die Homosexualität in der Literarischen Tradition*, 29.
    100. See Phillippe Jullian, *d'Annunzio* (London, 1972).
    101. Wolfdietrich Rasch, "Literary Decadence. Artistic Representations of Decay," *Journal of Contemporary History*, Vol. 17, No. 1 (January 1982), 205.
    102. See Martin Green, *Children of the Sun. A Narrative of "Decadence" in England after 1918* (New York, 1976).
    103. G. L. Mosse, *The Crisis of German Ideology*, (New York, 1964), 216.
    104. *Ibid.*, 175.
Ziemer and Hans Wolf, *Wandervogel* (Bad Godesberg, 1961), 261.
    106. Carl Boesch, "Vom deutschen Mannesideal," *Der Vortrupp*, Jahrg. 2, no. 1 (January 1, 1913), 3.
    107. *Ibid.*, 4.


CHAPTER 3

    1. Gert Mattenklott, *Bilderdienst, Ästhetische Opposition bei Beardsley und George* (Munich, 1970), 197–9.
    2. Friedrich Ludwig Jahn and Ernst Eiselen, *Die Deutsche Turnkunst* (Berlin, 1816), 244.
    3. *Nacktheit als Verbrechen, Der Kampf um #184 Strgb. in der Lüneburger Heide* (Egestorf, n.d.), 145.

4. See Mosse, *The Nationalization of the Masses*, 133.
5. Wolfgang R. Krabbe, *Gesellschaftsveränderung durch Lebensreform* (Göttingen, 1974), 13, 91. Sunburn was not prized in England before the industrial revolution; see Jenkyns, *The Victorians and Ancient Greece*, 146–7.
6. See Mosse, *Toward the Final Solution*, Chapter 2.
7. Heinrich Pudor, *Nacktkultur*, Vol. 1 (Berlin-Steglitz, 1906), 49.
8. Krabbe, *Gesellschaftsveränderung durch Lebensreform*, 98.
9. *Die Schönheit*, ed. Karl Vanselow, Jahrg. 1 (1903), 157.
10. See J. M. Seitz, *Die Nacktkulturbewegung* (Dresden, 1925), 35.
11. *Nacktheit und Verbrechen*, 9.
12. *Die Freude*, Jahrg. 1 (1923), 52.
13. *Die Schönheit* (1903), 557.
14. Seitz, *Die Nacktkulturbewegung*, 71.
15. *Ibid.*, 61.
16. Walter Flex, *Der Wanderer zwischen Beiden Welten* (Munich, n.d.), 22–3. Such ideals sometimes hid strong sexual drives as, for example, in the erotic phantasies of Fidus. Ulrich Linse has described how those itinerant prophets and self-proclaimed saviors who appeared in Germany directly after the First World War—linked to nudist and life-reform movements—hid their sexual promiscuities behind the mantle of a Christ-like purity. These people thought of their bodies as suffused with light, similar to the figures shown in Fahrenkrog's picture. (see plate 16). Ulrich Linse, *Barfüssige Propheten. Erlöser der zwanziger Jahre* (Berlin, 1983), 54.
17. See page 119.
18. See pages 119–120.
19. Krabbe, *Gesellschaftsveränderung durch Lebensreform*, 149ff.
20. Richard Ungewitter, *Nacktheit und Moral, Wege zur Rettung des deutschen Volkes* (Stuttgart, 1925), 10–11.
21. Seitz, *Die Nacktkulturbewegung*, 119.
22. Richard Ungewitter, *Die Nacktheit in entwicklungsgeschichtlicher, gesundheitlicher, moralischer und künstlerischer Beleuchtung* (Stuttgart, 1907), 122–3.
23. *Ibid.*, 130.
24. Mosse, *The Crisis of German Ideology*, 137.
25. Heinrich Pudor, "Die Schönheitsabende," *Sexual Probleme*, Jahrg. 4 (1908), 828.
26. *Ibid.*, 829.
27. See page 171.
28. Heinrich Pudor, *Nackende Menschen* (n.p., 1917?), 15.
29. *Der Vortrupp* (May 1, 1913), 279–80.
30. Krabbe, *Gesellschaftsveränderung durch Lebensreform*, 110.
31. See Chapter 5.
32. *Der Anfang* (September 1913), 138. This was a paper published by students of the Wickersdorf School—a community which had close ties to the left wing of the German Youth Movement.

33. Hans Blüher, *Die Rolle der Erotik in der Männlichen Gesellschaft*, Vol. 1 (Jena, 1921), esp. 4−7, 37, 181−2, and 204.

34. *Jahrbuch für Sexuelle Zwischenstufen*, Vol. 2 (1903), 921.

35. See Walter Z. Laqueur, *Young Germany* (London, 1962), 21−3; and Fritz Jungmann, "Autorität und Sexmoral in der freien bürgerlichen Jugendbewegung," *Studien über Autorität und Familie*, ed. Max Horkheimer (Paris, 1936), 5.

36. Ziemer and Wolf, *Wandervogel und Freideutsche Jugend*, 260−1.

37. See Chapter 8.

38. Jungmann, "Autorität und Sexualmoral in der freien bürgerlichen Jugendbewegung," 672.

39. Franz Schönauer, *Stefan George* (Hamburg, 1960), 102.

40. Dominik Jost, *Stefan George und Seine Elite* (Zurich, 1949), 63.

41. See George L. Mosse, *The Culture of Western Europe* (Chicago, 1961), 290−3.

42. Mattenklott, *Bilderdienst*, 198.

43. Ibid., 218ff.

44. Gabriele D'Annunzio, *The Flame of Life* (New York, 1900), 126.

45. Schönauer, *Stefan George*, 161−2.

46. See Richard Drake, *Byzantium for Rome, the Politics of Nostalgia in Umbertian Italy, 1878−1900* (Chapel Hill, N.C., 1980), 193.

47. The words are those of the painter Ernst Ludwig Kirschner, quoted in Wolf-Dietrich Dube, *The Expressionists* (London, 1972), 81.

48. Friedrich Nietzsche, "Die fröhliche Wissenschaft," *Nietzsche's Werke*, Vol. V, Part 1 (Leipzig, 1900), 41.

49. Lewis D. Wurgaft, *The Activists. Kurt Hiller and the Politics of Action on the German Left, 1914−1933* (Philadelphia, 1977), 15.

50. See Timothy d' Arch Smith, *Love in Earnest: Some Notes on the Lives and Writings of English "Uranian" Poets from 1889 to 1930* (London, 1970).

51. Reprinted in *Sexual Heretics, Male Homosexuality in English Literature from 1850 to 1900*, ed. Brian Reade (New York, 1971), 226.

52. Edward Carpenter, *Civilization; Its Cause and Cure* (London, 1889), 35, 39.

53. Edward Lewis, *Edward Carpenter: An Exposition and an Appreciation* (London, 1915), 67.

54. Margaret Waters, *The Nude Male* (Harmondsworth, Middlesex, 1979), 240.

55. See page 119.

56. Paul Fussell, *The Great War and Modern Memory* (London, 1975), 276.

57. Stephen Spender, *World within World* (London, 1951), 60.

58. Green, *Children of the Sun. A Narrative of "Decadence" in England after 1918.*

59. Charlotte and Dennis Primmer, *London. A Visitor's Guide* (New York, 1977), 112; S. Casson, "Rubert Brooke's Grave," *The London Mer-*

*cury*, Vol. II (May–October 1920), 715; and Paul Vanderbought, "Lettre aux Peuples de Skyros" (Chimay, Belgium, 1931), Foreword.
60. See Chapter 8.

## CHAPTER 4

1. Alfred Cobban, *In Search of Humanity* (London, 1960), 204.
2. For Auden and Isherwood to have sex together was the logical extension of a close friendship, according to Charles Osborne, *W. H. Auden, the Life of a Poet* (London, 1980), 46.
3. Helmut Möller, *Die Kleinbürgerliche Familie im 18. Jahrhundert* (Berlin, 1969), 201.
4. Denis Diderot's *The Encyclopedia*, ed. Stephen J. Gendzier (New York, 1967), 170.
5. Wolfdietrich Rasch, *Freundschaftskult und Freundschaftsdichtung im Deutschen Schrifttum des 18. Jahrhunderts* (Halle-Saale, 1936), 115.
6. H. Osterley, *Simon Dach seine Freunde und Johann Rohling* (Berlin and Stuttgart, 1876), xi.
7. Christian Fürchtegott Gellert, *Leben der Schwedischen Gräfin von G\** (Stuttgart, 1968; first published, 1750), 119.
8. James Milliot Servern, "Friendship, Its Advantages and Excesses," *The Phrenological Journal of Science and Health*, Vol. 106 (August–September 1889), 76.
9. Mme. de Tencin, *Les malheurs de l'amour* (Amsterdam, 1747), cited in Paul Kluckhohn, *Die Auffassung der Liebe in der Literatur des 18. Jahrhunderts und in der deutschen Romantik* (Tübingen, 1966), 52.
10. *Ibid.*, 76–7.
11. See pages 101ff.
12. Hans Dietrich Hellbach, *Die Freundschaftsliebe in der deutschen Literatur* (Leipzig, 1931), 29. Hellbach thinks that Gleim's poems do not show real love for a woman, but were bisexual fantasies; 30.
13. See *Der Göttinger Hain*, ed. Alfred Kelletat (Stuttgart, 1967), 404.
14. Rasch, *Freundschaftskult und Freundschaftsdichtung*, 187ff; for his soldiers' poems, see *Anthologie aus J. W. L. Gleim's sämtlichen Werken*, Zweiter Teil (Hildburghausen and New York, 1929), 42–3.
15. Thomas Abt, *Vom Tode für das Vaterland* (Berlin and Stettin, 1870), 17.
16. *Ibid.*, 16.
17. Christian Garve, "Einige Gedanken über die Vaterlandsliebe überhaupt, etc.," *Versuche über verschiedene Gegenstände aus der Moral, der Literatur und dem gesellschaftlichen Leben* (Breslau, 1802), 132, 203.
18. *Ibid.*, 148, 220, and 243.
19. *Jahrbuch der Preussischen Monarchie* (October 1801), 100.
20. Moses Mendelssohn, "Rezensionsartikel in der Bibliothek der Wissenschaften und der feinen Künste," ed. Eva J. Engel, *Gesammelte*

*Schriften, Jubiläumsausgabe,* Vol. 4 (Stuttgart-Bad-Canstatt, 1977), 332.
    21. Max von Schenkendorf, "Landsturmlied" (March 1913), quoted by *Die Befreiung, 1813, 1814, 1815,* ed. Tim Klein (Ebenhausen and Munich, 1913), 144.
    22. Theodor Körner, *Zwölf freie deutsche Gedichte* (Leipzig, 1814), 45.
    23. See George L. Mosse, "National Cemeteries and National Revival: The Cult of the Fallen Soldier in Germany," *Journal of Contemporary History,* Vol. 14 (1979), 1–20.
    24. *Theodor Körner's Sämtliche Werke in zwei Teilen,* ed. Wildenow, 120–1; Von Schenkendorf, "Landsturmlied," *Die Befreiung, 1813, 1814, 1815,* 144.
    25. Körner, "Mein Vaterland," *Theodor Körner's Sämtliche Werke in zwei Teilen,* ed. Wildernow, 113–14.
    26. Cited in Mosse, *The Nationalization of the Masses,* 14.
    27. Robert Minder, "Das Bild des Pfarrhauses in der deutschen Literatur von Jean Paul bis Gottfried Benn," *Kultur und Literatur in Deutschland und Frankreich* (Frankfurt-am-Main, 1962), 44–73.
    28. See George L. Mosse, "Death, Time and History: The Völkish Utopia and Its Transcendence," *Masses and Man* (New York, 1980), 69–87.
    29. Rasch, *Freundschaftskult und Freundschaftsdichtung,* 98.
    30. Heinrich von Kleist, *Geschichte meiner Seele: Ideenmagazin,* ed. Helmut Sembdner (Bremen, 1959), 286–7.
    31. J. Sjadger, *Heinrich von Kleist, eine Pathographische-Psychologische Studie* (Wiesbaden, 1910), 21, 55.
    32. *Ibid.,* 17.
    33. Rudolf Unger, *Herder, Novalis und Kleist. Studien über die Entwicklung des Todesproblems in Denken und Dichten vom Sturm und Drang zur Romantik* (Frankfurt-am-Main, 1922), 97, 104.
    34. *Ibid.,* 107.
    35. Klaus Lankheit, *Das Freundschaftsbild der Romantik* (Heidelberg, 1952), 182.
    36. Bloch, *Das Sexualleben unserer Zeit,* 605, n.9.
    37. *Ibid.,* 605.
    38. Alexander von Gleichen-Russwurm, *Freundschaft, Eine Psychologische Forschungsreise* (Stuttgart, 1912) 10, 77, 285.
    39. See Chapter 5, section III.
    40. Cf. Mosse, *Toward the Final Solution,* Chapter 2.
    41. Jean Murat, *Klopstock* (Paris, 1959), 296.
    42. Quoted in John R. Gillis, *Youth and History, Tradition and Change in European Age Relations 1770 to the Present* (New York, 1974), 157.
    43. Mosse, *The Crisis of German Ideology,* Chapter 11.
    44. See Thomas Nipperdey, "Verein als soziale Struktur in Deutschland im späten 18. und frühen 19. Jahrhundert," *Gesellschaft, Kultur, Theorien* (Göttingen, 1976), 174–205.
    45. Carl Euler, *Friedrich Ludwig Jahn* (Stuttgart, 1881), 122.
    46. Friedrich Jahn and Ludwig Eiselen, *Die Deutsche Turnkunst* (Berlin, 1816), 244.

47. C. Meiners, *Grundriss der Geschichte der Menschheit* (Lengo, 1785), 32, 21–30.

48. Friedrich Gottlieb Klopstock, *Wingolf*, ed. Jaro Pawel (Vienna, 1882), 40.

49. Klopstock to Gleim, June 23, 1750, *Klopstock's Sämtliche Werke* (Leipzig, 1830), 57.

50. Klopstock, "Hermann's Schlacht," *Klopstock's Sämtliche Werke* (Leipzig, 1823), 226.

51. J. W. L. Gleim, "An den Kriegsgott," *J. W. L. Gleim's Sämtliche Werke*, ed. Wilhelm Korte, Vol. 1, 90–1.

52. Murat, *Klopstock*, 366; Christoph Prignitz, *Vaterlandsliebe und Freiheit* (Wiesbaden, 1981), 28ff.

53. *Fichte's Reden an die deutsche Nation* (Berlin, 1912), eighth speech, 137.

54. Newsome, *Godliness and Good Learning*, 33.

55. Jonathan Gathorne-Hardy, *The Old School Tie. The Phenomenon of the English Public School* (New York, 1977), 172ff.

56. The phrase is from a sermon by Thomas Arnold quoted in Newsome's *Godliness and Good Learning*, 32. For a brief history of Thomas Arnold and the reform, see Gathorne-Hardy, *The Old School Tie*, Chapter 4.

57. Gathorne-Hardy, *The Old School Tie*, 101.

58. *Ibid.*, 90.

59. *Ibid.*, 103.

60. Michael Campbell, *Lord Dismiss Us* (London, 1967), 255.

61. *Ibid.*, 267.

62. Quoted in Newsome, *Godliness and Good Learning*, 35.

63. Charles Kingsley, *Westward Ho!* (London, 1899), 16.

64. Thomas Hughes, *Tom Brown's School Days* (New York, 1968), 270.

65. Ronald Hyam, *Britain's Imperial Century, 1815–1914* (London, 1976), Chapter 5.

66. Robin Maugham, *The Last Encounter* (London, 1972), 138.

67. Quoted in Thomas R. Metcalfe, "Architecture and Empire," *History Today*, Vol. 20, (December 1980), 9.

68. Lord Birkenhead, *Rudyard Kipling* (London, 1978), 363.

69. Cyril Connolly, *Enemies of Promise* (Harmondsworth, Middlesex, 1961; originally published, 1938), 234–5.

70. Richard Percevel Graves, *A. E. Housman, the Scholar-Poet* (London and Henley, 1979), 53.

71. George Orwell, "Boy's Weeklies," *Inside the Whale and Other Essays* (Harmondsworth, Middlesex, 1957), 180.

72. Richard Usburne, *Clubland Heroes, A Nostalgic Study of Some Recurrent Characters in the Romantic Fiction of Dornford Yates, John Buchan and Sapper* (London, 1953), 96–7.

73. *Ibid.*, 6.

74. For instance, *The Wizard* (September to December, 1922), 232. Usu-

ally these stories have an anti-Catholic twist, e.g., *Stories by A.L.O.E.* (Edinburgh, 1876).

75. Usborne, *Clubland Heroes*, 32.

76. Henry de Montherlant, *Les Garçons* (Paris, 1969, begun in 1929), 91.

77. *Ibid.*, 65.

78. Krafft-Ebing, *Psychopathia sexualis* (Stuttgart, 1898), 252.

79. Goldsworthy Lowes Dickinson, *The Autobiography and Other Unpublished Writing*, ed. Denis Proctor (London, 1973), 12.

80. See page 205, note 2.

81. Chushichi Tsuzuki, *Edward Carpenter 1844–1929. Prophet of Human Fellowship* (Cambridge, Engl., 1980), 20, 47, 68, and 77.

82. Hans Blüher, *Die Rolle der Erotik in der Männlichen Gesellschaft*, Vol. 1 (Jena, 1921), 70ff.

83. Mosse, *The Crisis of German Ideology*, 216.

84. H. Montgomery Hyde, *The Cleveland Street Scandal* (London, 1976), passim.

85. Louis Kronenberger, *Oscar Wilde* (Boston, 1962), 158.

86. Edward Carpenter, *My Days and Dreams, Being Autobiographical Notes* (London, 1916), 196.

87. *Two Friends, John Gray and André Raffalovich*, ed. Brocard Sewell (Ayleford, Kent, 1963), passim; Brocard Sewell, *Footnote to the Nineties, A Memoir of John Gray and André Raffalovich* (London, 1968), passim.

88. See Chapter 7.

CHAPTER 5

1. See Maurice Agulhon, *Marianne into Battle, Republican Imagery and Symbolism in France, 1789–1880* (Cambridge, Engl., 1981), 16.

2. *Ibid.*, 73.

3. *Courbet und Deutschland* (Katalog der Ausstellung in Hamburg und Frankfurt, 1979), 93.

4. See plate 124 in Siegmar Holsten, *Allegorische Darstellung des Krieges 1870–1918* (Munich, 1976).

5. Sigrid Bauschinger, "Die heiligen Julitage von Paris," *Frankfurter Allgemeine Zeitung* (January 20, 1983), 19.

6. Mona Ozouf, *La Fête Révolutionaire 1789–1799* (Paris, 1976), 120.

7. *Ibid.*, 120.

8. Margaret A. Rose, "The Politicization of Art Criticism: Heine's 1831 Portrayal of Delacroix's *Liberty*," *Monatshefte*, Vol. 73, No. 4 (Winter 1981), 406.

9. *Ibid.*, 409.

10. Richard A. Soloway, "Reform or Ruin: English Moral Thought During the First French Republic," *The Review of Politics*, Vol. 25, No. 1 (January 1963), 113.

11. Richardson, *Pamela*, Vol. 1, (London, 1935), 463.

12. Mosse, *The Nationalization of the Masses*, 177.

13. Jost Hermand, *Sieben Arten an Deutschland zu leiden* (Königstein-Taunus, 1979), 128.

14. Angelika Menne-Haritz, "Germania: Die deutsche Nationalallegorie in den Kriegsgedichten von 1870–71," *Carleton Germanic Papers*, No. 8 (1980), 60.

15. Hans-Joachim Ziemke, "Zum Begriff der Nazarener," *Die Nazarener*, Städsche Gallerie im Städelschen Kunstinstitut, Frankfurt-am-Main (April 28–August 28, 1977), 17–27; Sigrid Metken, " 'Nazarener und Nazarenisch' Popularisierung und Trivialisierung eines Kunstideals," *ibid.*, 365–70.

16. M. Spahn, *Philipp Veit* (Bielefeld and Leipzig, 1901), 75.

17. *Ibid.*, 88; Philipp Veit had perfect romantic credentials. He was the son of Dorothea Veit and the stepson of Friedrich Schlegel.

18. See R. Eylert, *Die Gedächtnissfeyer der verewigten Königin Luise von Preussen* (Berlin, 1812), 211; and E. Mensch, *Königin Luise von Preussen* (Berlin and Leipzig, n.d.), 93.

19. Paul Seidel, "Königin Luise im Bild ihrer Zeit," *Hohenzollern Jahrbuch*, Vol. 9 (1905), 150.

20. *Ibid.*, 148.

21. Wulf Wülfing, "Eine Frau als Göttin: Luise von Preussen—Didaktische Überlegungen zur Mythisierung von Figuren in der Geschichte," *Geschichts-Didaktik*, Heft 3 (1981), 265, 269.

22. *Ibid.*, 258, 261.

23. Cited in Hans Peter Bleuel, *Das Saubere Reich* (Bergisch-Gladbach, 1972), 18.

24. See page 160.

25. Paul Bailleu, "Königin Luise's letzte Tage," *Hohenzollern Jahrbuch*, Vol. 6 (1902), 48.

26. Seidel, "Königin Luise im Bild ihrer Zeit," 148.

27. Cited in Hermann Dreyhaus, *Königin Luise* (Stuttgart, 1926), 219.

28. See Walter Hinck, "Die Krone auf dem Haupt Germania's, Der Kölner Dom und die deutschen Dichter," *Frankfurter Allgemeine Zeitung* (October 25, 1980).

29. Quoted in Hans-Ernst Mittig, "Über Denkmalskritik," *Denkmäler im 19. Jahrhundert*, ed. Ernst Mittig and Volker Plageman (Munich, 1972), 287; Frank Otten, "Die Bavaria," *ibid.*, 109–10.

30. See Randolph Trumbach, *The Rise of the Egalitarian Family* (New York, 1978), 132.

31. There exists no historical account of Britannia, just as there is a paucity of accounts of Germania as well. For Britannia, see only *Notes and Queries* (January 9, 1964), 36–7; (April 3, 1909), 274; (August 3, 1903), 84; and (June 28, 1947), 282.

32. John Edwin Wells, "Thomson's Britannia: Issues, Attributions, Dates, Variants," *Modern Philology*, Vol. XL, No. 1 (August 1942), 43–56.

33. James Gough, *Britannia, A Poem* (London, 1767), 21–3.

34. Holsten, *Allegorische Darstellung des Krieges*, 38.

35. *Ibid.*, 48.

36. Angelika Menne-Haritz, *Germania*, 49.
37. Marianne Thalmann, *Der Trivialroman des 18. Jahrhunderts und der romantische Roman* (Berlin, 1923), 173.
38. Novalis, *Heinrich von Ofterdingen*, Zweiter Teil (Stuttgart, 1965), 11–12.
39. Thalmann, *Der Trivialroman des 18. Jahrhunderts*, 200, and Jutta Hecker, *Das Symbol der Blauen Blume im Zusammenhang mit Blumensymbolik der Romantik* (Jena, 1931), 11.
40. Wulfing, "Eine Frau als Göttin: Luise von Preussen," 259.
41. Spahn, *Philipp Veit*, 69.
42. Eric Trudgill, *Madonnas and Magdalens, The Origins and Development of Victorian Sexual Attitudes* (New York, 1976), 259.
43. Eckart Bergmann, *Die Prä-Raffaeliten* (Munich, 1980), 27, 105.
44. Scott, *Ivanhoe*, 238.
45. Major Z. D. Noel, *Die deutschen Heldinnen in den Kriegsjahren 1807–1815* (Berlin, 1912), passim.
46. Rudolf Schenda, *Volk ohne Buch* (Munich, 1977), 391ff; 393, n. 340.
47. *Ibid.*, 394.
48. Cf. Gathorne-Hardy, *The Old School Tie*, 248–50.
49. See Chapter 8, section IV.
50. Gathorne-Hardy, *The Old School Tie*, 177–8.
51. See Chapter 6.
52. See A. J. L. Busst, "The Image of the Androgyne in the Nineteenth Century," *Romantic Mythologies*, ed. Ian Fletcher (London, 1976), 38.
53. *Ibid.*, 67.
54. Max L. Bäumer, "Winckelmann's Formulierung der Klassischen Schönheit, *Monatschefte*, Vol. 65, No. 1 (Spring 1973), 69.
55. Jean-Pierre Guicciardi, "L'Hermaphrodite," *Dix-Huitième Siècle*, Vol. 12 (1980), 57, 76.
56. Thalmann, *Der Trivialroman des 18. Jahrhunderts*, 200, 298–9.
57. Quoted in Mario Praz, *The Romantic Agony* (New York, 1956), 205–06.
58. Busst, "The Image of the Androgyne in the Nineteenth Century," 51.
59. Hirschfeld, *Sexualwissenschaftlicher Bilderatlas zur Geschlechtskunde*, 490.
60. L. S. A. M. V. Römer in *Jahrbuch für Sexuelle Zwischenstufen*, Vol. 5, Part 2 (Leipzig, 1903), 921.
61. Mattenklott, *Bilderdienst. Äesthetische Opposition bei Beardsley und George*, 101.
62. Voltaire, "Amour Socratique," *Dictionnaire Philosophique*, Vol. 1; *Oeuvres Complètes de Voltaire*, Vol. 33 (Paris, 1819), 254.
63. Raymond De Becker, *The Other Face of Love* (New York, 1964), 125.
64. *Ibid.*, 134.
65. Jonathan Katz, *Gay American History* (New York, 1976), 340.
66. *Ibid.*, 554.
67. Günther Gollner, *Homosexualität, Ideologiekritik und Entmytho-*

*logisierung einer Gesetzgebung* (Berlin, 1974), 167.

68. See Annemarie Wettley, *Von der "Psychopathia sexualis" zur Sexualwissenschaft,* 58, and Lillian Faderman, *Surpassing the Love of Men* (New York, 1981), 241ff.

69. Jeannette H. Foster, *Sex Variant Women in Literature* (London, 1958), 81.

70. *Ibid.,* 63.

71. *Ibid.,* 65.

72. *Ibid.,* 83.

73. Quoted in Ilse Kokula, *Weibliche Homosexualität um 1900* (Munich, 1981), 27.

74. *Ibid.,* 22–3.

75. Wilhelm Hammer, *Die Tribadie Berlins* (Berlin and Leipzig, 1906), passim.

76. Wilhelm Hammer, "Über Gleichgeschlechtliche Frauenliebe mit besonderer Berücksichtigung der Frauenbewegung," *Monatsschrift für Harnkrankheiten und sexuelle Hygene,* Vol. IV (Leipzig, 1907), 396.

77. Edward J. Bristow, *Vice and Vigilance. Purity Movements in Britain since 1700* (London, 1977), 53.

78. Renée Vivienne, *A Woman Appeared to Me* (New York, 1979; first published, 1904), 34, 54.

79. Colette, *The Pure and the Impure* (New York, 1966), 73.

80. Jean Pierrot, *The Decadent Imagination 1880–1900* (Chicago, 1981), 14.

81. Colette, *The Pure and the Impure,* 69.

82. Mattenklott, *Bilderdienst,* 71.

83. Wolfdietrich Rasch, "Literary Decadence, Artistic Representations of Decay," *Journal of Contemporary History,* Vol. 17, No. 1 (January 1983), 208.

84. *Lesbian-Feminism in Turn-of-the-Century Germany,* ed. Lillian Faderman and Brigitte Eriksson (Iowa City, 1980), 12, 65ff.

85. *Ibid.,* 51.

86. Rasch, "Literary Decadence," 201ff.

87. Quoted in Richard J. Evans, *The Feminist Movement in Germany* (London, 1976), 76.

88. Bristow, *Vice and Vigilance,* 220.

89. See, for example, Evans, *The Feminist Movement in Germany,* 130ff.

90. See Chapter 2.

91. Judith R. Walkowitz, *Prostitution and Victorian Society* (Cambridge, Engl., 1980), 245.

92. Amy Hackett, "The German Woman's Movement and Suffrage, 1890–1914: A Study of National Feminism," in *Modern European Social History,* ed. Robert J. Bezucha (Lexington, Mass., 1972), 366.

93. *Ibid.,* 371.

94. *Ibid.,* 377.

95. Marlitt (pseudonym for Eugenie John), *Im Hause des Kommerzienrates* (Leipzig, n.d.), 41, 218 ("gleichmässiges, Harmonisch-inniges Familienleben").

96. Nataly von Eschstruth, *Hofluft*, Vol. 2, (Leipzig, n.d.), 284.

97. Gabriele Strecker, *Frauenträume, Frauentränen. Uber den unterhaltenden deutschen Frauenroman* (Weilheim, Oberbayern, 1969), 117.

98. *Ibid.*, 129.

99. *Ibid.*, 160.

100. Körner, "Aufruf" (1813), *Theodore Körner's Sämtliche Werke in zwei Teilen*, ed. Wilderow, 120.

CHAPTER 6

1. Brian Finney, *Christopher Isherwood* (London, 1979), 53.

2. Christopher Isherwood, *Lions and Shadows* (London, 1938), 74.

3. Samuel Hynes, *The Auden Generation* (Princeton, 1972), 21.

4. See, for example, *Der Weltkrieg im Bild* (Minden, n.d.), Vorwort (Foreword).

5. Ernst Jünger, *Der Kampf als inneres Erlebnis* (Berlin, 1983), 34ff.

6. Isherwood, *Lions and Shadows*, 79.

7. Jean-Jacques Becker, *1914, Comment les Français Sont Entrés dans la Guerre* (Paris, 1977), 574–5.

8. Paolo Nello, *L'Avanguardismo Giovanile alle Origini del Fascismo* (Bari, 1978), 12.

9. Becker, *1914*, 574.

10. Bill Gamage, *The Broken Years, Australian Soldiers in the Great War* (Canberra, Australia, 1974), 270.

11. Adolf Hitler wrote a brief foreword to the novel—Hans Zöberlein, *Der Glaube an Deutschland* (Munich, 1931), 268–9.

12. Ulrich Sander, *Das feldgraue Herz* (Jena, 1934), 29ff.

13. Douglas Reed, *Insanity Fair* (London, 1938), 22.

14. Eric J. Leed, *No Man's Land, Combat and Identity in World War I* (Cambridge, Engl., 1979), 39ff; Rupert Brooke, "Peace," *The Collected Poems of Rupert Brooke with a Memoir* (London, 1918), 298.

15. *The Collected Poems of Rupert Brooke with a Memoir*, xxvii.

16. *Ibid.*, ciii; John Lehmann, *Rupert Brooke, His Life and Legend* (London, 1980), 106.

17. Werner Schwipps, *Die Garnisonskirchen von Berlin und Potsdam* (Berlin, 1964), 92.

18. Ernst Jünger, *Der Kampf als inneres Erlebnis*, 89; Giovanni Boine, *Discorsi Militari* (Florence, 1915), 99.

19. Erich von Tchischwitz, *Blaujacken und Feldgraue gen Oesel, Walter Flex's Heldentod* (Mylan, 1934), 81.

20. Fussell, *The Great War and Modern Memory*, 277; Lyn Macdonald, *Somme* (London, 1983), 200–03.

21. Walter Flex, *Der Wanderer Zwischen Beiden Welten* (Munich, n.d.), 10–11, 31, 37.

22. *Ibid.*, 19, 41.
23. *The Diary of Virginia Woolf*, ed. Anne Olivier Bell, Vol. 1 (New York, 1977), 172.
24. Flex, *Der Wanderer Zwischen Beiden Welten*, 46.
25. Fussell, *The Great War and Modern Memory*, 299.
26. *Ibid.*, 246.
27. Sir Frederic Kenyon, *War Graves, How the Cemeteries Abroad Will Be Designed* (London, 1918), 13.
28. Rupert Brooke, *The Collected Poems* (1918), 245.
29. See Stanley Casson, *Rupert Brooke and Skyros* (London, 1921), 10, and Gabriel Boissy, *Message sur la Poésie Immortelle*, prononcé a Skyros pour l'inauguration du monument dedié à Rupert Brooke (Paris, 1931), n.p.
30. T. E. Lawrence, *The Seven Pillars of Wisdom* (New York, 1976; first printed privately, 1926), 28.
31. *Ibid.*
32. Quoted in Mosse, *The Crisis of German Ideology*, 26.
33. Ernst Jünger, *The Storm of Steel*, (New York, 1975), 255, 263.
34. Quoted in Tidrick, *Heart-Beguiling Araby*, 19.
35. Phillip Knightley and Colin Simpson, *The Secret Lives of Lawrence of Arabia* (London, 1962), 21.
36. Cited in Mosse, *Masses and Man*, 53.
37. Lawrence, *The Seven Pillars of Wisdom*, 92, 98.
38. Donald Hankey, *A Student in Arms* (New York, 1916), 61.
39. Flex, *Der Wanderer Zwischen Beiden Welten*, 47.
40. See Jenkyns, *The Victorians and Ancient Greece*, 338.
41. Flex, *Der Wanderer Zwischen Beiden Welten*, 46.
42. Max von Schenkendorf in *Die Befreiung, 1813, 1814, 1815*, 144.
43. Karl Prümm *Die Literatur des soldatischen Nationalismus der 20er Jahre (1918–1933)*, Vol. 1, (Kronberg/Taunus, 1974), 155.
44. *Ibid.*, 152.
45. *Ibid.*
46. *Ibid.*, 193.
47. *Ibid.*, 154.
48. Hannjoachim W. Koch, *Der Deutsche Bürgerkrieg* (Frankfurt-am-Main, 1978), Chapter 2 passim.
49. Former volunteers have written autobiographies, one of the most typical being Marc Augier (Saint-Loup), *Les Voluntaires* (Paris, 1963). For the best discussion of one group of volunteers, see G. A. Marylen, "Soldats français sous Uniforme Allémande," *Revue d'histoire de la deuxième guerre mondiale*, No. 108, (October 1977).
50. Ulrich Sander, *Das feldgraue Herz*, 35.
51. See Toni Ashworth, *Trench Warfare 1914–1918* (London, 1980), 155.
52. Leed, *No Man's Land*, 88ff.
53. Franco Sapori, *La Trincea* (Milan, 1917), 285–6.
54. Michael Golbach, *Die Wiederkehr des Weltkriegs in der Literatur* (Kronberg, 1978), 183; Jacques Pericard, *Face à Face* (Paris, 1917), 75.

55. Sapori, *La Trincea*, 17.

56. Fussell, *The Great War and Modern Memory*, 57.

57. Ernest Raymond, *Tell England* (London, 1973; first published, 1923), 300.

58. See H. C. Fischer and E. X. Dubois, *Sexual Life during the World War* (London, 1937).

59. Thor Goote, *Glühender Tag, Männer in der Bewährung* (Gütersloh, 1943), 84.

60. Leed, *No Man's Land*, 161.

61. Ludwig Tugel, *Die Freundschaft* (Hamburg, 1939), 14, 23.

62. R. K. Neumann, "Die Erotik in der Kriegsliteratur," *Zeitschrift für Sexualwissenschaft*, Vol. 1 (April 1914–March 1915), 390–1.

63. Till Kalkschmidt, "Kameradschaft und Führertum an der Front," *Dichtung und Volkstum*, Heft 2, Vol. 39 (1938), 180, 182.

64. Henry de Montherlant, *Les Olympiques* (Paris, 1939; first published, 1924), 148, 11–12, 74, 83, and 103.

65. Pierre Sipriot, *Montherlant* (Paris, 1975), 55.

66. Marie-Louise Scherer, interview with Philippe Soupault, *Der Spiegel* (January 3, 1983), 131.

67. Simone de Beauvoir, "Die Frau im Werke Montherlants," *Das Buch*, Vol. 3, No. 9 (1951), 19–21.

68. Finney, *Christopher Isherwood*, 54.

69. Cf. L. Riefenstahl, *Kampf in Schnee und Eis* (Leipzig, 1933), passim.

70. Nello, *L'Avanguardismo Giovanile*, 23.

71. Hynes, *The Auden Generation*, 23.

72. Cf. George L. Mosse, "La sinistra europea e l'esperienze della guerra," *Rivoluzione e Reazione in Europa, 1917–1924*, Convegno storico internazionale—Perugia, 1978. Vol. 2 (Milan, 1978), 151–69.

73. Egmont Zechlin, *Die deutsche Politik und die Juden im Ersten Weltkrieg* (Göttingen, 1969), 527.

74. *Lila Nächte, Damenclubs in den Zwanziger Jahren*, ed. Adele Meyer (Berlin, 1981); Hirschfeld, *Berlins Drittes Geschlecht*.

CHAPTER 7

1. See Mosse, *Toward the Final Solution*, Chapter 1, and Adolf Hitler, *Mein Kampf* (Munich, 1934), 63.

2. Friedrich Dukmeyer, *Kritik der reinen und praktischen unvernunft in der gemeinen verjudung* (Berlin, 1892), 11.

3. Jean Recanati, *Profils Juifs de Marcel Proust* (Paris, 1979), 142.

4. Sander L. Gilman, *Viewing the Insane* (New York, 1982), xi.

5. *Ibid.*, 82.

6. Friedrich Christian Benedict Avé-Lallemant, *Das Deutsche Gaunertum*, Vol. 2 (Wiesbaden, n.d.), 4–5.

7. Alexandre Raviv, *Le Problème Juif aux Miroir du Roman Francais l'Entre Deux Guerres* (Strasbourg, 1968), 4; George L. Mosse, "Die NS Kampfbühne," *Geschichte im Gegenwartsdrama*, ed. Reinhold Grimm

and Jost Hermand (Stuttgart, 1976), 35; Schopenhauer, *Die Welt als Wille und Vorstellung, Sämtliche Werke*, ed. Arthur Hubscher, Vol. 2 (Wiesbaden, 1949), 648.

8. Helmut Jenzsch, *Jüdische Figuren in deutschen Bühnentexten des 18. Jahrhunderts* (Hamburg, 1971), 158; Oscar Wilde, *The Picture of Dorian Gray*, quoted in Jeffrey Myers, *Homosexuality and Literature* (London, 1977), 24.

9. Bertrand-Rival, *Tableaux Historiques et Morales*, 34; J. F. Bertrand-Rival, *Précis Historique* (Paris, 1801), 309.

10. Ambroise Tardieu, *Die Vergehen gegen die Sittlichkeit* (Weimar, 1860), 140ff.

11. See Jan Goldstein, "The Hysteria Diagnosis and the Politics of Anticlericalism in Late Nineteenth-Century France," *The Journal of Modern History*, Vol. 54, N. 2 (June 1982), 221.

12. Wolfgang Schievelbusch, *Geschichte der Eisenbahnreise* (Munich, 1977), 55ff; Nordau, *Degeneration*, 37.

13. Anson Rabinbach, "L'age de la fatigue, énergie et fatigue à la fin du 19e siècle," *Vribi*, N. 2 (December 1979), 33–48.

14. Bloch, *Die Perversen*, 28; Moll, *Ärtzliche Ethik*, 46.

15. Edouard Drumont, *La France Juive*, Vol. 1 (Paris, 1944), 107; Luis Neustadt, *Josef Streblicki, ein Proselyt unter Friedrich dem Grossen* (Breslau, 1841), 9.

16. Friedrich Berthold Loeffler, *Das Preussische Physikatsexamen* (Berlin, 1878), 221.

17. Balzac, "Scènes de la Vie Parisienne," *La Comédie Humaine, Oeuvres Complètes de M. de Balzac*, Vol. 9 (Paris, 1843), 236; John H. Gordon, *NewYorkitis* (New York, 1901), 120.

18. Marcel Proust, *A La Recherche du Temps Perdu*, Vol. IV: *Sodom et Gomorrhe*, Vol. 1 (Paris, 1921), 276.

19. Bibliography about homosexuality and animals in *Jahrbuch für Sexuelle Zwischenstufen*, Vol. 2 (1900), 126–55.

20. Trudgill, *Madonnas and Magdalens*, 31.

21. Proust, *Sodom et Gomorrhe*, 269; Isabel V. Hull, *The Entourage of Kaiser Wilhelm II, 1888–1918* (Cambridge, Engl., 1982), 136.

22. Marc-André Raffalovich, *Uranisme et Unisexualité* (Lyons and Paris, 1896), 184.

23. Walter Pater, *The Renaissance. Studies in Art and Poetry* (London, 1900), 193ff.

24. Quoted in Wolpert, *Die Nackten und die Toten des Dritten Reiches*, 158.

25. "Der Riese, Friedrich Nietzsche," *Pan*, Jahrg. 1, Heft 2, 89.

26. Glen B. Infield, *Leni Riefenstahl, The Fallen Film Goddess* (New York, 1971), 141.

27. Johann Jakob Schudt, *Jüdische Merkwürdigkeiten*, Vol. 1 (Frankfurt-am-Main, 1715), 219.

28. Miklos Nyiszli, *Auschwitz, A Doctor's Eyewitness Account* (New York, 1960), 175.

29. P. Möbius in *Jahrbuch für Sexuelle Zwischenstufen*, Vol. 4 (1904), 499.

30. Weeks, *Sex, Politics and Society*, 133.

31. *Auf Hieb und Stich. Stimmen zur Zeit am Wege einer deutschen Zeitung*, ed. Günther d'Alquen (Berlin and Munich, 1937), 264.

32. Brief an Jung, November 2, 1911, *Freud und Jung Briefwechsel* (Frankfurt-am-Main, 1974).

33. The correspondence lies already edited in the Bundesarchiv at Koblenz, but has never been published.

34. Thus Hermann Ahlwart attempts to prove that Jews corrupt Christian girls even while admitting that Jewish family life is exemplary—*Der Verzweiflungskampf der arischen Völker mit dem Judentum* (Berlin, 1890), 220.

35. Quoted in *Vorurteile gegen Minderheiten, die Anfänge des modernen antisemitismus in Deutschland*, ed. Hans-Gert Oomen (Stuttgart, 1978), 62.

36. Quoted in Sander L. Gilman, "Sexology, Psychoanalysis, and Degeneration," *Degeneration*, ed. Sander L. Gilman (New York, forthcoming).

37. *Das Schwarze Korps* (March 4, 1937), n.p.

38. Sander L. Gilman, "What Looks Crazy. Towards an Iconography of Insanity in Art and Medicine in the Nineteenth Century," *The Turn of the Century, German Literature and Art 1890–1915*, ed. Gerald Chapple and Hans H. Schulte (Bonn, 1981), 74; Mosse, *Toward the Final Solution*, 216–20.

39. C. Wilmans, *Die "Goldene Internationale" und die Notwendigkeit einer socialen Reformpartei* (Berlin, 1876), 195.

40. Otto Weininger, *Geschlecht und Charakter* (Vienna and Leipzig, 1920), 106–7.

41. Emil Lucka, *Otto Weininger, Sein Werk und Leben* (Vienna and Leipzig, 1905), 109.

42. Weininger, *Geschlecht und Charakter*, 94.

43. Hermann Swoboda, *Otto Weininger's Tod* (Vienna, 1923), 117.

44. David Abrahamsen, *The Mind and Death of a Genius* (New York, 1946), 173; Lucka, *Otto Weininger, Sein Werk und Leben*, 83.

45. Abrahamsen, *The Mind and Death of a Genius*, 173.

46. Friedrich Christian Benedict Avé-Lallemant, *Das Deutsche Gaunertum*, Vol. 1 (Wiesbaden, n.d.), 7.

47. F. Luba, *Enthüllung über die internationale russisch-jüdische Gaunerbande* (Berlin, 1892), passim; Richard Mun, *Die Juden Berlins* (Leipzig, 1924), 69. The link between Jews and bands of thieves was made by one of the most notorious Nazi racists, Johann von Leers, in *Judentum und Gaunertum* (Berlin, 1944).

48. Anklage Dr. Schumann (December 12, 1969), Landesgericht Frankfurt-am-Main (Yad Vashem Archives, Jerusalem, JS 18-69).

49. Mosse, *Toward the Final Solution*, 84.

50. Gilman, *Viewing the Insane*, 102; Sir Charles Bell, *Essays in the Anatomy of Expression*, 1806, quoted in Gilman, "What Looks Crazy. To-

wards an Iconography of Insanity in Art and Medicine in the Nineteenth Century," 60.

51. John McManners, *Death and the Enlightenment* (Oxford, 1981), 315.

52. Jacques Charon, *Death and Modern Man* (New York, 1964), 99.

53. Emil Ludwig, *Goethe: Geschichte eines Menschen*, Vol. 3 (Stuttgart, 1922), 458.

54. Quoted in Pascal Hintermeyer, *Politiques de la Mort* (Paris, 1981), 87.

55. *Ibid.*, 94, 96.

56. McManners, *Death and the Enlightenment*, 362–3.

57. Wilhelm Stoffers, *Juden und Ghetto in der Deutschen Literatur bis zum Ausgang des Weltkrieges* (Graz, 1939), 385.

58. Drumont, *La France Juive*, 122.

59. Schudt, *Jüdische Merkwürdigkeiten*, Vol. 2, 25.

60. Maria Teresa Pichetto, *Alle Radici dell'Odio, Prezioso e Benigni Antisemiti* (Milan, 1983), 77.

61. Renzo de Felice, *Storia degli Ebrei Italiani Sotto Il Fascismo* (Turin, 1961), 291.

62. Hintermeyer, *Politiques de la Mort*, 17.


CHAPTER 8

1. See George L. Mosse, *Germans and Jews* (New York, 1970), 153.

2. *Der Frontsoldat. Ein Deutsches Kultur und Lebensideal*, Fünf Reden von Theodor Bertram aus dem Jahr 1919 (Berlin-Templehof, 1934), 29.

3. The youthful S.A. illustrates how the predilection for violence became a cult within National Socialism. Otis C. Mitchell, *Hitler Over Germany. The Establishment of the Nazi Dictatorship (1918–1934)* (Philadelphia, 1983), 189.

4. Ferdinando Cordova, *Arditi e Legionari Dannunziani* (Padua, 1969), 17.

5. Ernst Jünger, *Der Kampf als inneres Erlebnis* (Berlin, 1933), 33, 56.

6. Jünger, *The Storm of Steel*, 109.

7. See page 129.

8. Ernst Jünger, *Der Arbeiter, Herrschaft und Gestalt* (Hamburg, 1932), 22, 57, 251.

9. George L. Mosse, "The Genesis of Fascism," *Journal of Contemporary History*, Vol. 1, No. 1 (1966), 14–27.

10. Paolo Nello, *L'Avanguardismo Giovanile alle Origini del Fascismo* (Rome and Bari, 1978), 18, 23.

11. NS Frauenwarte, Jahrg. 2 (July 2, 1940), 36–7; Alexander de Grand, "Women under Italian Fascism," *The Historical Journal*, Vol. 19, No. 4 (1976), 960, 967.

12. A picture of Mussolini sitting listening to a suffragette is reprinted in Renzo de Felice and Luigi Goglia, *Mussolini. Il Mito* (Rome and Bari, 1983), plate 129.

13. Margherita G. Sarfatti, *Mussolini. Lebensgeschichte* (Leipzig, 1926), 334.

14. Maria-Antonietta Macciocchi, *Jungfrauen, Mütter und ein Führer, Frauen im Faschismus* (Berlin, 1979), 31; Paolo Monelli, *Mussolini Piccolo Borghese* (Milan, 1983), 190–92. Monelli was a journalist who first believed in Mussolini and then became disillusioned. His descriptions of Mussolini's attitudes toward women, especially Claretta Petacci, carry a great deal of conviction. The book was first published in 1950.

15. See Niccolo Zapponi, *I Miti e Le Ideologie. Storia della Cultura Italiana 1870–1960* (Naples, 1981), Chapter 2.

16. Emilio Gentile, *Le Origini dell' Ideologie Fascista* (Bari, 1975).

17. Franz Seidler, *Prostitution, Homosexualität, Selbstverstümmelung, Probleme der deutschen Sanitätsführung 1939–1945* (Neckargemünd, 1977), 202; *Hitler aus nähster Nähe, Aufzeichnungen eines Vertrauten 1929–1932*, ed. H. A. Turner, Jr. (Berlin, 1978), 200–01.

18. Otis Mitchell, *"Clear the Streets." Hitler's Storm Troops, 1918–1933* (forthcoming).

19. Peter Nathan, *The Psychology of Fascism* (London, 1941), 14.

20. Ottmar Katz, *Prof. Dr. Med. Theo Morell* (Bayreuth, 1982), 122.

21. Seidler, *Prostitution, Homosexualität, Selbstverstümmelung*, 203.

22. Hans-Georg Stumke and Rudi Finkler, *Rosa Winkel, Rosa Listen, Homosexuelle und 'Gesundes Volksempfinden' von Auschwitz bis heute* (Reinbeck bei Hamburg, 1981), 190–96.

23. George L. Mosse, *Nazi Culture* (New York, 1966), 31.

24. *Ibid.*

25. See Chapter 5.

26. Lydia Ganzer-Gottschewski, "Nacht auf der Nehrung," *N.S. Frauenwarte*, Jahrg. 8 (July 1, 1934), 16.

27. Adolf Sellmann, *50 Jahre Kampf für Volkssittlichkeit und Volkskraft. Die Geschichte des Westdeutschen Sittlichkeitvereins von seinen Anfängen bis heute (1885–1935)* (Schwelm i, Westf. 1934), Vorwort (Foreword); Hans Peter Bleuel, *Sex and Society in Nazi Germany* (Philadelphia, 1973), 5.

28. Dorothee Klinsieck, *Die Frau im NS-Staat* (Stuttgart, 1982), 94.

29. See Jill Stephenson, *The Nazi Organization of Women* (Totowa, N.J., 1981), 89–90.

30. See note 26.

31. Lydia Gottschewski, *Männerbund und Frauenfrage* (Munich, 1934), 39.

32. *Ibid.*, 43.

33. *Ibid.*, 40–1.

34. Irmgard Weyrather, "Numerus Clausus für Frauen-Studentinnen im Nationalsozialismus," *Mutterkreuz und Arbeitsbuch* (Frankfurt-am-Main, 1981), 138–9.

35. *Der Schild*, Jahrg. 13, No. 14 (April 20, 1934); Hildegard Brenner, *Die Kunstpolitik des Nationalsozialismus* (Reinbeck bei Hamburg, 1963), 65ff.

36. Johnpeter Horst Grill, *The Nazi Movement in Baden, 1920–1945* (Chapel Hill, N.C., 1983), 311.
37. See pages 167ff.
38. Cited in Martin Klaus, *Mädchen in der Hitlerjugend* (Cologne, 1980), 169.
39. *Ibid.*
40. *Auf Hieb und Stich. Stimmen zur Zeit am Wege einer deutschen Zeitung,* ed. D'Alquen, 262.
41. Hans Peter Bleuer, *Das Saubere Reich* (Bergisch Gladbach, 1979), 286.
42. While this office is mentioned briefly in most accounts of National Socialism and homosexuality, no one has yet been able to find its records —if any survive. See also Hans Günther Hockerts, *Die Sittlichkeitsprozesse gegen Katholische Ordensangehörige und Priester 1936–37* (Mainz, 1971), 11.
43. Gollner, *Homosexualität. Ideologiekritik und Entmythologisierung einer Gesetzgebung,* 175.
44. Peter Löwenberg, *Decoding the Past* (New York, 1983), 217.
45. Bradley F. Smith, *Heinrich Himmler: A Nazi in the Making, 1900–1926* (Stanford, Calif., 1971), 116. Himmler was "a strangely rigid and nongrowing personality, overburdened with crochets—a near-sighted visionary"—Robert Lewis Koehl, *The Black Corps. The Structure and Power Struggles of the Nazi SS* (Madison, Wis., 1983), 295.
46. Löwenberg, *Decoding the Past,* 221.
47. Smith, *Heinrich Himmler,* 115.
48. Hans Günther Hockerts, *Die Sittlichkeits Prozesse gegen Katholische Ordensangehörige,* 91, n. 220.
49. Stumke and Finkler, *Rosa Winkel, Rosa Listen,* 190–200.
50. Seidler, *Prostitution, Homosexualität, Selbstverstümmelung,* 222.
51. *Ibid.,* 223.
52. *Kriminalität und Gefährdung der Jugend. Lageberichte bis zum Stand vom 1. Januar 1941,* Hrsg. vom Jugendführer des Deutschen Reiches, bearbeitet W. Knopp (Berlin, n.d.), 96. On the importance and confidentiality of this report, see Brigitte Geisler, *Die Homosexuellen-Gesetzgebung als Instrument der Ausübung politischer Macht, mit besonderer Berücksichtigung des NS Regimes,* Unpublished magister dissertation, Göttingen, 1968, 55–56. I am grateful to James D. Steakley for providing this reference.
53. *Kriminalität und Gefährdung der Jugend,* 223ff.
54. *Ibid.,* 227.
55. *Ibid.,* 87–8.
56. *Rede des Reichsführer-SS anlässlich der Gruppenführer Besprechung in Tölz, am 18. 11. 1937,* Institut für Zeitgeschichte, Munich, Archiv MA 311 BL 818 (cited hereafter as Himmler, Bad Tölz Speech), 53.
57. Himmler, Bad Tölz Speech, 24.
58. *Ibid.,* 55.

59. C. Kirkpatrick, *Nazi Germany, Its Women and Family Life* (Indianapolis and New York, 1938), 141–2.

60. Himmler, Bad Tölz Speech, 56.

61. *Ibid.,* 44.

62. *Ibid.,* 45.

63. *Ibid.* Hitler also used what was no doubt an obvious analogy between homosexual patronage of congenial men and the hiring of pretty secretaries regardless of their efficiency; see, e.g., Rudolf Diels, *Lucifer ante Portas* (Zurich, n.d.), 277. Rudolf Diels was briefly the head of the political police and the Gestapo after the Nazi seizure of power.

64. *Ibid.,* 47.

65. *Ibid.,* 47ff.

66. The fear of imputations of homosexuality proved on one occasion greater than the desire to take revenge on a Jew—even though as a matter of policy the deportation of the Jews took precedence over the persecution of homosexuals, for example, in occupied Holland (see Chapter 9, note 26). The murder of the German diplomat Von Rath by Hershel Grünspan in Paris in 1938 was the occasion for the "Kristallnacht"—the burning down of synagogues all over Germany, and the arrest of many Jews—though Grünspan was never brought to trial and perhaps survived the Second World War. Apparently the Nazis feared that a homosexual relationship between Grünspan and Von Rath had led to the murder, rather than Grünspan's desire to avenge the Nazi persecution of his parents. Helmut Heiber, "Der Fall Grünspan," *Vierteljahrshefte für Zeitgeschichte*, Jahrg. 5 Heft 2 (April 1957), 134–72.

67. Himmler, Bad Tölz Speech, 47.

68. *Ibid.,* 50–2.

69. *Ibid.,* 58.

70. Barry D. Adam, *The Survival of Domination, Inferiorization and Everyday Life* (New York, 1978), describes Himmler's cure and then claims that the same cure is still used today, 40, 41; see also Heinz Heger, *Die Männer mit dem Rosa Winkel* (Hamburg, n.d.), 137.

71. Himmler, Bad Tölz Speech, 53.

72. *Ibid.*

73. See Chapter 7.

74. Himmler, Bad Tölz Speech, 59.

75. *Ibid.*

76. Klaus, *Mädchen in der Hitlerjugend,* 89.

77. Klinksieck, *Die Frau im NS-Staat,* 65.

78. *Kriminalität und Gefährdung der Jugend,* 208.

79. Reprinted in Adolf Sellmann, *50 Jahre Kampf für Volkssittlichkeit und Volkskraft,* 108.

80. Ordinance of July 8, 1935, reprinted in *Für Zucht und Sitte, Die Verfolgung der Homosexuellen im III. Reich* (Osnabrück, n.d.), 12.

81. Wolbert, *Die Nackten und die Toten,* 186.

82. Hans Surén, *Gymnastik der Deutschen, Körperschönheit und Schulung* (Stuttgart, 1938), 62.

83. Ibid., 65.

84. Mosse, The Nationalization of the Masses, Chapter 8.

85. Jenkyns, The Victorians and Ancient Greece, 146; Wolbert, Die Nakten und die Toten, 188.

86. Arno Breker, Im Strahlungsfeld der Ereignisse (Preussisch-Oldendorf, 1972), 134.

87. Ibid., 362.

88. V. G. Probst, Der Bildhauer Arno Breker (Bonn and Paris, 1978), 28.

89. Proclamation by Hitler to the "Party Day of Unity," Nüremberg, 1934, The Speeches of Adolf Hitler April 1922–August 1939, ed. Norman H. Baynes (New York, 1969), 329.

90. Rolf Gödel, "Kameradschaft über den Tod hinaus," Völkischer Boebachter (August 18, 1940), 3.

91. See Chapter 6; Wolbert, Die Nackten und die Toten, 192.

92. Zeev Sternhell, Ni Droite, Ni Gauche. L'Idéologie Fasciste en France (Paris, 1983), 21.

93. Robert Brasillach, Notre Avant Guerre (Paris, 1941), 272.

94. Ibid., 282.

95. Robert Soucy, Drieu La Rochelle (Berkeley, 1979), 203.

96. Henry de Montherlant, Les Olympiques (Paris, 1939; first published, 1914), 70, 103, 110, and 111.

97. Soucy, Drieu La Rochelle, 326.

98. Brasillach, Notre Avant Guerre, 230.

99. Robert Brasillach, Comme le temps passe (Paris, 1983), 72, 142–52.

100. Jacques Isorni, Le Procès de Robert Brasillach (Paris, 1946), 139.

101. Jean Guéhenno, Journal des Années Noires (1940–1944) (Paris, 1947), 123.

102. Drieu La Rochelle, Gilles (Paris, 1939), 455. The Dutch National Socialist Party attracted some homosexuals, and its leader, Anton Mussert, was accused of tolerating them in the party. However, probably Mussert's contained no more homosexuals than any other Dutch political party, although one prominent member was convicted for homosexual practices in 1938 and committed suicide while in prison. Pieter Koenders, Homoseksualiteit in Bezet Nederland (S-Gravenhage, 1983), 69–70.

103. Klinksieck, Die Frau im NS-Staat, 107, 109.

104. Klaus, Mädchen in der Hitlerjugend, 58.

105. Klinksieck, Die Frau im NS-Staat, 50; see also "The Ideal of Womanhood," in Mosse, Nazi Culture, 39–47.

106. Wolbert, Die Nackten und die Toten, 49.

107. See pages 128–129.

108. Quoted in W. v. Owen, Mit Goebbels bis zum Ende, Vol. 1 (Buenos Aires, 1949), 40.

109. See Chapter 7.

110. Kurt Klare, Briefe für Gestern und Morgen, Gedanken eines Artztes zur Zeitwende (Stuttgart and Leipzig, 1934), 119.

111. Kurt Klare, Introduction to Wilhelm Hildebrandt, Rassenmischung und Krankheit (Stuttgart, 1935).

112. Stumke and Finkler, *Rosa Winkel, Rosa Listen*, 223. For an analysis of Klare's crusade against homosexuals, see Rüdiger Lautmann and Erhard Vismar, *Pink Triangle. The Social History of Anti-Homosexual Persecution in Nazi Germany* (mimeographed, 1983, hopefully soon to be published in the United States), 14ff.

113. *Ibid.*, 227.

114. Klare, *Briefe für Gestern und Morgen*, 112.

115. Nathan, *The Psychology of Fascism*, 78.

CHAPTER 9

1. L. Trenker, *Alles Gut Gegangen* (Hamburg, 1959), 77.

2. See Mosse, *The Crisis of German Ideology*, 15ff.

3. See Chapter 2.

4. Hendrik van Oyen in *Probleme der Homophilie*, ed. Theodor Bovet (Bern and Tübingen, 1965), 119.

5. E. P. Thompson, *The Making of the English Working Class* (London, 1965), Chapters 11 and 12. There were about 2 million working-class children enrolled in Sunday Schools in 1850. One such school was run by Sarah Trimmer. Thomas Walter Laqueur, *Religion and Respectability, Sunday Schools and Working Class Culture 1780–1850* (New Haven and London, 1976), 47, 191.

6. Karl Marx and Friedrich Engels, *The German Ideology* (New York, 1939), 87ff; Wolfgang Essbach, *Eine Studie über die Kontroverse zwischen Max Stirner und Karl Marx* (Frankfurt-am-Main, 1982), passim.

7. Anon., "Demos und Libertas, oder Der Entlarvte Betrüger," *Aus den Anfängen der Sozialistischen Dramatik*, ed. Ursula Münchow, Vol. 1 (Berlin, 1964), 93. Many of the other plays included in this collection draw similar moral conclusions.

8. August Bebel, *Woman under Socialism* (New York, 1971), 81–2.

9. Jacob Israel de Haan, *Open brief aan P. L. Tak* (Amsterdam, 1982), 47.

10. W. U. Eisler, *Arbeiterparteien und Homosexuellenfrage* (Berlin, 1980), 40, 42. John Lauritsen and David Thorstad, *The Early Homosexual Rights Movement* (New York, 1974), 58–9.

11. Wilhelm Reich, *Die Sexuelle Revolution* (Frankfurt-am-Main, 1971; originally published, 1930), 169.

12. Cited in *ibid.*, 179.

13. Manfred Herzer, "Gay Resistance Against the Nazis 1933–1945," *Among Men, Among Women*, Gay Studies and Women's Studies, University of Amsterdam Conference, June 22–26, 1983, 330.

14. *Ibid.*, 325–7.

15. Elke Kerker, *Weltbürgertum-Exil-Heimatlosigkeit, die Entwicklung der politischen Dimensionen im Werke Klaus Mann's von 1924–1936* (Meisenheim-am-Glan, 1977), 101.

16. Radclyffe Hall, *The Well of Loneliness* (London, 1982), 412, 513; Hirschfeld, *Berlin's Drittes Geschlecht,* 27ff, 40–1.

17. See the 1920s Berlin lesbian bars described in *Lila Nächte,* ed. Adele Meyer (Berlin, 1981), passim.

18. Wettley, *Von der "Psychopathia sexualis" zur Sexualwissenschaft,* 87.

19. James D. Steakley, *The Homosexual Emancipation Movement in Germany* (New York, 1975), Chapter 3.

20. See Vera Brittain, *Radclyffe Hall: A Case of Obscenity?* (New York, 1929), passim.

21. Hall, *The Well of Loneliness,* 393.

22. "Christa Reinig über Christa Winsloe," Christa Winsloe, *Mädchen in Uniform* (Munich, 1983), 241–8.

23. *Ibid.,* 217.

24. B. Ruby Rich, "Mädchen in Uniform, from Repressive Tolerance to Erotic Liberation," *Jump Cut, A Review of Contemporary Cinema,* No. 24–25 (1983), 44–50.

25. *Lila Nächte,* 38.

26. Mosse, *Toward the Final Solution,* 223–4. The precedence given to the persecution of Jews over all other groups is documented in Nazi-occupied Holland , where the prosecution of homosexuals was left to the Dutch local police, while the German authorities themselves directed the rounding up and deportation of the Jews—Peter Koenders, *Homoseksualiteit in Bezet Nederland* (Gravenhage, 1983), 141.

# Index

# 230 Index